AF737658

The Psychology Industry under a Microscope!

David B. Stein

University Press of America,® Inc.
Lanham · Boulder · New York · Toronto · Plymouth, UK

Copyright © 2012 by
University Press of America,® Inc.
4501 Forbes Boulevard
Suite 200
Lanham, Maryland 20706
UPA Acquisitions Department (301) 459-3366

10 Thornbury Road
Plymouth PL6 7PP
United Kingdom

All rights reserved
Printed in the United States of America
British Library Cataloging in Publication Information Available

Library of Congress Control Number: 2012940810
ISBN: 978-0-7618-5956-7 (clothbound : alk. paper)
ISBN: 978-0-7618-5962-8 (paperback : alk. paper)
eISBN: 978-0-7618-5957-4

™ The paper used in this publication meets the minimum requirements of American National Standard for Information Sciences—Permanence of Paper for Printed Library Materials, ANSI Z39.48-1992

Dedication

My children,
Alex, Kevin, and Heidi,
and my grandchildren,
Caydence and Addalynne

Table of Contents

TABLES AND FIGURES

ACKNOWLEDGEMENTS

This book would not have been possible were it not for giants upon whose shoulders I have tried to climb. It was their writings from long ago that planted the seeds for the content of this book, which were first introduced to me while I was a doctoral student in the 1970s. In my morning classes, I was being taught psychological testing, theories, and methods of counseling, while in the afternoons, classes consisted of scientific literature reviews which where highly critical and even condemning of the morning's materials. It was the literature classes that initiated my earliest inquiries into "What is wrong with this picture!" Gradually, I began to make sense of the quagmire and convoluted thing known as clinical psychology. The literature materials made sense, but the theory and practice course made little or no sense. Oddly, the reader will soon learn that not much has changed in the curricula of psychology graduate training. The authors who have most influenced me are Walter Michele, Neal Miller and John Dollard, H. J. Eysenck, Leon Festinger, Albert Ellis, Aaron Beck, Thomas Szasz, and William Glasser. Since then, other voices have chimed in with even more convincing critical commentaries. Sadly, it seems that the validity of what these critics were saying have not and are not receiving the attention within psychology that they should.

In the years following graduate school, I had trouble wondering why I was seeing this picture and almost all practicing clinicians were not. Why are the clinical psychology masses clinging to fiction, while only a very few are not? Why was I the only graduate in my class to see this, but none of the others were? These questions plagued me, but fortunately I had a friend and former chair of my psychology department, Dr. Ed Smith. He lost the battle with cancer seven years ago. His encouragement and support has kept me going. He was a quiet person who had the rare skill to say something important in the shortest and most succinct manner. When I first joined the department, I stepped into his office and asked him, "Why am I seeing the problems within clinical psychology, but most of the others aren't?" He looked up from his desk and quietly replied, "Leon Festinger's

Effort Justification." It was a lightning bolt from the sky. Epiphany at last! The testing and theoretical practicing courses took so much energy to master that over time the clinical graduate students had to believe that which they worked so hard to learn and reject any information that was contradictory and might cause them discomfort, confusion, consternation, and even vexation. Professor Smith, thank you for being an important part of my life and career.

I give special thanks to my sons, Alex and Kevin. Special thanks to Courtney and Liz, and to my granddaughters, Caydence and Addalynne, for giving me so much joy, a joy which sustains me during the long, lonely hours of writing. I must, once again, thank my former mother-in-law, Opal Bristow, for being a bedrock for both family life and ethics. My friends also sustain me, even though I am a certified curmudgeon: Barry Kudlowitz, Laura Birdsong, Dona Briggs, Ira Rakoff, Jill Rakoff, and Lois Rakoff.

My executive assistant, Grisel Campbell, not only helps with the hard work, but she also tolerates my outlandish humor.

INTRODUCTION

The Roman poet, Syrus, once wrote, "The pain of the mind is greater than the pain of the body." Patients usually go to psychologists seeking relief from mental pain. Sometimes the pain may be self-perpetuated, as with depression and anxiety, or sometimes the pain may be relational, as with struggling with a child or a teen, and sometimes the pain may be from a faltering relationship in a marriage. It is incumbent with the practice of psychology to offer the best talent possible in order to help patients, just as it is critical for the practicing surgeon to apply his craft with the greatest skill possible. However, as complex as surgery is, healing the pain of the mind is far more daunting and makes medicine pale by comparison. Psychology has been wrestling for hundreds of years to find the path into the human mind in its quest to heal. Unfortunately, it has a long history of not being able to find the exact right path. Many possible paths have been proposed, with many offering some good ideas. However, the psychology industry has a track record that is far from stellar. It is an industry that sees itself as succeeding, but, alas, as we will explore, it is not. Why is the quest so difficult? Why have some of the keenest minds who ever lived been unable to find a truly productive path?

Deepak Chopra, physician and spiritualist, often says that the mind is more complex than the universe. Perhaps this is true, and perhaps it is not. The main point is that there is no question that the human mind is extraordinarily complex. We then add to the equation the problem of which may be the best approach for studying the mind. Indeed, this issue has reigned since Plato and Aristotle. On the one side is the position that the mind can best be decoded through the tools of science, i.e., Aristotle, and on the other side is the argument that the mind does not lend itself to the mechanistic determinism philosophy of science but can only be understood through sound logic, i.e., Plato. This is known as the mind versus brain controversy. The "brain" does permit scientific inquiry. It is a physical thing that lends itself to the cornerstone of science, which is observation. The mind, on the other hand, is invisible. We observe only a small portion of the consequences of the mind in observable behavior, but behavior alone does not define the essence of the mind. Humans have events that go on in the mind which are private and may never be revealed. Thus, the question remains whether or not we can apply science to the study of the mind. We pursue this quest not merely for intellectual inquiry, but perhaps more because we wish to alleviate the suffering which can be produced by the mind.

Historically, and perhaps unwittingly, psychology has taken a dual approach to studying the mind, with one part being scientific, or Aristotelian, and the other part being philosophical, or Platonic. Thus, if we observe any introductory textbook in psychology, we readily discover that half the book is based upon science, such as topics of sensation and perception, memory, learning, and physiology. The other half is purely philosophical, such as theories of personality, assessment, and many so-called treatment modalities, such as Freudian, Adlerian, Jungian, and so forth. Often, the young student taking introductory psychology is not told that this switch takes place, but, instead, he is told, "Psychology is the scientific study of behaviors." The reality is that it is not all science; it is part science and part philosophy. This book explores the fact that psychology is a mixture of science and philosophy, and that the scientific part may, in fact, be sadly compromised by greed and ignorance. If this is so, then is it any wonder that treatment of the suffering of the mind has not proven to be an easy thing?

There are over two thousand theories of personality. Why? They are philosophical, and therefore anyone with a logical mind can argue for one position or another, and such disputation can, and has been, going on forever. Has this proven fruitful for alleviating suffering? This book will argue that the answer seems to be—not very well. It has contributed some, but as we shall see, not enough.

What about the scientific wing of psychology? Has this proven effective in alleviating mental suffering? Again, as will be argued throughout this book, some, but not very well.

One cannot fault science for the complexities involved in attempting to study the mind, even if the science is rigorous and exacting, which it is not. If we compare the study of cancer to the study of the mind, the complexity of the endeavor becomes clearer. Science searches for cause and effect relationships, i.e., c – e. Any dictionary defines science as the search to predict and control natural phenomenon, which is to find the c – e, cause – effect, of a natural event. Once this relationship is discovered, then these events lend themselves to prediction, i.e., to observe the cause and predict the event that will follow, and also to potential control, i.e., to block the outcome of the effect by manipulating the cause, which we can call 'treatment'. If we apply our comparison to the search for the c – e of cancer, we find that all the potential causes of cancer may number in the millions. The search is indeed daunting. However, nature makes things even more complex, because cancer is an effect that occurs from a precise combination, or permutation, of causes. The trick then becomes finding this precise combination of causes from among the millions. The number of potential permutations would then be staggering. Is it any wonder that we cannot find the precise permutation for cancer? This is proving to be so difficult that, thus far, the answer seems to keep eluding science.

If we now turn back to the study of the mind, as will be discussed in chapter 8 where we look at the complexity of all the variables which may come together in order to form a single thought, we will discover that the potential causes for a mere thought are gigantic, which are way beyond those for cancer. The potential causes for complex or sophisticated thought become even more mind-boggling. We are unable to find the cause – effect relationship for cancer, so is it any wonder that science has also failed to find ways to predict and control, i.e., alleviate the suffering of the mind?

Thus, the science of the mind is struggling. The problem is made worse when close examination reveals that the practices of scientific inquiry in psychology are riddled with flaws, i.e., bad science, and, even worse, the practices may be riddled with political and economic agendas which are leading scientific inquiry in psychology down a path of deliberate manipulation to distort the data in the interest of financial gain. This will be explored throughout this book.

Matters may be made worse, and the evidence is mounting that something is indeed really wrong with the *practice* of psychology. Patients, for the most part, are not getting many benefits from seeing therapists. Even when there is good research in psychology, we are finding that the research is not making its way into the offices of clinicians, and is, therefore, not being used to treat patients. Walter Mischel, one of the finest scholars in the history of psychology, was quoted in a *Newsweek* article (October 2, 2009), "The disconnect between what clinicians do and what science has discovered is an unconscionable embarrassment," and he stated that there is a "widening gulf between clinical practice and science." A major article by Baker, McFall, and Shoham (2008) seems to have been a recent catalyst for exposing the widening gap between treatments found to be effective in the research laboratories, from the actual training of psychologists to the actual practices within the offices of psychologists.

This book is not aimed at denigrating psychology. It is aimed at perhaps assisting psychology to evolve in a better way. Historically, psychology has run into incalculable blind alleys in its quest to alleviate human suffering, and, at this very moment, it is bogged down in the deepest blind alley ever. We will explore treatment efficacy rates, only to find that they are low. However, suggestions will be made in Chapter One and Chapter Two to place more focus on human problems and hopefully for more efficacious treatment practices. We will examine the training of psychologists, only to find out that it is ill-defined and poorly focused. The accreditation criteria of the American Psychological Association for doctoral programs may be based on a model that is arcane and out of date; this will be discussed at length in Chapter Two, where the actual course content of doctoral programs will be scrutinized. This is something that has never been done before. This overview may help open the reader's mind as to why the practicing psychologist may not being doing well. Suggestions will be made for an overhaul of the course content of doctoral programs, hopefully to improve the skills of the practitioner. We will explore diagnostic issues, only to find that agreement rates for diagnoses are close to zero. However, here, too, suggestions will be made to perhaps find a more productive route. Chapter Seven explores a hidden cognitive pattern in diagnosis which may help improve the diagnostic system and the application of diagnosis to improve treatment. A new, more sensible diagnostic system will be proposed. Psychology is finding a growing market in the court systems, but new court decisions on expert testimony, which will be explored in Chapter Three, may place psychology in an embarrassing position. These court precedents will expand and permeate the court system, and, thus, result in psychologists not being allowed through the front door in many court cases. Perhaps psychology needs to face its limitations and learn to simply say, "I do not know for certain."

Psychology has returned to the disease model, which permeated diagnosis and the manner in which mental problems were viewed in the early twentieth century. In Chapter Four and Chapter Six, we will explore the new onslaught of disease etiologies, examine why the research is inundated with flaws, and why the sheer volume of poor research is convincing both the professional community and the public of diseases of the mind that are unfounded. Chapter Nine discusses how the profit motive may be underlying the misinformation and disinformation permeating the industry about so-called new evidence supporting the diseases of mental problems. Suggestions will be made for improving the system which will help ferret out "junk science" and will cleanse psychology of the blemish of tons of research. These may be serving as propaganda for the greedy, rather than serving the needs of scientific inquiry toward the nobler goal of alleviating mental suffering. Psychology has lacked a model which unifies its wide variety of bits and pieces. Such a model would, perhaps, facilitate or expedite psychology's evolution. Chapter Five offers a three-dimensional model called 'The Pyramid' to fill this void. This model makes clear how different response modalities, which have historically been studied in a loose, chaotic manner, are all part of one equation. Thus, different theories emphasizing different aspects of human responding can now be better understood and better integrated to produce multimodal treatments. This new model clearly shows where behavioral treatments fit in, where pharmacological interventions fit in, where cognitive methods fit in, where stress management fits in, where affective therapies fit in, and how each treatment modality can be blended, not as eclectic, hodgepodge therapies, but as truly unified and comprehensive treatment packages for a wide variety of ailments of the mind. The model clarifies how to best select, or emphasize, a treatment modality in different circumstances and for different and specific human problems. Physics has not yet found its integrating theory of everything, but perhaps this model does the job for psychology.

It is hoped, therefore, that the material in this book will not be viewed as an attack on psychology, but rather as an attempt to open eyes and suggest new roads so that we may help better alleviate the torment of the minds and the suffering which too many people are enduring. Finally, Chapter Ten suggests which important roles psychologists can best play, while at the same time fully understanding and accepting the many limitations within psychology which may not necessarily ever be erased.

CHAPTER ONE

Exploring the Course Content of American Psychological Association Accredited Doctoral Programs:

Does APA Accreditation Make Sense, or is it Outdated?

This chapter explores several issues surrounding the American Psychological Association's accreditation process for doctoral training of clinical psychologists. The actual course content of 115 accredited programs will be closely scrutinized. This is something that has never been done before. It will be shown that the course content of doctoral programs is not evolving sufficiently to produce highly effective clinicians. Instead, we will see how many hours of training are being wasted on time-consuming and unessential topics. We will address the question as to whether or not there is enough time in the student's few doctoral school years to train clinicians to be both researchers and clinicians. Furthermore, many clinical courses themselves are filled with material which has been repeatedly proven to be arcane, inaccurate, misleading, and even dangerous. Finally, we will explore why there needs to be change made in the course content to better prepare clinicians for helping patients with real-life problems. Four issues will be addressed in this chapter: first, the issue of treatment efficacy rates will be explored; second, the validity and reliability of psychological tests will be reviewed; third, we will explore whether or not it still makes sense, or even if there is sufficient time, to train clinicians in both human problems *and* research and statistical methods; and fourth, the actual course content of 115 American Psychological Association approved doctoral programs will be reviewed. There are four hypotheses to be addressed:

1. Psychosocial treatment efficacy rates are low for most human problems. There may be a few bright sparks, but they appear to be the exception.
2. Validity and reliability of psychological tests are low, almost worthless, and are, therefore, considered dangerous and misleading. It is also hy-

pothesized that current reviews indicate that tests which were previously favored and were considered fairly valid are more recently viewed by updated research as invalid and unreliable, most notably the MMPI. Additionally, it is hypothesized that the examination of current course content indicates that the vast majority of graduate schools are still teaching assessment courses with a foundation of invalid and unreliable test materials.

3. Courses in statistics and research methodology may be appropriate for doctoral candidates who wish to be teachers and researchers but are not essential for students who wish to be clinicians.
4. Doctoral training has changed little in thirty years, clinging to a model that is mostly theoretical, abstract, and arcane, with little emphasis on treatment strategies for specific human problems.

Controversy over Treatment Efficacy Rates

Eysenck (1952, 1961) upset the psychological world when he pioneered research on psychological treatment efficacies. His research indicated that individuals with a host of behavioral and emotional problems improved better over time when they did not visit a therapist, while those who sought psychological help did worse. Numerous studies followed, with most supporting his findings. A recent attempt at a large-scale meta-analysis by Lipsey and Wilson (1993) does not seem to clear the confusion over efficacy rates. On the one hand, the authors make the following statement:

> "It is a distressing observation that, over recent decades, the results of treatment research and reviews of that research have not yielded convincing support for the efficacy of many psychological, educational, and behavioral treatments." (p. 2)

However, Lipsey and Wilson later conclude that there are some positive effects with some of the treatments, namely, cognitive/behavioral, but only within the closed doors of academic research projects, but these methods do not seem to be crossing the threshold into real world clinical practice. Thus, treatment efficacy rates in clinicians' offices are appalling low.

Rossi and Wright (1984) concluded that:

> "Similar controversy has characterized intervention in social work, counseling, education, criminal justice, organizational development, and a host of related areas echoed many reviewers in these areas when described evaluation research as a 'parade of close-to-zero effects'." (p. 348)

The Lipsey and Wilson (1993) meta-analysis seems to indicate that cognitive/behavioral treatments fared best in the academic world. However, a study by

Baker, McFall, and Shoham (2008) indicates that the actual practices of therapists who claimed to practice cognitive/behavioral treatments were not faithfully practicing the methods espoused in the text and research literature, such as the cognitive/behavioral methods of Beck (1961, 1979), Ellis and Harper (1975), Meichenbaum (1977), Maultsby (1984), and Kendall and Hollon (1981). In fact, it appeared that most were practicing a more homespun, common sense, and *made up at the moment* variety. Eclectic would be insufficient to describe the observations. It was previously stated that an article in the November 2, 2009 issue of Newsweek, where the author interviewed prominent and respected researchers and writers, supports the hypothesis that currently the practices of psychological clinicians are not faring well at all.

Table 1.1 Approximations of Some Treatment Efficacy Rates

Efficacy – How effective are psychological/psychiatric treatments?

Problem	Efficacy
sex offenders	.05 (Hagen, 1997; Dineen, 2000)
physical abusers	.37 (Hagen, 1997)
criminals, general	.20 (Barlow & Durrand, 2006)
alcohol and drug abuse including AA	.20 (Peele, 1995)
marriage counseling	.33 (McGraw, 2000; Wilson, 2002)
counseling, general	.30 (Eysenck, 1952; Dineen, 2000)
oppositional teens	.20 (Stein, 2004)
conduct disorders	.17 (Stein, 2004)

Table 1.1 gives a brief idea of treatment efficacy rates for some of the more common forms of human problems. More extensive reports can be found in the Lipsey and Wilson (1993) meta-analysis where some efficacy rates are reported as being higher, i.e., cognitive/behavioral in pure academic form at .61, while others are reported as being even lower. Overall, treatment efficacy in the *field or real world* appears to be discouraging. Hagen (1997) reports that when making threat assessments, psychologists are wrong two out of three times. Something is very wrong, and it is believed that a considerable part of the problem is in the actual course content of doctoral graduate training, which will be reviewed shortly.

Behavior Modification – A Response to the Eysenck Studies

It is interesting to note that following the Eysenck studies in the 1960s, it was suspected that the problem lay in non-empirically-based treatments (Barlow and Durrand, 2006). Therefore, attention turned to the one treatment modality that spawned from learning theory research and later evolved into researched-based treatments known as Behavior Modification and Behavioral Therapy (Kanfer and Phillips, 1970). Later, as a result of Meichenbaum's (1977) recognition of

Ellis' Rational/Cognitive approaches, behavioral devotes adopted the cognitive concepts, and Cognitive/Behavioral Therapy resulted.

At first, it appeared as if psychological therapies were finally on an empirically-based track; however, enthusiasm seemed to wane after some initial promising approaches appeared, such as with children (Patterson, 1971); Becker, Engelmann, and Thomas (1971), with desensitization for phobias (Wolpe, 1958), or Bandura's (1969) modeling approaches. It seemed that this enthusiasm was short-lived. A few treatment approaches have remained as standard, but for the most part, treatment efficacy rates with children and teenagers actually declined (Stein, 2001a), while other methods, such as covert sensitization (Barlow, Leitenberg, and Steinbrook, 1969) did not prove as promising as originally thought. When asked what went wrong with the behavioral movement, one of the early pioneers, Eisler, simply responded that, "They ran out of ideas." (In a personal communication, September 28, 1997). Thus, the behavioral movement is still around, but it has not proven to be the panacea to save the treatment efficacies of psychology. However, there is still hope that more and more research in the cognitive/behavioral arena for *specific human problems* will still prove to be more promising, and, even more importantly, the work that now exists may be more incorporated into the training and reading requirements within doctoral programs.

The Lack of Validity and Reliability of Psychological Tests?

Psychology tests, or what constitutes a *so-called battery of psychological tests,* can be divided into three parts (Lilienfeld, S. O., Lynn, S. J., and Lohr, J. M., 2003):

- One part is composed of *educational tests* that purportedly measure specific learning skills, such as reading, math, and writing, and the overall measure of *intelligence,* which is usually reported in the form of I.Q., intelligence quotient score(s).
- Second are the so-called personality tests, which, in turn, are divided in subjective personality tests and objective personality tests.
- Third are the questionnaire rating scales, used to measure a plethora of things, such as attention deficit disorder, ADD; attention deficit hyperactivity disorder, ADHD; oppositional defiant disorder, ODD; conduct disorders; depression; and anxiety, all of which only scratches the surface at the countless number of questionnaires being produced at factory line rates.

Educational Tests

Educational tests can measure weaknesses in a child's academic skills, but, unfortunately, these weaknesses are increasingly being viewed as psychiatric diseases. Please note that the term 'disorder' is often used, but modern lexicon has made this term, for most intents and purposes, synonymous to both the public and professional communities with the term 'disease' (Stein, 2001a, 2001b). In order to clarify this issue, children who score poorly in math skills may be labeled as having *dyscalculia,* meaning that they are not just weak at math but that they have some MBD, minimal brain damage, that causes this problem. Oddly, no one has identified which area of the brain is involved, but, nevertheless, that does not deter psychologists from *believing* that it is a disease, or, by modern vernacular, it is one of the *learning disabilities* (Strauss and Lehtinen, 1947). A poor reading skill becomes *dyslexia.* Sloppy handwriting becomes *dysgraphia or agraphia,* and on and on goes the issue. Thus, fancy vocabulary connotes diseases as a replacement for hard scientific evidence. Interestingly, whether viewed as a weak skill or as a disease, the remedy is almost always the same, which is to enlist a tutor to use what are called *multi-sensory learning methods* in order to properly relearn the fundamentals (Becker, W. C., Engelmann, S., and Thomas, D. R., 1971). It is the failure of not properly paying attention when the fundamentals are taught, which, according to the World Health Organization, is the main reason children are weak in certain specific skills, but, nevertheless, the disease concept is now the *paradigm du jour.* The multi-sensory method simply means, at its most basic level, that the teacher writes a word out with glue, pours sand over it, and lets it dry, and then the child traces the word with his finger, i.e., tactile sense, says it out loud, i.e., auditory sense, all while looking at the word, i.e., which is the visual sense. Thus, a simple method of relearning the fundamentals is given a fancy name and made to look as if it were some form of complex learning approach designed to ameliorate a diseased brain. There are other, more sophisticated methods, but they are still fairly similar. No one has as yet explained to where this diseased part of the brain disappears once a child catches on to the fundamentals and resumes work at a pace equal to the other children. Identifying and ameliorating academic weaknesses is a good thing, but labeling them as diseases is dangerous because too many children come to believe that such a disease is a permanent condition that they will have to live with for the rest of their lives. (Stein, 2001a; 2001b)

Intelligence tests can also serve a useful purpose if they are properly used, but here, too, psychology bends the truth. The first intelligence test was developed by Alfred Binet and Theodore Simon, in 1904, in France, in order to estimate how well a child *might* do in an academic setting, and, therefore, assist with the best class placement of a child. However, the I.Q., intelligence quotient, has over the years taken on a life of its own where it has come to mean that it becomes a true and accurate assessment of how intelligent a child actually is (Barlow and Durand, 2006), and once made, this label often sticks to the child for the rest of his life. The reader is asked to consider how well an average farmer might do on such a test. Not well, one might guess, and yet the running of a farm requires nothing short of brilliance, since it is such a complex endeavor, but once given, such labels tend to stick. Stein (2001a, 2001b, 2005) suggests that the term 'Intelligence Quotient', i.e., I.Q., be replaced simply by R.Q., i.e., 'Readiness Quotient', which is more appropriate and has considerably less stigma attached to it. Barlow and Durand (2006), two of the most respected names in psychology today, make the following statement:

> "One of the biggest mistakes non-psychologists [and a distressing number of psychologists] make is to confuse IQ with intelligence. . . . An IQ score significantly higher than average means that the person has a significantly greater than average chance of doing well in our educational system." (p. 75)

In sum, educational tests do measure specific skills and can be useful for identifying academic weaknesses, but the paradigm is in drastic need of changing, moving away from pejorative and disease connotations.

Personality Tests

We now enter the *Twilight Zone* of psychology. Hundreds of theories of personality exist, but no one has yet successfully identified, or even defined, what personality is (Hall and Lindzey, 1957). Thus, there exists a myriad of psychological tests that measure something, but no one seems to quite know what it is. The first test which was introduced was the Rorschach Inkblot test, a *Projective Personality Test,* introduced in 1921 by Swiss psychiatrist Hermann Rorschach, which consists of ten inkblots supposedly *carefully designed* in order to serve as psychology's equivalent to the X-ray (Wood, Nezworski, Lilienfeld, and Garb, 2003). This, of course, begs the question of, "X-ray of what?" which is something which no one seems to know. It has no validity, with measures ranging between .03 and .28, which means that it does not predict behavior (Mischel, 1996; Wood, et al, 2003), and it does not match with how individuals give self reports. It also has no reliability (Mischel, 1996; Lilienfeld, Wood, and Garb, 2001a; Woods, et al, 2003), which means that when individuals retake the test, they do not yield the same personality profiles. Ray (1968), one of the great historical figures in statistical analysis, points out that validity and reliability measurements below .40 are considered to be of little worth or of no worth at all. Validity and reliability are reported as correlations, which, in statistics, is '*r*', the correlation coefficient. It may be helpful to better interpret correlations by calculating what proportion, or percent of the time the two measures, i.e., which means test with behavior, for validity, and test with a retest or a different psychologist, i.e., reliability, agree. There are many measures of correlation that can be made in psychological testing, but the measure of most concern is how well tests correlate with actual behaviors (Mischel, 1996), or how well the test might predict behavior, validity, how well test results will be repeated, or be repeated with different test administrators, i.e., reliability. Furthermore, different psychologists scoring the tests will proffer completely different personality profiles, i.e., extremely poor reliability (Anastasi, 1988; Mischel, 1996). Apparently, these tests fare extremely poorly for both validity and reliability. Ray (1962) and Edwards (1967) point out that if *r* is squared, then we obtain this proportion, which is called the '*coefficient of determination*'. Thus, as Ray (1968) points out, a correlation for either validity or reliability below .40 is poor, which means that the proportion, or percent of agreement is 16%. This makes it clear why psychological testing is being presented in this book as extremely poor, and perhaps dangerous. The highest validly for the *Rorschach is* .28, which means that, at its best, it predicts behavior at less than a rate of 8%. Is the reader now beginning to fully understand the skepticism expressed in this book about psychological testing? If psychologists are still using these tests in their practices, one wonders if they understand what has just been pointed out. Let's see if other tests fare any better than the *Rorschach.*

Table 1.2 Psychology Tests Validity Coefficients

1. Projective personality tests:	
A. Rorschach	
B. TAT – Thematic Apperception Test	
C. Draw a Person Test	.03 - .28
2. Objective personality tests:	
A. MMPI – Minnesota Multiphasic Personality Inventory	.29 - .37
3. Educational tests:	.44 - .85
A. IQ Tests as an issue	

The TAT, or Thematic Apperception Test, is the second most widely used projective test. It was developed in 1935 by Morgan and Murray at the Harvard Psychological Clinic. This test consists of a series of purportedly ambiguous drawings, for which the test subject makes up a story and reports his feelings earlier, presently, and in the future, that are related to the story. The examiner subjectively looks for themes and then reports his conclusions. The interpretation of this test is far less uniform than the Rorschach and turns out to be even less valid and less reliable. (Lilienfeld, Wood, and Garb, 2000)

One hundred percent of the 115 graduate programs researched for this paper still teach courses in *Rorschach* and other projective testing techniques. Why? They are used eighty percent of the time by school psychologists (Lilienfeld, Wood, and Garb, 2000), one third of the time in clinical practices, and approximately over eighty percent for custody hearings, abuse and neglect hearings, and criminal trials (Lorandos and Campbell, 2005). Why?

Presently, psychology is seeking to readopt the medical model in order to gain prescription writing privileges, but if an analogy is applied to medicine, then the psychology industry would have us believe that projective personality tests are analogous to X-rays, but empirical data clearly indicates that this analogy is totally unfounded and improper (Lorandos and Campbell, 2005). Teaching testing with a lower than 16% accuracy rate makes no sense at all and merits a plea to the American Psychological Association to review this as a criteria for graduate school accreditation.

A different approach to personality testing was made with the introduction of *objective personality inventories.* This category of testing supposedly had a more empirical foundation. They were composed of specific questions which were made objective by administering and standardizing them against clinically-based normative groups. An individual's answers were then compared to the normative group responses, yielding a supposedly *objective* profile. The most notable of these tests is the MMPI, Minnesota Multiphasic Personality Inventory, introduced by Hathaway and McKinley in 1943. Initially, the MMPI offered considerable promise as psychology's *X-ray* into the personality of subjects. However, one of the most prolific writers on psychological tests, Anne Anastasi (1988), began to question the validity of the test. She states, "The test manual and related publications now caution against literal interpretation of the clinical scales." (p. 530) Lilienfeld, Lynn, and Lohr (2003) report validity coefficients ranging from .29 to .37, which, to those familiar with correlation coefficients, really means that they are meaningless (Hagen, 1997) and even lower than a 13% accuracy rate. Anatasi (1988) stated, "The MMPI is essentially a clinical instrument whose proper interpretation calls for considerable psychological sophistication," (p. 531). However, this is not consistent with Lilienfeld, Lynn, and Lohr's (2003) more recent statement, "That is, clinicians with more MMPI experience and knowledge were no more accurate in their interpretations pf MMPI data than were clinicians with significantly less MMPI experience and knowledge." Dawes (1994) points out that in the clinical arena, secretaries perform just as well as clinicians with years of experience. Again, Lilienfeld, Lynn, and Lohr (2003) point out that, "Similarly, experienced clinicians are generally no more accurate than advanced graduate students." (p. 24)

Hagen (1997) states, "In fact, the authors of the MMPI gave up the original attempt to use the test to diagnose various kinds of mental disorders almost before the ink was dry on the first edition." (p. 31)

Other less popular tests have fared even worse (Anastasi, 1988). All of this begs the questions as to why psychologists are wasting so much valuable training time on arcane, unproductive, invalid, unreliable, and inaccurate courses. Cannot their time be better spent reading intensely the literature that is available on specific human problems, where the student becomes intimately familiar with the all aspects of the problem, such as precipitants, effects on the family constellation and interactions, effects on the individual, the resulting cognitive and behavioral impairments, and treatment methods which empirically appear to be the most productive? What is taking so long for tenacious adherence to tradition to die out? Medicine has evolved since 1900, why has not psychology?

Thus, there are no medical tests and no psychological tests to make or confirm almost all diagnoses and which fail to predict actual behaviors, with the exception of very few, such as retardation, and Alzheimer's.

Rating Scales and Questionnaires

Rating scales and questionnaires are being mass-produced at factory production line rates (Stein, 2004). Rating scales and questionnaires are merely uniform interviews; they are not tests that yield insights into the human psyche, brain, mind, or soul. Most of them are used merely to approximate diagnoses from the DSM-IV, the *Diagnostic and Statistical Manual – Fourth Edition* (1994). In 1998, at an American Psychological Association press conference, Stein argued that there seemed to be little need for the plethora of manufactured rating scales, which are intended to merely approximate a DSM diagnosis. He stated, "Wouldn't it be easier to just use the DSM criteria as a checklist instead of beating around the bush." He further argued that instead of using rating scales, which are checklists, the diagnostic criteria in the DSM-IV are also merely checklists, and the need for more and more checklists is not really necessary. Thus, the checklists are used to justify the invalid and unreliable checklists of the DSM-IV. The problem is further complicated by the fact that there is little reliability between clinicians for making specific diagnoses (Davison and Neale, 1994; Lorandos and Cambell, 2005). The inter-rater reliability statistics in the DSM-III were so low and embarrassing that the compilers of the DSM-IV handle the problem by merely eliminating all of the inter-rater statistics, and without reliability, there can be no validity. (Lorandos and Campbell, 2005)

Unfortunately, questionnaires and rating scales are snuck into the so-called battery of psychological tests, resulting in pronouncements to patients or parents of child or adolescent patients that they *have such and such a disorder*. Naïve patients and parents are not told the truth, that none of the tests were of any use in making such pronouncements, and that it was the questionnaire or rating scale that they filled out that formed the foundation for any diagnoses (Stein, 2005). Thus, questionnaires or rating scales which approximate a system of invalid and unreliable diagnoses make matters even more confusing and chaotic. (Lorandos and Campbell, 2005)

If there are no medical tests or psychological tests to make or confirm almost all psychiatric diagnoses, then how can questionnaires and rating scales accurately approximate that which does not exist? In addition, Hagen (1997) points out that in the research for these measuring instruments, "Any participant in one of these studies would have to be completely brain-dead to miss what the researchers are getting at with their questionnaires." (p. 37)

Human Problems

Before reviewing the course content of all APA accredited schools, it may prove useful to list some of the numerous problems with which the human race must cope:

1. Marriage
2. Divorce
3. Grief
4. Parenting

5. Daily hassles or stresses
6. Work related stresses
7. Communication and effective listening skills
8. Assertiveness
9. Coping with physical illnesses
10. Anxieties
11. Religion(s)
12. Death and dying
13. Terrorism
14. Homeland security
15. Crime and criminology
16. The elderly
17. Coping with having a handicapped child
18. Delinquency
19. Spousal abuse
20. Child abuse
21. Anger and temper tantrums
22. Sexual dysfunction(s)
23. Depression and sadness
24. Existential and philosophical problems, such as finding a meaning and purpose for life
25. Irrational and cognitive dysfunction
26. Obesity and other eating disorders
27. Substance abuse and addictions
28. Process addictions, i.e., addiction to behaviors, such as gambling, sex, pornography, and excessive partying
29. Prejudice, racial, and ethnic hatreds
30. Conflict resolution
31. Effective behavior modification and therapies for specific problems, such as autism, retardation, and phobias
32. Psychopharmacology, with an emphasis on deleterious complications and side effects
33. Overcoming growing up with a highly dysfunctional family
34. Crisis intervention
35. Sociological problems of urban and rural living
36. Gangs
37. Cults
38. Prostitution
39. Gender issues for men and women
40. Overcoming shyness
41. Cultural, ethnic, and minority issues

(This list is generated in part from Santrock, Minnett, and Campbell, 1994.)

The list is not complete, and it can go on and on. Readings for almost any of these problems are plentiful and inexhaustible. In addition, there are countless research and scientifically-based studies in cognitive and behavioral psychology that already exist for each of these problem areas, but clinicians either do not know the material, are not trained in the material, or are ignoring the material pertaining to what they practice (Begley, 2009). *Courses involving extensive reading and extensive practice and rehearsal for dealing with as many of these problems as possible should consume the limited years that doctoral students have. Alas, such is not the case!*

Course Content of 115 APA Accredited Doctoral Programs

This section is devoted to an extensive and comprehensive review of the course content of 115 APA, American Psychological Association, accredited doctoral programs. Data for five programs was not available. Hopefully inaccuracies were avoided, but because this is such a formidable project, it is certain that some error has occurred. However, the overall course patterns are apparent, and it is judged that a few oversights would not alter the interpretation and analysis for the reader. The reader is asked to review the tables with care.

The first column lists the type of courses, and the right column lists the number of doctoral programs offering the courses. Please note that Assessment and Psychometrics upon close examination appear to mean the same thing, i.e., the administration of psychological tests.

Table 1.3 Total Core Course Offerings by all APA Accredited Doctoral Programs

N = 115

University Courses Offered	Total
Assessment	98
Psychopathology	94
Psychological Intervention	86
Psychometrics	59
Research Design	78
Research Methods	79
Statistics	78
Learning	47
Physiological Psychology	59
History and Systems	54
Social Psychology	63
Developmental Psych	58
Ethics	75
Practicum	81
Dissertation	71
Health Psychology	16
Personality Theories	50
Neuropsych	49
Neuropharmacology	18
Cognition	57
Advanced Human Memory	6
Child Psychology	6

Perception	32
Doctoral Project	3
Theory and Philosophy	30
Psychology as a Profession	13
Psychopharmacology	19
Personal Counseling	1
Motivation	12
Psycholinguistics	13
Group and Organizational Dynamics	8
Ego Psych	2
Object Relations	1
Animal Behavior	5
Community Psych	7
Psychophysics of Hearing	3
Drugs and Behavior	1
Visual Processes	5
Decision Making Process	6
Comparative Psych	3
Experimental Psych	3
School Psych	5
General Psych	1
Helping Skills	1
Needs Assessment Techniques	1

Table 1.4 Total Elective Course Offerings by all APA Accredited Doctoral Programs

N = 115

University Courses Offered	Total
Cognitive Psychology	18
Perception	12
Motivation and Emotion	10
Developmental Psychology	19
Learning Processes	13
Social Psychology	18
Group Dynamics	7
Cardiology Seminar	1
Personality Theories	11
Neuropsychology	18
Theory and Research in Emotion	2
Dynamics of Pain	1
Seminar in Language Development	2
Health Psychology	9
Human Brain Behavior Relationships	1
Neurophysiology	16
Animal Behavior	3
Invertebrate Psychology	1
Design of the Mind	2
Drugs, Brain, and Behavior	6
Animal Human Communication	3
Language Acquisitions	7
Psycholinguistics	4
Moral Development	3
Social Influence	2
Behavioral Medicine	7

Table 1.5 Total Specialty Course Offerings by all APA Accredited Doctoral Programs

N = 115

University Courses Offered	Total
Teaching of Psychology	16
Rehabilitation Psychology/Vocational Rehab	2
Psychology of Aging	17
Motor Control after Stroke/Neurological Issues	2
Psychology of Addiction	14
Interviewing and Behavioral Observation	23
Behavioral Assessment	20
Interpersonal Psychotherapy	18
Behavior Therapy	32
Family/Marital Therapy	44
Child and Adolescent Psychotherapy	43
Forensic Psychology	8
Anxiety and Anxiety-Based Disorders	3
Organizational/Staffing/Personnel	23
Developmental Disabilities	8
Ethnic and Minority Issues in Psych/Diversity	49
Psychology of Sex Differences and Similarities/Gender	23
Sleep and Sleep Disorders	3
Youth and Violence	3
Psychology of Death and Loss	4
Issues in Rural Health	3
Stress, Coping, and Health	12
Law, Psychology, and Policy	9
Current Issues/Topics in Psychology	26
Supervision and Management	9
Psychology in the Community	26
Case Conference	3
Consultation Methods	8
Group Psychotherapy	32
Developing Scales/Instruments	3
Human/Computer Interaction	6
Expectations and Prevention of School Failure	1
Publication Seminar	1
Health Assessment and Major Illnesses	6
Health Education and Promotion	3
Crisis Intervention	3
Emotions and Health in Clinical Practice	2
Nonverbal Behavior	1
Intro to Roschach	2
Hypnotherapy	2
Brief Psychotherapy	4
Bio Medical Data Programs	1
Play Therapy	1

Identification of Child Abuse	2
Psych and Deafness	1
Psych of Career Development	3
Minnesota Multiphasic Personality Inventory	1
Behavior Disorders of Childhood and Adol	1
Attitude and Attitude Change	12
Depression	4

Table 1.3 focuses on a summation of the core courses, which are usually taken during the first one or two years of doctoral work. The next two tables, Table 1.4 and 1.5 are summations of the overall course content of the 115 programs. Specifically, Table 1.4 focuses on a summation of elective courses, which means that there is no assurance about which courses any individual doctoral student may have taken. Table 1.5 focuses on a summation of specialty course offerings, and again, what any individual student may have taken cannot be ascertained.

It Is Evident that Courses are Abstract, Theoretical, and Fail to Focus of Specific Human Problems.

Immediately, it is apparent that extensive training in most of the human problems previously listed are absent in most programs. Psychological interventions may cover some of the topics, but interviews with numerous colleagues seems to indicate that these courses were mostly surveys of the more philosophical forms of therapies, such as Freudian, Adlerian, Jungian, Behavioral, and so forth, with little in the way of in-depth and extensive readings and training for treating any of the specific human problems listed. Psychologists may argue that this problem is now remedied in almost all fifty states by requiring yearly continuing education courses in order to maintain licensure. However, the rebuttal consists of two parts. The first involves the development of mindsets, or rather a fixed way of looking at things, which is often engrained during the first years of training. Indeed, it is this very mindset which may also be called 'hegemonic thinking', a paradigm, or a prevailing *Zeitgeist,* that continues to permeate the dogged adherence to an arcane and ineffective training model in the first place. Festinger (1977) aptly calls this *effort justification,* which means if one exerts considerable effort into learning a skill, then one is going to cling tenaciously to what he or she has learned, excluding any information that may contradict their ingrained paradigm. New or contradictory evidence that contradicts what the individual believes he knows makes him so uncomfortable and confused that the new information usually gets rejected as somehow being flawed or of being prejudiced. The individual fails to see that it is he who is prejudiced. It is similar to combating or challenging someone who has a fixed delusion. Whether or not such mindsets can be altered with weekend or online abbreviated post-doctoral courses is, of course, an empirical question, but common sense observations seems to indicate that the tradition of the old curriculum model is being tenaciously clung to and is, therefore, most likely responsible for psychology not changing and not adapting to a more productive training curricula. The second part of the rebuttal consists of the idea that abbreviated weekend courses or quickie online courses cannot possibly cover each of the specific life problems with sufficient depth. Thus, the APA accreditation requirements are in dire need of reform, but there seems to be little chance of that happening any time soon. Doctoral programs are not doing a very good job, which is made apparent by the weak showing of treatment efficacies.

The second glaring problem one may notice is that the most frequently required course is *assessment or psychometrics.* Why? We have already looked at the assessment problem, and as Walter Mischel (1996) points out in an astute and scholarly fashion, we are doing very poorly at predicting behaviors in specific settings, and we are not very well at matching assessment to diagnosis, a diagnostic system that is greatly in need of re-conceptualization anyway. Why is the most frequently offered course a course consisting of teaching and training in content which is repeatedly and empirically proven to be invalid and unreliable misinformation and disinformation? The argument that it is *useful information* as part of the evaluation process is absolutely wrong. How can wrong information be useful? In fact, if such information is used in the courts for custody hearings, criminal culpability, and so forth, then it is downright dangerous (Faust, Anderer, and Ziskin, 2001; revision in press). This practice is unconscionable.

A third problem seems to be the extreme emphasis on statistic and research methodology. Is this a pragmatic use of graduate school training time or sufficient time for learning to treat specific human problems, for which we identified 41 different types of problems? Cognitive/behavioral treatments offer fairly well-researched concepts and methods for dealing with many of these problems, and the self-help book market is replete with lots of valuable material for dealing with these same problems (Santrock, J. W., Minnett, A. M., and Campbell, B. D., 1994). This would consume every spare minute for the trainee. Research courses consume too much time and should be electives for those students who know they wish to be academicians or researchers. Medical students do not spend time studying research. They are exclusively devoted to mastering treatments for clinical problems. The argument may be made that the Psy.D., i.e., doctorate of psychology degree remedies this excessive emphasis on research. No, it does not! Those programs are included in these summary tables and indicate that their courses are the same as for the Ph.D programs. It does eliminate the dissertation, and more course work is substituted, but two problems remain. First, too much time is still spent on research courses, and second, the courses that are added still consist of more abstract, arcane, and esoteric subject matter.

An overview of the course offerings, whether core, specialty, or elective, reveals that they have little to do with the understanding and amelioration of specific human problems. They are filled with abstraction, philosophical psychology, research, and so forth. In other words, they are collectively a more in-depth study of *introductory psychology*. Again, this is analogous to a medical student taking and retaking all of his introductory biology courses. Psychology must make up its mind whether its doctoral training is academically oriented, which seems to fulfill the needs of only 15% of those taking the clinical degree, or whether it is a practicing degree, which seems to be the needs of 85% of its students (Zimbardo, Weber, and Johnson, 2000). The discipline must be separated. Time does not permit continuing the tradition of trying to do both at the same time.

It is unethical to continue this practice (Hodgson, 2007 in a personal communication, August 29, 2007), because we are dealing with people's lives. When they come to us in our clinical offices, they are in pain and/or in need, and yet, we are mostly unqualified to handle whatever the presenting problem may be. When we testify in the courts, again, we are lacking the requisite training to make declarations and reports of bogus findings which will affect people's lives. In most states, clinical psychologists are required to take ethics courses in order to maintain their licenses, and yet they practice unethically on a daily basis. Worst of all, no one seems to *get it*.

It is only in the third cluster of courses that we begin to see some evidence of problem-based courses. However, the numbers are discouraging. Only 44 schools, or 38%, offer specialty courses in family/marital therapy. This is unconscionable and unacceptable. How can we release clinicians, most of whom have never had in-depth training in marital counseling techniques. This is at the high end of course offerings in a specific human problem, and the other forty problems are addressed even more infrequently. Is it any wonder that marriage counseling fails two-thirds of the time? Only 43 programs, or 38%, have training in adolescent and child therapy. Is it, therefore, any wonder that we have to increasingly rely on psychiatric drugs with childhood and adolescent disorders? Two-thirds of us are clueless about what it takes to effectively use psychosocial techniques to ameliorate patients' problems. In other words, most psychologists do not know what they are doing.

We are playing an increasing role in the criminal court system (Dawes, 1994; Dershowitz, 1994; Hagen, 1997) and yet only eight schools, or 7%, offer forensics courses, and much of these are filled with misinformation because they emphasize psychological assessment (Faust, et al., 2001), which as we already discussed is filled with invalid and unreliable material. The FBI had to develop its own diagnostic system (Douglas, Burgess, Burgess, and Ressler, 1997) to help categorize, profile, and understand criminal conduct, because psychology has almost completely neglected this very important arena. It is the discipline of sociology that adopted criminal justice; psychology dropped the ball. Nine programs have courses in law, psychology, and policy, which is again another 7%. Only four programs, or 3.5%, have courses in youth and violence. This is inadequate. This is unacceptable. Crimes, gangs, and drugs are growing problems which are consuming the fabric of this country, and psychology seems to fail to take notice. Every jail and every prison has either staff psychologists or consulting psychologists, and yet few doctoral programs have any training. Research needs to be done to explore what it is that the *shrinks* are doing in these institutions. Certainly most of them are unprepared and unqualified to deal with the criminal mentality. (Samenow, 2007)

Only 32 programs, or 28%, have courses in behavior therapy, which is one of the few therapeutic modalities that is built on a foundation of empirical evidence. Is it any wonder that the treatment efficacy rates with ADD/ADHD is 44% (NIH report, 1998), 20% with ODD (Flick, 2004), and about 0% with delinquents (Samenow, 2004)? Is it any wonder that the popular behavioral treatment approaches are poorly designed, that theoretically they should not work, and realistically they do not. (Stein, 2004)

Only 49 programs, or 43%, offer ethnic and minority issues courses. Do we give lip service to diversity? Are we going to remedy this situation, or are we going to continue to teach more sensation and perception courses?

The Boulder model (Wedding and Mengel, 2004) has been dominating training practices for over seventy years, which emphasizes the course content covered in the tables. It does not work. It is broken. It needs to be fixed. We need to recognize this as a fact. The matrix model of Snyder and Elliott (2005) perpetuates the same, old, same old. Close examination of the model seems to indicate that it is not very different than the Boulder model. This model also fails to focus on specific human problems. Is the problem that psychology professors stick to tradition because it is easier than doing the enormous work necessary to develop expertise in even one specific human problem? Is it that psychology professors stay fixed in their comfort zones rather than investing long hours, hard work, and even anxiety in order to develop expertise in specific problems? Is this attachment to old dogma the result of Festinger's (1977) *effort justification*, where they enormous effort and work that it took to make it through graduate school has locked psychologists into a mindset from which they cannot extricate themselves?

Medical schools are constantly updating what they teach. New findings must be incorporated into their course content. Medical professors must stay current. Why are psychology professors not doing the same? Clinical psychology, on the one hand, seems to aspire to the medical model, but on the other hand, it refuses to relinquish the old to make way for the new. There is a wealth of literature for almost all of the topics previously mentioned, and yet few clinical psychology students are doing required readings in most of the topics, and, of course, their professors, out of ignorance, laziness, or addiction to dogma, are not requiring such in-depth reading.

A look at one problem immediately makes it apparent how much the clinician needs to know. Child sexual abuse usually does not involve only the abuse itself. Abuse does not occur in a vacuum. The clinician needs to be familiar with all of the other potential problems surrounding such abuse (Sgori, 1982). Let us say, for pedagogical purposes, that the father is the abuser, which occurs in the majority of cases. What is the mother's role? What is the likelihood that she has always known it is going on? What help does *she* need? What about the abuser's control of the family? What about the secrecy that all members of the family must maintain? How does secrecy affect a child's peer relationships? What does an abused child do with precocious sexual knowledge? How does it affect a child's behavior in school? What effects accrue when human services, the police, and the courts intervene? Are there treatments for the abusers that are effective (No!)? What does the child experience if he/she reveals what has been going on? What role can the therapist play in helping the child deal with making revelations and possible guilt feelings for the breakup of the family? One can go on and on, but the point is obvious. In this problem alone, the therapist must have a vast amount of knowledge if he is to help all members of the family, and the sad part is that courses in this topic are mostly absent in the graduate training programs. Nay, instead, we waste precious time on invalid assessment courses, on endless statistics and research methodology courses, on theoretical falderal, on studying systems of treatment that do not work, and on courses that are mere repetitions of introductory psychology.

Recently, Stein (the author) introduced a proposal for a new course in his department for the *Psychology of Terrorism and Homeland Security*. It took two and one-half years of difficult and meticulous preparation to make ready for teaching the course. Countless hours were spent reading. Countless hours were spent reviewing media materials. The author had the good fortune of having police security clearance, and therefore could attend private government meetings on terrorism and homeland security. Wherever possible, he took courses at police training academies. Preparations were difficult and sometimes even painful. Staying current on the topic requires even more diligence. But this is what it will take for graduate professors to develop expertise in most of the human problem issues. Thus far, few seem willing to invest the time and energy in order to make the transition in modernizing graduate clinical training. It is so much easier to stay in the comfort zone and maintain tradition.

We will help humans with specific human problems when we begin learning what those problems are and what it takes to ameliorate them. It may turn out that even if course content is modernized into the twenty-first century that treatment efficacy rates will not improve, simply because humans stubbornly refuse to change, but this is an empirical question that will not be answered until psychology itself changes, We are not, as the introductory texts would have us believe, *scientific practitioners*. We can't seem to find what it is that we are. It is time that we start to better define the training and practice of clinical psychology. It is time for the APA to re-examine its traditional criteria for accreditation, consider requiring intensification of training in cognitive/behavioral methods for *all* human problems, and eliminate or streamline courses which are not essential for helping patients in emotional and relational distress. We must separate clinician training from academic research training. We must eliminate courses filled with material that is invalid and unreliable.

Tracks in Graduate Training

More and more graduate schools are offering specialty tracks, such as child treatment or forensics. However, the problem appears to be that the courses are still filled with the same old invalid and unreliable assessment courses. The treatment courses are still problematic because students are supervised by professors from a wide variety of theoretical perspectives, which only confuses students and is counterproductive for training only in scientifically-based treatment modalities. The track approach needs considerably more refining.

The next chapter will look at the evolution of court decisions on expert testimony that will slowly require major changes in the training of psychologists. That which is invalid and unreliable will no longer be permitted in the courts. That which is theoretical and lacking in empirical foundations will be barred from the courts. That which is based on years of practice and subjective opinions will be barred from the courts. The new decisions will permeate the court systems in the coming years, and psychology had better be prepared.

CHAPTER TWO

RECENT COURT RULINGS MAY BE TARGETING PSYCHOLOGY AND MAY BE THE DRIVING FORCE FOR REFORM

In this chapter, we will review a number of court decisions which have occurred just prior to and after the new millennia, ranging from district courts, the appellate courts, and all the way to the Supreme Court. These court decisions may force the psychology industry take a hard look at itself and realize that unless change occurs, psychology may embarrassingly be barred from participating in much of the legal process. This may prove to be painful, because many practicing psychologists have made a cottage industry from testifying in the courts, sometimes on insanity defenses, but also on mitigating circumstances, custody cases, psychic damage resulting from post traumatic stress, being crime victims, being abused as children, and so on, and so forth. Much is at stake for the psychology industry, and the discussion in this chapter is aimed at highlighting the ways in which the profession may be failing to adapt.

Psychiatry has been the more frequent target, because of its long history of simplistic and scandalous medically-based treatments, such as lobotomies, electric shock, insulin shock, a flawed commitment history, and powerful drugs, which have frequently been considered risky for contributing to a wide range of iatrogenically produced illnesses in patients (Breggin, 1991; Johnston, 2000; Whitaker, 2002; Valenstein, 1998). Extensive criticisms of psychiatry have already been written countless times, and, therefore, will not be repeated here. Psychology's weaknesses and why it is being targeted by court reform is the focus of this chapter.

Is Psychology the Science it Claims to Be?

Most introductory textbooks in psychology open with the cliché, "Psychology is the science of behavior and the mind," (Zimbardo, Weber, and Johnson, 2000). Perhaps when the literature is examined more closely, psychology may be a "science" in its animal experimental efforts, but it is far from being good science, or any science at all, when its efforts in the clinical arena are exposed. (Hagen, 1997; DeGrandpre, 1999A Brief History of Psychology

Psychology began as an academic exercise by Wundt in 1870 and James in 1875. Psychology wanted to begin its birth by being accepted as a science within the "other" scientific disciplines, such as chemistry, biology, and physics; it wanted to establish itself as a legitimate and accepted academic discipline (Lefton, 2000). In order to facilitate acceptance in the academic world, psychology borrowed concepts from other disciplines that were already establish as 'real' scientific subjects. The *Structuralists* borrowed from atomic theory, i.e., the structure of atoms; the *Functionalists* borrowed from Darwinian concepts, i.e., what functions for survival the senses play. The *Behaviorists* borrowed its methodology from all the already established sciences where objective observation was the only legitimate method for the new science of psychology and where verbal reports, i.e., introspection, had no place for a burgeoning science. Behaviorism sought to limit itself to the study of learning by measuring observable behaviors. (Lefton, 2000)

The clinical arm of psychology had a very different beginning. Some trace the beginnings of clinical psychology to Annie Sullivan, who some credit as initiating the first behavioral treatment when she worked with Helen Keller. The first scientific attempt at *treatment* is perhaps traced to one of J. B. Watson's students at John's Hopkins University, namely the counter conditioning method introduced by Mary Cover Jones (Kanfer and Phillips, 1970). Today, little reference is made of her work, and, in fact, much of what she did was reintroduced many years later by Joseph Wolpe, who coined the term '*systematic desensitization*' (Barlow and Durand, 2008). One cannot say for certain if Wolpe deliberately failed to give credit to Dr. Jones or if it was an oversight. However, the archives of Temple University, where Wolpe spent most of his career, seem to indicate that he used introductory psychology texts which cited Mary Cover Jones' work, and, therefore, he either made a glaring oversight or a deliberate obfuscation by not citing her work in many instances or minimizing her influence on his work. Further digression into this matter will only detract from the focus made here about the attempt to start the discipline of psychology as an accepted science.

Patient treatment during the early days, however, lay predominantly in the hands of psychiatry. No attempt will be made here to become embroiled in the heinous beginnings and even the current practices of psychiatry as a treatment arm of medicine. There are some outstanding books already on this topic, such as the prolific writings of Thomas Szasz (1961), the scathing books by Peter Breggin (1991), the writing of Lucy Johnstone (2000), and the most recent superb writings of journalist Robert Whitaker (2002). This chapter, as previously stated, is focused on the world of psychology.

Psychology seemed to enter the clinical arena in the 1930s and 1940s with the development of psychological tests, such as the *Rorschach Inkblot Test* and the *Thematic Apperception Test.* The weaknesses of these tests were discussed at length in the previous chapter. Thus, psychology entered the clinical arena as *handmaidens* to psychiatrists (Roback and Kierman, 1969). Psychiatrists who practiced treatment methods not biologically or medically based, i.e., the *talk therapies* also known as *psychosocial therapies* (Bregin, 1991) introduced by Freud, Jung, Adler, and other neo-Freudians, were sparsely utilized at first. Nevertheless, it was these forms of talk therapies that became popular and entrenched in both the European and American psychiatric communities (Roback and Kierman, 1969). It was at this time that psychologists proceeded to develop tests based on the concepts promoted by these forms of therapies. (Barlow and Durand, 2008)

It did not take long, as pointed out in the previous chapter, before these therapies came under scrutiny. When these methods were closely scrutinized scientifically, it became apparent that they did not work, and the tests that the psychologists developed around these theories were mere measures of hypothetical constructs, were found to be equally mercurial, and were found to be actually measuring nothing. (Mischel, 1996)

Sadly, naïve young college students are mistakenly being led to believe that the psychologist is a *scientific practitioner* (Lefton, 2000), and this belief continues even after the student completes doctoral training and enters the world of the clinician. (Hagen, 1997)

Matters became more intense in the late 1960s and throughout the 1970s when a series of events led to the growth of the psychology industry (Dineen, 2001; Hagen, 1997). Psychiatry began facing humiliating revelations in the news media when the horrors of psychiatric hospitals were exposed, making citizens afraid to go to psychiatrists (Breggin, 1991). It was then psychology doctoral programs began to proliferate. Psychologists began to be licensed to "treat" patients with the various talk therapies and were allowed to receive third-party insurance payments for their fifty-minute sessions. The American Psychological Association exploded to become larger than the American Psychiatric Association (Barlow and Durand, 2008). Psychology even confronted the psychiatrists by insisting that it participate in the development of the next diagnostic manual, which appeared in 1980 as the DSM-III, Diagnostic and Statistical Manual, 3rd edition.

Many psychologists acknowledged the poor treatment efficacy rates, but in the 1960s and 1970s, a furor burst forth that this flaw could be remedied by turning to the one approach that had some degree of scientific legitimacy, namely, the behavioral methods. Prior to this onslaught, Behavior Modification had been developed in only a few universities, such as Yale, Harvard, and the University of Chicago. However, in the 1960s and 1970s, it came into vogue. It enjoyed only a brief period of popularity, which has since subsided. It seemed that behaviorism offered some promise for some disorders, such as phobias and child misbehaviors, but it did not offer answers for too many of the other disorders. Behavioral treatment efficacy rates seemed to have declined since the 1970s, mostly because the behaviorists abandoned well-established principles and instead began popularizing methods that violated these principles, and, therefore, they theoretically should not work, and, in reality, they do not work (Stein, 2005). There are many behaviorists who deny this, but one need only look at the successes of Lovaas during the 1960s and 1970s with autism, which are now fading away, or the early successes in parenting with out of control children by Becker, Engelmann, and Thomas (1971) and Patterson (1971), successes that were properly designed but are now yielding to lower efficacy rates because of the prevailing *Zeitgeist* based on the shoddy treatment designs of Barkley (1995). The early promise of counter conditioning treatment successes with alcoholics and addicts are now proving to have been unfounded (Peele, 1996). However, cognitive therapies are proving to be valuable, but as previously pointed out, they are not finding their way into the clinical practices of psychologists.

An Avalanche of Criticism Is Emerging

An extensive list of books has appeared since the early 1990s exposing both psychology's and psychiatry's weaknesses. A few are listed here:

Breggin, P. (1991). *Toxic Psychiatry.* New York: St. Martin's Press.

Boyle, M. (2002). *Schizophrenia: A Scientific Delusion.* New York: Taylor and Francis.

Dawes, R. M. (1996). *House Of Cards: Psychology And Psychotherapy Built On Myth.* New York: The Free Press.

Dineen, T. (2001). *Manufacturing Victims: What The Psychology Industry Is Doing To People.* New York: Robert Davies Publishing.

Glasser, W. (2003). *Warning: Psychiatry Can Be Hazardous To Your Health.* New York: Harper Collins Publishers.

Hagen, M. A. (1997). *Whores Of The Court: The Fraud Of Psychiatric Testimony And The Rape Of American Justice.* New York: Regan Books.

Johnstone, L. (2000). *Users And Abusers Of Psychiatry: A Critical Look At Psychiatric Practice.* Philadelphia, PA: Taylor and Francis.

Joseph, J. (2003). *The Gene Illusion: Genetic Research In Psychiatry And Psychology Under The Microscope.* UK: PCCS Books.

Lorandos, D. & Cambell, T. (2005). *Benchbook In The Behavioral Sciences: Psychiatry –Psychology – Social Work.* Durham, NC: Carolina Academic Press..

Mischel, W. (1996). *Personality And Assessment.* Mahwah, NJ: Lawrence Erlbaum Associates.

Peele, S. (1995). *The Diseasing Of America: How We Allowed Recovery Zealots And The Treatment Industry To Convince Us We Are Out Of Control.* San Francisco, CA: Wiley, Jossey-Bass.

Valenstein, E. (1998). *Blaming The Brain: The Truth About Drugs And Mental Health. New York: Free Press.*

Whitaker, R. (2002). *Mad In America: Bad Science, Bad Medicine, And The Enduring Mistreatment Of The Mentally Ill.* Cambridge, MA: Perseus Publishing.

Wood, J., Nesworski, T., Lilienfield, S. & Garb, H. (2003). *What's Wrong With The Rorschach?* San Francisco, CA: Wiley, Jossey-Bass Publishers.

But, nothing seems to be changing in psychology. However, new rulings in the courts may precipitate or even force psychology to re-examine itself, or else psychologists will face the embarrassment of being barred from the courts. (Lorandos and Campbell, 2005)

Enter the Courts

Psychology is *not* adapting. It is failing to attend to its weaknesses. It seems to not even be aware that its weaknesses even exist. The sledge hammer for change may be coming from an unexpected direction, the courts.

A contradiction exists in psychology's relationship with the courts. On the one hand, very few doctoral programs offer any courses in forensic psychology (Stein, 2009). The few programs that offer any courses focus on administering "the same old, same old" tests, which again have neither validity nor reliability, and they are rendering diagnoses which also have no validity nor reliability (Lorandos and Campbell, 2005). Criminal Justice has been adopted across the country by Sociology Departments, while Psychology Departments seemed to have missed the importance of studying criminal behavior. Criminal Justice is now an "exploding" major in universities across the country, e.g., Virginia State University started with five majors in 2003 and expanded to six hundred majors by 2008. No adequate explanation seems to exist to explain psychology's oversight. Curiously, psychology seems to be evolving as a growing industry for use by the court systems (Dershowitz, 1994; Hagen 1997). Melton, Pertrila, Poythress, and Slobogin (1997) list the expanding uses of psychologists in the courts:

1. nine types of competency examinations, i.e., for different purposes;
2. six mental health defenses;
3. five types of sentencing evaluations;
4. eight civil commitment exams,
5. and eighteen "other" evaluations routinely requested the courts.

The obvious contradiction is that few psychologists have formal, or for that matter, adequate doctoral training in dealing with court issues, and yet they are increasingly making money as so-called "experts" in the court system.

Psychology and the Legal System

One can say that the insanity defense *has been driving the courts nuts*. Psychology has a long history of confusing the legal process by mixing the issues of culpability and responsibility during the fact-finding or substantive issues of trials with the issue of mental responsibility. Stated a bit differently, the facts of whether or not the defendant committed the crime, the guilt or innocence for the commission of the crime, is contaminated with the issue of the defendant's state of mind at the time of the crime, i.e., *Mens Rea.* (Wrightsman, Nietzel, and Fortune, 1994)

What is it that psychologist get into in the legal system? First is the *insanity defense.* The idea which involves psychologist is the issue of *free will.* Psychologist, it would seem, have a keen ability to know when the offender has lost his or her free will. This gets somewhat sticky, because no one has made clear where exactly the line of demarcation is. Insanity is a legal term that does not have a precise equivalent to any given psychological diagnosis. The word psychosis is a psychological term where a whole bunch of diagnoses may or may not qualify. Sometimes schizophrenia means psychosis, but sometimes it does not. Sometimes bipolar disorder means psychosis, but sometimes it does not. Sometimes delusional disorder means psychosis, but sometimes it does not. Oddly, rarely does dissociative disorder, or the multiple personality, mean psychosis, but most of the time it does not. Matters are made even more complicated when an offender may be judged psychotic by the psychologist but does not meet the criteria for being insane in the legal sense. So confusing is all of this that it has driven the legal system *nuts.*

The second thing that psychologists do is have a magical ability to convince the courts that the offender committed the crime(s) because of mitigating circumstances, such as being abused. The fact that most people who have been abused, even severely, never hurt anyone does not seem to matter to the psychologists. It is the psychologist who has to convince the court that this offender had special life experiences that excuse or exonerate him or her from culpability, and that he or she had the right to take the law into his or her own hands. Prominent Harvard law professor, Alan Dershowitz (1994) has written a book, *The Abuse Excuse,* expressing disdain for the role psychologists have been playing in the courts for getting offenders off with an emotional appeal to the judge or jury that the son of a bitch who was killed deserved it at the hands of the offender. The offender does not deserve to be punished because he or she had special circumstances to justify the violent revenge. Super attorney Jerry Spence (Communicated on FOX News, November 12, 2009) has frequently pointed out during his numerous media appearances that trials are not won by facts; they are won by emotion. The point taken here is that psychologists are muddling up trials with providing the very emotional appeals and excuses defense attorneys love. Please remember that the psychologists opinions on the state of mind of the offender are based mostly on years of clinical experience, as we shall see is usually extremely inaccurate, and by a battery of tests, which we have already well established have no validity and no reliability. Rarely is a psychologist's testimony based upon hard science (Lorandos and Cambell, 2005). We will discuss shortly whether or not psychologists have any business testifying during the substantive, or fact finding, stages of trials, because they have a long history of mucking up the trials by contaminating mental issues with the facts of guilt or innocence. In other words, they confuse the judges and the juries and make a mess of the legal system.

A Brief History of Criminal Cases

The landmark for the earliest recorded case appears to be 1794 for considering a defendant's mental state during a violent crime with the case of Edward Arnold. The defendant was found guilty, but the presiding judge commented that Arnold "did not know more than an infant, than a brute, or a wild beast."

In 1800, in the case of one James Hadfield, in England, he was found not guilty because he was insane. The verdict was predicated only on *the feelings of the jury.*

The year 1843 represents the first real insanity defense with the case of James McNaughton, also in England. He was believed to be acting on a delusion that the prime minister was plotting against him. He murdered the prime minister's secretary. Nine medical "experts", including an American psychiatrist, Isaac Ray, testified that he was insane. Their opinions prevailed. Queen Victoria was outraged and demanded a stricter interpretation of insanity, which prevails even to today in many states (Wrightsman, Nietzel, and Fortune, 1994). This case will be explored in more detail later in this chapter.

In 1954, the Durham Rule was introduced. Monte Durham had a long history of both crimes and mental hospitalizations. By this time, psychiatry had become an "accepted" branch of medicine and psychiatrists were permitted to testify. The presiding Judge Brazelton was himself outraged by the doctors' testimony and the trial outcome of Not Guilty by Reason Of Insanity. Now it appeared that doctors magically knew the criminal state of mind at the time of the crime, *Mens Rea (guilty mind),* and that all criminals were insane by mere repetition of crimes, known as the *products test.* Thus, if this ruling had stayed in effect, then all criminals would be found to have a mental illness simply by any history of repeatedly committing crimes. Anarchy would reign on the streets, and the prisons would be empty if this power remained with the psych-experts. (Wrightsman, Nietzel, and Fortune, 1994)

In 1972, Judge Brazelton was given an opportunity to redeem himself by disallowing the products test and by applying the American Law Institute's standards of appreciating the wrongfulness of his act, and by being unable to conform his behavior to the requirements of the law as a result of having a mental disease. This became known as the Brawner rule, which became very similar to the McNaughton rule.

However, in 1981, John Hinckley was found Not Guilty By Reason of Insanity after shooting President Reagan, Press Secretary Brady, and a Secret Service Agent. The country was outraged. Few people seem to be aware that Hinckley is now permitted weekends with his parents in Williamsburg, Virginia. After this trial, states sought to once again tighten the insanity defense. (Wrightsman, Nietzel, and Fortune, 1994)

The issue of psych-expert testimony was *not* only not resolved after Hinckley, but it has become worse. New issues of mitigating circumstances and a multitude of excuses are evolving which are leading to an increasing reliance on psych-experts in the courts and an increasing contamination of the fact-finding responsibility of trials with mental excuses. (Lorandos and Campbell, 2005)

These issues include *abuse excuses* (Dershowitz, 1994), mitigating circumstances (Dershowitz, 1994), and a renewed expansion of classifying emotional and behavioral problems as diseases and mental illnesses (Breggin and Cohen, 1999). Presently, the use of psych-experts has become a huge and growing cottage industry (Melton, et al, 1997). Now, as pointed out earlier, the use of psych-experts appears in a wide variety of court cases, way beyond the criminal arena, and once again these "experts" are confusing juries and judges by intermingling the issues of fact finding with mental state. (Lorandos and Campbell, 2005)

The Frye – Downing and Daubert Trilogy Evolution

The evolution of court standards has been aimed at all disciplines, e.g., forensics, blood spatter, DNA evidence, autopsy testimony, and so forth. The series of decisions requires that the highest standards of science be required for any and all expert testimony. Collectively, these decisions are known as *'The death of junk science'* (Lorandos and Campbell, 2005). Why? Anglo-Saxon law is devoted to the protection of the innocent:

> It is better that 5, 10, 20, or 100 guilty men go free than for one innocent man to be put to death. This principle is embodied in the presumption of innocence. In 1895, the U.S. Supreme Court, in a decision in the case Coffin v. United States, 156 U.S. 432; 15 S. Ct. 394, traced the presumption of innocence earlier than England, Ancient Greece, and Ancient Rome, and, at least, according to Greenleaf, to Deuteronomy. (www.CrimeLeft.com/The History of the Presumption of Innocence, p. 1)

Thus, expert testimony should not harm the innocent, but it is equally important that it should not aid the guilty by contaminating the substance or facts of the case or the minds of the jurors. Thus, as we previously noted, nothing in the history of jurist-prudence has contaminated the finding of fact more than the testimony of psych-experts (Lorandos and Campbell, 2005). Perhaps the best protection of the innocent is the accurate presentation of facts and that these facts are presented in such a manner that the average jury can clearly understand their meaning. (Lorandos and Campbell, 2005)

Presently, all federal courts in all states are required to impose the *Daubert Trilogy* standards for any and all expert testimony, and thirty-three states have adopted these standards for their state courts; the remaining seventeen states are using the *Frye – Downing* standards.

A Brief History of *Daubert* and *Frye* in the Courts

These new Supreme and Appellate Court standards under both rules require that any expert testimony:

1. be based on good quality scientific research;

2. that the expert is truly an expert in the area they are addressing in the trial by having a history of solid research in the area and that the research has been published by refereed journals, which means that they are monitored by other experts in the field;

3. that the testimony be presented in such a fashion that it can be readily understood by a jury of ordinary citizens.

4. The *Daubert Trilogy* adds two additional requirements: first, that the attorneys for either side of the trial that is introducing evidence will pre-submit the expert's testimony to the judge in the form of briefs, i.e., a *in limine brief* is submitted by the trial attorney, while an *amicus brief* can be submitted by an outside friend of the court attorney,

5. and, that the judge serve as the trial *gatekeeper*, having the responsibility to make certain that the pre-submitted materials fulfill the standards for scientific rigor and that testimony during the trial maintain the judge's approved standards.

The Frye – Downing Standard

The *Frye Standard* dates back to the invention of the polygraph in 1917 by William Moulton Marston, who was also the creator of the *Wonder Woman* comic strip. The use of the polygraph in the courts was tested in 1923 in *Frye v. United States*. James Frye was being heard for an appeal from a lower court decision of murder when he used the polygraph to support his claim of innocence. Research was introduced that the polygraph could be manipulated. The result was that the polygraph did not meet the requisite standard for scientific accuracy within the court system, and, thus, the bar was raised for admittance of scientific expert testimony, i.e., the testimony of a polygraph expert.

It was not until 1985 that standards for experts started to seriously escalate. In the *United State v. Downing,* Downing was accused of mail fraud. Twelve eyewitnesses testified against him. The defense attorney wanted to introduce an expert psychologist on the lack of validity and reliability of eye witnesses. The lower court rejected the expert's testimony on the grounds that the jury had sufficient tools to assess their testimony and the expert would not serve the purpose of *helpfulness,* and that the expert would only usurp the function of the jury, and cross examination would be all that was necessary. However, the Appellate Court overturned the lower court and found that the expert did qualify as an expert and that his testimony would *help* the jury who are not typically versed on the science of eyewitness validity and reliability. It should be noted that this type of research can compare eyewitness statements to the outcomes of trials, which can serve as a fairly concrete and reliable data source. In other words, it is pretty decent science. Thus, correlations could be made between the eyewitnesses and the hard proof from the trial outcome of what actually occurred. Most *clinical research* does not rise to a standard for such solid comparisons.

The Daubert Trilogy

The *Daubert* standards began to be established by a series of court decisions beginning with *Daubert v. Merrell Dow Pharmaceuticals,* 509 U S 579, 113 S Ct 2786 (1993). Joyce Daubert had borne a child with a deformed limb after taking Merrell Dow's morning sickness drug Benedectin. The main elements of law that emerged from this case include:

> "in order to qualify as 'scientific knowledge', an inference or assertion must be derived by the scientific method."
>
> This is interpreted to mean that the foundations of expert assertions are based on either controlled research or correlation research that has a foundation of a connection with a well established, verifiable, and valid phenomenon, similar to the earlier *Downing* criteria.
>
> "scientific knowledge that will assist the trier of fact will be whether it can be [and has been] tested."

A second component of the *Daubert Trilogy* seems to be aimed at psychiatry and psychology where the courts make a statement against the abuses of *junk science.* Indeed, psychiatry and psychology have long been a thorn in the side of the courts by proffering testimony supported by the psych community but which does not fly in the face of good sense. (Lorandos and Campbell, 2005)

General Electric v. Joiner, 864F. Supp. 1310 – 1314 (N.D. Ga. 1994).

> 1) Robert Joiner and his wife sought damages for his lung cancer that was allegedly caused by on-the-job exposure to biphenyls (PCPs).
>
> 2) The eleventh circuit emphasized that the judge's role is to assure that an experts' opinions are based on relevant scientific methods, processes, and data, and not on mere speculation, and that they apply to the facts at issue.
>
> 3) This strengthens *Daubert* and is known as the "tombstone for junk science" in the courtroom.

This part of the trilogy is whether or not the expert's testimony will be *helpful* to the jury or the judge, or whether it would only serve to confuse the facts of the case. It seems that if one reviews the history of psych-expert testimony that often the lawyers, the judges, and just about everyone seems to be baffled by what psych-experts' proffer, but often they seem embarrassed to admit this. The *tested* part generally means whether or not the research upon which the expert relies is verifiable by other scientists. In the *junk science* of psychology (DeGrandpre, 1999), considerable verification comes only from other researchers who are in a state of financial conflict, such as having allegiances to pharmaceutical companies. Verification must be made by independent scientists of good reputation with a strong commitment to the ethics of research.

One of the most difficult obstacles that psych-experts face is that the testimony they present must not only be based on science, but it must be accepted by the psychological community. However, since psychology is inundated with junk science, then testimony accepted by the community may not prove sufficient for the courts (Lorandos and Campbell, 2005). The possible solution for circumventing this problem lies in *replication* of relevant studies by researchers whose work is clearly not tainted by loyalties to potential contaminating organizations, such as the pharmaceutical companies. This problem has not yet been resolved, and it will remain an issue for the courts to resolve when challenges to specific testimony occur and when the courts render opinions.

The third component is the courts' requirement that the scientific evidence being proffered is directly relevant to the case before the court. Generalist meanderings will no longer succeed in the courts.

Kumho Tire Company, Ltd. v. Carmichael, 526 U S 137; 119 S. Ct. 1167 – 1171.

1. Carmichael was claiming that a flaw in the tire's design caused a fatal car accident.
2. It was found that the so-called tire expert insufficiently connected his findings to the specific case.
    a. The Court must determine both the validity of the expert's qualifications and the reliability of the testimony, i.e., is it based on real science and is it specifically relevant to the case?

Roadblocks

Problems emerge in psych-expert testimony more than in any other field. Psych-experts have long relied on *years of experience* in order to qualify as expert witnesses, such as a psychologist who has worked in the prison system for many years believing that he has the expertise to testify in criminal trials. Research clearly shows that years of experience for psych-experts do not improve the standards of their testimony (Lorandos and Campbell, 2005), and also reliance of anecdotal experiences to support testimony is extremely inaccurate and unscientific. (Mischel, 1996)

Unfortunately, there is a bigger problem in the arena of psych-expert testimony. Clinical and counseling psychology research literature is overwhelmingly overloaded with *junk science* (Hagen, 1997). Researchers and/or professors of psychology and psychiatry may have long illustrative careers where they have numerous refereed published studies, may have risen to high ranks, such as full professor, even at prestigious universities, may have served as editors or associate editors of several professional journals, and may have been voted as leaders in several professional organizations, all of which may be predicated on a career of doing nothing but *junk science.*

How Psychology and Psychiatry have become Permeated with Junk Science

There are over three to four hundred journals in psychology and psychiatry. These journals are a business, meaning that they must operate at a profit, professors want promotions and increased salaries; researchers often seek the prestige and financial rewards of being speakers and presenters; lucrative consultant positions can be enticing; serving on the boards of pharmaceutical companies can offer powerful financial rewards as well as access to luxurious vacation condominiums, and gaining a position, especially psychology and psychiatry academic appointments, may require that the applicant bring with her large research grants. The combination of seduction by appointments and money, blind ambition, indifference to ethics, and a profession where clear definitions are often lacking and concepts are often obscure, have paved the way for psych-experts confusing the courts. The latest set of rulings have not as yet permeated the courts because of the lack of training of lawyers and judges, but this is changing, and as the courts modernize less and less, shrinks will be permitted to make *definitive statements based on dubious data.* (Stein, 2007)

Psychology Misses a Vital Chance – The Oversight of Criminal Justice

Criminal Justice is exploding as an academic discipline. However, its adoption is within Sociology (Schmalleger, 2006). Psychology has offered little in the study of criminals, penology, and even criminal profiling (Lorandos and Campbell, 2005). Instead, as pointed out earlier, psychology has interfered with the legal system, making a mockery of the insanity defense and confusing trials with a barrage of mitigating circumstances (Dershowitz, 1994), which, in turn, has forced the courts to make "an end run" around psychology by elevating the criteria for admitting all expert testimony, with the hidden agenda being to almost completely exclude psychological testimony from the courts (Lorandos and Campbell, 2005). Psychologists have traditionally proffered testimony based on tests that have no validity (Hagen, 1997), and with only a couple of nebulous, overly-broad, and sweeping diagnoses, i.e., antisocial personality disorder, borderline personality disorder, and delusional disorder, which offer little or no insight into the full workings of the criminal mind (Hagen, 1997; Lorandos and Campbell, 2005). Law enforcement had to take it upon itself to develop better insights into the criminal mind. (Douglas, Burgess, Burgess, and Ressler, 1992)

Perhaps it is for the best that psychology has been mostly remiss in its attention to criminal justice. If it had adopted the discipline then, this too would be open fodder for the pseudoscience of the psychology industry (Lilienfeld, Lynn, and Lohr, 2003). The embarrassment of the 1954 *Durham Rule* might still dominate the courts, curtailing the recent court decisions that almost exclude psychological testimony. This exclusion has not yet taken place, because only 4% of judges and very few trials attorneys are well trained in the new standards (Lorandos and Campbell, 2005), but, nevertheless, this exclusion is coming at psychology like a speeding train. In addition, with psychology accepting the extremely bad science of mental diseases, every criminal act would be a disease and almost all criminals would be exculpated from responsibilities for their actions, and the embarrassing *products test* excluded by Judge Brazelton in 1979 might still be in effect. (Wrightsman, Nietzel, and Fortune, 1994)

Forensic psychology still consists of testing, testing, and more testing, none of which are valid or reliable (Dawes, 1996; Hagen, 1997). Worse is the fact that the tests are aimed at diagnosing according to the DSM, which as stated earlier is also filled with inaccurate and unreliable diagnoses, ergo, we have a system of invalid and unreliable tests matching invalid and unreliable diagnoses. No test has as yet been developed to match the classification system used by the FBI's Crime Classification System (Douglas, Burgess, Burgess, and Ressler, 1997). Sociology, instead, focuses on the complex social circumstances that mold criminals and rejects the simplistic biomedical model of criminal behavior (Schmalleger, 2006). Thus, psychology's oversight seems to be a blessing in disguise.

A Better Definition of Insanity

The inconsistencies with the insanity defense are outrageous. Why was Andrea Yates, after killing her five children, found not guilty by reason of insanity, but Susan Smith, who killed her two children, was found guilty? Why was John Hinckley found not guilty by reason of insanity, while serial killer and cannibalist Jeffrey Dahmer was found guilty? Why were the testimonies of seven different psych-experts in the Dahmer trial so completely divergent and inconsistent? Why was David Berkowitz diagnosed by several psych-experts as paranoid schizophrenic, when in recent years, he has admitted that he faked his symptoms? Why was one of the most prolific serial killers ever known, Ed Gein, found not guilty by reason of insanity, while Mark David Chapman, who killed only one person, John Lennon, was found guilty? One could go on and on about the absence of consistency for psychological standards on insanity and for the testimonies of psych-experts in trials, but the main idea is quite simple, which is that no one seems to know what they are doing! This includes the shrinks, the judges, and the lawyers, who are all dependent upon the testimony of the shrinks.

As discussed earlier, the term 'insanity' is a legal term, while the term 'psychotic' is a loosely defined psychiatric term. The courts are guided by a variety of precedents for the insanity defense, and, therefore, the criteria will vary from state to state, where some adhere to the McNaughton standards, some to the Brawner, or even to the ALI standards, but the main components include the following:

1. The suspect must have a diagnosable psychiatric condition.

2. The suspect must have an irresistible impulse that he or she could not control.

3. The judgment of the suspect must be so markedly impaired that he or she cannot tell the difference between right and wrong, or stated another way, that he or she could not *appreciate* the wrongfulness of his or her action. (Wrightsman, Neitzel, and Fortune, 1994)

Two issues are interfering with precisely clarifying when insanity and psychosis mean the same thing, i.e., when is a defendant to be held not guilty by reason of insanity? The first issue involves which specific diagnosis in psychology would equate to insanity in the law. The second issue involves better understanding of a symptom called *delusion.*

The solution to this dilemma lies in the FBI's work on criminal profiling. The FBI considers all serial killers, rapists, arsonists, etc. as being mentally ill, but only one type would fit the legal description of insane, namely, the disorganized serial killer, rapist, or arsonist. In the interest of brevity, we will focus on the serial killer.

The disorganized killer is so completely decomposed and malfunctioning that he cannot plan his attack; he cannot cover the evidence he leaves, and, in fact, he makes no attempt to hide any evidence; he cannot plan to bring his implements of death to the crime scene, and, therefore, with no forethought or planning, he uses whatever is available at the crime scene; he does not function well enough to try to hide or distort the crime scene in order to protect his identity, which is known as 'staging'; his act is one of impulse; he has no cogent identity for a possible victim, but instead attacks an immediate target of opportunity. His inability to function carries over to his private life, where his home is messy, his clothing unkempt, his hygiene poor, where he cannot work at a skilled job, and his car is also dirty and unkempt. If he is caught, he will be difficult to interview because his thoughts are so illogical that he is likely to babble a string of unintelligible epithets. In other words, his global functioning is totally impaired. (Holmes and Holmes, 2002)

If we explore the psychology classification system, then only one diagnosis fits these criteria, namely, schizophrenia. If accurately diagnosed, the schizophrenic has a host of symptoms that equate to the disorganized killer. He has hallucinations where he senses stimuli that are not present, and sometimes, especially in acute case, these hallucinations terrify him. The most common hallucinations are auditory and visual, but others can be present. He has illusions, which are distortions of perception, where stimuli are present but become distorted when the brain tries to interpret them. Again, the auditory and visual delusions are most common. He has illogical thoughts, which prevent him from coherent planning, preparation, and forethought, i.e., the hallmark of the disorganized killer. He may have delusions, which are false beliefs that he will act upon and for which a logical argument will not get him to abandon his beliefs. He cannot control his behaviors, which can take on a variety of forms. He may demonstrate rapid speech, which when coupled with illogical thought represents incoherence. (Barlow and Durand, 2008)

When these two disparate diagnoses are examined side by side, they match, with the legal side being insane, and with the psychological side being the psychotic disorder of schizophrenia.

It is important to note that the terms 'psychosis' and 'insanity' do not match that of the organized killer. A good case in point is where, for example, postpartum depression with psychotic features only has some of the symptoms, such as hallucinations and delusions, but logical thought is still intact, illusions are not typically reported, speech is intelligible, behavior is controlled, and speech may be slow and measured. Delusions may be present, but so what! A delusion may cause an irresistible impulse to kill, if the content is violent, but if the killing is organized, then planning went into it, preparations were made to do the killing, and the organization reflects a desire to hide the crime. The individual may admit the crime, but he is sufficiently in control to plan and hide the crime so that he may complete the act, which is a telltale giveaway that he knows the crime is wrong. *In other words, he knows right from wrong.*

Andrea Yates received this diagnosis, and yet her crime was highly organized. She was sufficiently in touch with reality to prepare for the crime, wait for her husband to leave for work, and then, in a highly organized fashion, she systematically killed her five children. She hid her intentions because she knew it was wrong. She may have had an irresistible impulse, but she knew that what she was doing was wrong. After the killings, she called her husband to come home, and then she called the police, clearly indicating that she knew she had done something that was terribly wrong. Is it possible that her call to her husband was the result of anger and revenge? She was a nonassertive and highly compliant woman with little or no backbone to stand up to her droning husband. Her husband, Rusty, was not abusive in the typical sense of abuse, but the news media present him as the type of person who would drone on and on, relentlessly, until he got his way, which was to make her stay at home and cope with five children. He loved his kids, and Andrea knew this. Is it possible that she planned this crime as an act of revenge to destroy what he loved the most? Was Andrea crazy or cunning? Many writers point out that she may be in a mental institution for the rest of her life. This writer never thought that John Hinckley, who got bullets into the body of the President of the United States, the Press Secretary, and a Secret Service agent, would ever walk the streets, but now he goes home to Williamsburg, Virginia for weekend visits with his parents. In other words, there is a good chance that Ms. Yates will also one day be free, because legally she is not guilty.

The diagnosis of postpartum depression with psychotic features may be accurate for Andrea Yates, but does it truly fit the limited and restricted criteria proposed here for insanity? No! Does this diagnosis fulfill the criteria that match a disorganized killer that law enforcement views as truly insane. No! If Hinckley is free to leave the hospital, what reason is there to keep Ms. Yates?

What about bipolar disorder as qualifying for the insanity defense. After the previous discussion about Andrea Yates, the depressive phase of a bipolar cycle would not qualify. What about the manic phase? Hyper behavior is present; hallucinations are sometimes present; illusions are sometimes present; flight of ideas or rapid speech is common, and delusions may be present. Mania is referred to as a high or a feeling of euphoria (Barlow and Durand, 2008). The patient if filled with pleasure and is not likely to kill anyone. However, most notable is the fact that the manic's behavior, although agitated, is organized. They can function sufficiently enough to go on a shopping spree, count money, wait for change, clean the house, and so forth. In other words, they are sufficiently in touch with reality to know what they are doing. On rare occasions, the bipolar person may have a short period of irritability, which occurs at the end stages of the manic phase. During this brief time, the defense of insanity may be applicable because the symptoms are almost identical to acute schizophrenia. It is during this brief period that the person's functioning is totally impaired and would reflect a disorganized crime scene. If observed only during this phase, a psychologist could not distinguish the symptoms of the irritable phase of mania from paranoid schizophrenia. Thus, the argument of disorganization for legal insanity still applies. One could view the brief stage of the manic phase as a transitory period of schizophrenia, and, therefore, they may qualify for not guilty by reason of insanity only if a murder is committed during this brief time window.

Delusional disorder is perhaps the most frequent thorn within the courts for the insanity defense. This disorder is marked by one primary symptom, namely, delusion. *This is the one diagnosis that has disrupted the courts perhaps more than any other and is the most controversial in the insanity defense.* This is the diagnosis that ticks off prosecuting attorneys, delights defense attorneys, confuses juries and judges, and creates a huge cottage industry for the shrinks. This is the diagnosis that wreaks havoc on the insanity defense. The delusional individual may have some bizarre social behaviors and may be a recluse, but this does not in the least qualify for the insanity defense. Often, they function well and fit in with regular society. They may fit the irresistible impulse criteria, but they do know right from wrong, which is clearly reflected in the crime scene. If they commit a murder as a consequence of a delusion with violent composition, it would not, and should not, qualify for the insanity defense.

The delusional disorder individual would most likely commit a highly organized crime, reflecting enough deceit and clandestine behavior as to hide their intentions in an effort to not get caught, i.e., knowing right from wrong. If they commit a crime, or killing, and the crime scene is organized, then the insanity defense must not be allowed to prevail. Their thoughts are logical; there are no hallucinations; there are no illusions; speech is not rapid, and behavior is controlled and measured. It is the job of the judge to act as gatekeeper and prevent any psych-expert from bamboozling the jury with hocus-pocus about delusional disorder equating to the legal defense of insanity. It does not even come close, but so convincing can be the psych-experts that the insanity defense could mistakenly prevail; that is, if it gets past the judge in the first place. If a psychologist-profiler, namely the author, thinks about it, almost every serial killer, rapist, arsonist, and whatever, would fit the criteria for delusional disorder.

Is Profiling Admissible?

Profiling and polygraphs are not admissible in the courts. However, whether a crime scene is organized or disorganized is a matter of forensic science and therefore is admissible. Whether or not the organization of the crime reflects insanity crosses the line into inadmissibility, because the interpretation is then profiling. However, it is not specific profiling. No specific criminal typology or personality is being proffered. It is hoped that the courts will allow testimony on the relationship of organization and disorganization of a crime scene as reflecting the issue of insanity into the courts. Extreme disorganization of a crime is most likely in a state of schizophrenia, which is then psychological diagnosis and should therefore be admitted into the trial. In other words, it is not a profile that is being proffered in the courts but rather the connection is being made of crime scene behaviors with a psychological diagnosis. This will help bridge the huge and obvious gap between the legal definition of insanity and the psychological definition of psychosis, and whether or not one is not guilty by reason of insanity. All the confusion and obfuscation in trying to admit all types of disorders and diagnoses as justification for the insanity defense will disappear, leaving only true, severe episodes of schizophrenia and the possible last stages of mania, which is viewed as a brief period of schizophrenia, as qualifying for insanity in the courts. All other diagnoses would therefore not qualify for the insanity defense! Thus, much of the mysticism that has enshrouded the insanity defense will evaporate, and much of the confusing testimony of psychologists will be limited to far better defined parameters. It is time for this to happen.

Thus, it is the schizophrenic and only the schizophrenic, during a full episode that fulfills *all* the criteria for the defense of Not Guilty by Reason of Insanity. All other diagnoses, even with some psychotic features, are able to perform organized crimes indicating that they are enough in touch with reality to know right from wrong. They may be diagnosed with a psychiatric condition and they may have an irresistible impulse, but they do not fulfill the criteria for not knowing right from wrong. Case closed!

A great deal more will be discussed about the mystery that surrounds delusions in Chapter Seven, when we explore a phenomenon called cognitive diversion. In the next chapter, we explore the issue of accuracy and meaningfulness of psychiatric diagnoses.

CHAPTER THREE

UNRAVELING THE DIAGNOSIS FIASCO: THE WHOLESALE MANUFACTURING OF MENTAL DISEASES AND A CONFUSING AND CHAOTIC DIAGNOSTIC SYSTEM

Psychiatric/psychological diagnosis is not the same as medical diagnosis. This is a fact that not only eludes the public but the psychiatric/psychological community as well. Psychiatric diagnoses are in a state of utter confusion. This chapter is aimed at pointing out where the confusion lies and what may help unravel the confusion.

The *American Heritage Dictionary* (2000) defines diagnosis as, "The act or process of identifying or determining the nature and cause of a *disease* [italics added] or injury through evaluation of patient history, examination, and review of laboratory data," (p. 500). In medicine, the majority of diagnoses are made after a review of "hard data". The physician makes his/her diagnostic conclusion based on blood tests, urinalysis, X-rays, MRIs, PET Scans, CT scans, microscopic observations, physical exams, and so forth. There are a few instances where a diagnosis is made in the absence of hard data. Examples might be CFIDs, Chronic Fatigue Immune Disorder, or, perhaps, lower back pain. However, such diagnoses are exceptions, and for the vast majority of medical diagnoses, some type of hard evidence is available that, indeed, a disease is present. This is not the situation in psychiatry/psychology, where diagnoses are usually made based, not on hard data, but more on "highfalutin", twisted, contorted, fancy, and obfuscated vernacular (Smail, 1998), which John Rosemond (2001) has often called "psychobabble".

The confusion in psychiatric/psychological diagnosis lies in the fact that its diagnostic system weaves in and out of real diseases, with the vast majority of diagnoses being factitious (Lorandos and Campbell, 2005). This means that diagnoses are not diseases, but merely convenient labels that are descriptors of clusters of behaviors. The official diagnostic manual for psychiatry/psychology is called the DSM-IV, TR, Diagnostic and Statistical Manual Revised, fourth edition, revised. There are hundreds of diagnoses in the DSM-IV, TR, but only for a very few does hard data and real clinical tests exist to prove that they are diseases; these include most forms of mental retardation, dementias, Alzheimer's, and brain damage *resulting* from trauma or chronic use of drugs or alcohol. Alcohol and drug abuse are not primary causes or diseases, i.e., where they are a consequence of anatomical anomalies or chemical imbalances as the causes the abuse of drugs (Peele, 1995). Thus, having a few legitimate disease diagnoses seems to open the floodgates where all diagnoses are increasingly being considered diseases. Even the use of the term '*diagnosis*' and '*symptoms*' illegitimately *connotes* the existence of a disease. This is known as '*reification*' (Stein, 2005) where the mere *labeling* of behaviors evolves into declaring it as real.

Only hard laboratory evidence should be available in order to support the presence of a real disease. The correct terms instead of 'symptom' in psychiatry/psychology should be restricted to *labels* used as convenient descriptors of *behaviors or behavior patterns*. That is the crucial point, because hard laboratory evidence does not exist for the overwhelming majority of psychiatric/psychological diagnoses. Even the term 'disorder' has become misleading, because it has also come to connote disease, when, in fact, it too is merely a convenient label used for the purpose of communication.

There is presently a propaganda campaign orchestrated by the pharmaceutical companies to convince the lay and professional communities that disease data does exist, when, in fact, it does not (Baughman, 2006). Real medicine, as distinguished from psychiatry and psychology, is sadly beginning to accept the massive volume of bad research that is being factory line and mass-produced throughout the psychiatric and psychological journals. DeGrandpre (1999) calls it "junk science," while Stein (2001, 2004) calls it "unethical science". It seems that the overwhelming *volume* of bogus research is succeeding in replacing fact in psychiatry and psychology. However, the confusion is proving to be contagious, because physicians, psychiatrists, and psychologists are, unfortunately, accepting this volume of junk science as gospel (Stein, 2004). The pharmaceutical companies would love to get everyone to believe that psychiatric/psychological diagnoses, disorders, and symptoms are synonymous with the term disease because it sells pills, i.e., lots of pills. It is essential to explore how this campaign is being waged.

Why the Concern?

Why is the issue of diagnosis of such concern? In medicine, diagnosis usually sets the stage for medical interventions, usually involving medication or surgery, i.e., a physical problem is corrected by physical intervention. Medications and surgeries are intended to heal, to exorcise, to remove, to eliminate, to correct, or to control the clearly identified disease entity. In psychiatry/ psychology, this is not the case. Viewing psychiatric/psychological diagnoses as diseases often leads to risky and dangerous treatments. If diagnosis were to lead to relatively safe procedures, such as psychosocial interventions or talk therapies, then there would be little need for concern. However, this is not the case. Psychiatry is the "bad boy" of medicine and has had a most questionable and dubious history, where the treatments are often more insane than the patients. Medical psychiatry has a long history of abuses that include such things as cutting brain tissue, called lobotomies, placing patients at great risk with insulin shock, damaging brain tissue with electric shock, tormenting patients into submissive behavior with prolonged immersions in ice baths, and more recently has led to the staggering escalation of prescribing toxic psychiatric drugs, which are especially dangerous in the developing bodies and brains of children. (Breggin, 1991; Valenstein, 1998)

Psychology, distinguishing it from psychiatry, has had a relatively less innocuous history. It tried to develop more safe talking techniques (Smail, 1998), or behavioral correction techniques (Barlow and Durrand, 2008), but sadly, psychologists, probably wanting recognition as "real doctors", are now fighting, state by state, for the power to write psychiatric drug prescriptions, and are increasingly accepting medication as an answer for behavioral and emotional problems (Stein, 2004). At one time, during the 1960s and 1970s, psychologists even fought the use of any diagnoses, viewing them as being nothing more than simplistic descriptors for complex mind and behavioral issues (Kanfer and Phillips, 1970), but today, they are increasingly accepting diagnoses as real diseases, and, therefore, as sacrosanct.

The reality is that for the issue of diagnosis, psychologists, physicians, educators, and the public are "being had" by powerful and nefarious forces orchestrating a campaign to make psychiatric/psychological diagnoses as real, and medicines as the logical solution for all that ails us (Baughman, 2006). Nowhere is this issue more crucial than when the well-being of our children is at stake.

A Brief History of Psychiatric/Psychological Diagnosis

The disease concept of abnormal behavior can be traced to the ancient Greeks, germinating from the beliefs of the father of medicine Hypocrites (460-357 B.C.E.). This was only conjecture with no basis in any known facts. A pedantic debate ensued that has lasted for thousands of years, even extending to today, when still no proof exists.

The more modern controversy can be traced to three threads. The first thread is attributed to physician Emil Kraeplin (1898; 1899) who, at the turn of the twentieth century, introduced the first comprehensive psychiatric diagnostic system. We can immediately see Kraeplin's weaknesses in logic. It had been observed that patients in the third stage of syphilis behaved insanely. Kraeplin, adopting the new and popular germ theories of Louis Pasteur, assumed that the same bacteria caused this insanity. He extrapolated, without any merit or justification, that all mental disorders had some type of disease or medical basis. At that time, treatment of the insane was the exclusive domain of physicians. Psychology was emerging as a strictly academic discipline, and treating patients was not, as yet, a consideration. The syphilis theory was soon completely disproved, but that did not deter psychiatry from equating diagnosis with medical causesA second twist developed during the 1930s and 1940s when deliberate campaigns emerged to convince the public and professional communities that alcoholism was a disease. The two founders of Alcoholics Anonymous, known as Bob and Bill, in the 1930s, simply declared alcoholism a disease, perhaps because one of them was a physician, and/or perhaps to alleviate out of control drunks from responsibility for their behaviors. It seems that no one knows for certain their motives. A second disease movement for alcoholism can be traced to a group of Yale psychiatrists who formed a public relations organization called the National Council on Alcoholism, NCA, to "convince Americans that alcoholism is a diseased and the alcoholic is a sick person who needs help and treatment," (Peele, 1995, p. 45). Even though there was not a shred of proof for this declaration, the campaign has been so successful that today ninety percent of the public believes that alcoholism is a disease (Peele, 1995). No science should rest on conjecture. In proper science, real research is essential to support claims. Unsupported claims are the domain of philosophy and do not belong as stated "fact" in any science.

The third part of the disease argument evolved around attempts to understand the behavior of children who were inattentive and highly misbehaving. No one dared suggest that inept parenting might be the cause; instead, disease was again used to explain inappropriate behaviors. A physician, George Still, in 1902, was the first to publicly state that children who behaved in such a manor were diseased. Once again, a declaration was made without scientific evidence. Notice that it was physicians who were making all these disease claims; perhaps it was because physicians were trained to see things from a medical perspective, or perhaps there was an underlying desire to avoid permitting any other social agencies from treating abnormal behaviors and instead to keep such responsibility within the domain of medicine.

The fire was further fueled in 1923 when an encephalitis epidemic left numerous children with this same pattern of inattentiveness and hyperactive behavior. Again, there was the leap of logic made by physician F. G. Ebaugh that the encephalitis virus was responsible. The falsehood of this type of logic was demonstrated in the eighteenth century by mathematician L. Euler who developed what are known as Venn diagrams. This is known as making a *universal affirmation,* which is true, but the converse is not true. An example might be:

All Hawaiians are good swimmers. However, the converse of this is not necessarily true that all good swimmers are Hawaiians.

Look at the Venn diagram below:

Figure 3.1 Example of Logic

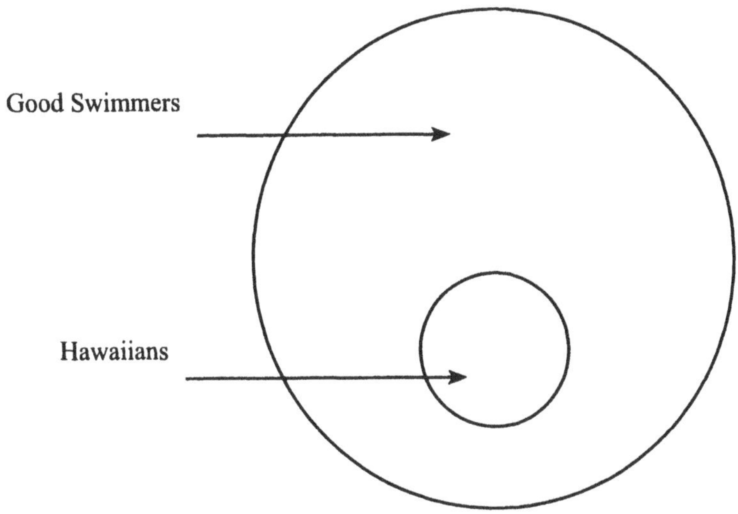

Thus, the logic that all kids who have encephalitis become inattentive and hyperactive is not accurate the other way around, that all kids who are inattentive and hyperactive have encephalitis.

It is this poor use of logic which has helped make much of diagnosis into psychobabble. The problem is that the public and many mental health professionals accept this false logic as true and acceptable. No science can properly develop with such poor use of logic and language. In science, we must endeavor to be precise and accurate, but, sadly, this has not been the case in the history of psychological/psychiatric diagnosis.

The next major goof in logic had, and to some degree still has, a major influence in the development of the disease theory of psychological/psychiatric diagnosis. In 1937, Dr. Charles Bradley noticed that stimulant drugs seemed to subdue the behavior of highly active and inattentive children. He called this a paradoxical effect and claimed that this was proof of inattentiveness and hyperactivity as being medical conditions, more specifically, that the effectiveness of the drugs served as proof that there is a chemical imbalance that is being corrected. Even some professionals still accept this incorrect use of logic. Research clearly shows that stimulant drugs produce the same effect on almost everybody, adults or children. The falsehood of this logic can be easily demonstrated. If one drinks whiskey, which is a sedative, and he rapidly feels calm, does this mean that he has a disease that causes anxiety? In the science of drugs, this type of logic is completely unacceptable. Two leading pharmacologists have given this type of illogic different names; Baldessarini (1985) calls it allopathic logic, while Valenstein (1998) calls it ex juvantibus. Despite the contradictory research and the use of illogic, there are still some professionals, and an even larger number of the public, who buy into this type of babble as being proof of diseases in psychology/psychiatry.

In 1947, Strauss and Lehtinen proposed the idea that the cause of inattention and hyperactivity in children was Minimal Brain Damage, MBD. However, so minimal is this so-called brain damage that even with sophisticated modern medical machines, no one can find it. This has not stopped dozens of researchers from claiming that they have found this damage, and even though every one of these studies has been refuted, the sheer volume of these studies, numbering in the hundreds, is succeeding in winning converts to the disease theories. More will shortly be said about this issue.

In 1968, the American Psychiatric Association arbitrarily decided in the then newer diagnostic manual, the DSM-III, to call active and inattentive children hyperkinesis, which means excessive movement. The term sounded like a scientific disease, and, therefore, it stuck for a while. But that was all there was to it. Once again a term merely had the connotation of disease, and that was satisfactory for the psychiatric community. These were physicians in search of patients, and mystifying, scientific sounding terms helped their cause.

The Diagnosis Wars Escalates: The 1960s to the 1990s

During the 1960s and 1970s, the separate worlds of psychiatry and psychology turned upside down, and conflict arose between the separate disciplines, over treatment methods and especially over diagnosis.

In the 1970s, psychiatry almost disappeared as a practicing profession and as a discipline within medicine (Breggin, 1991). Revelations of patient mistreatment at the hands of psychiatry began to be made public. Books and movies began to appear exposing the abuses of psychiatry. University professors made these books required readings and began showing exposé movies about conditions in psychiatric hospitals in their classes. Students were outraged at what, for many years, had been kept hidden from the public. The public also began to become aware of what had been going on. Revelations poured forth about patients being hospitalized by psychiatrists, against their will, for an average of thirteen years, and sometimes for life (Breggin, 1991; Whitaker, 2002). Records indicated that patients frequently saw a psychiatrist an average of one time during their incarceration. Incarceration was often based on unsubstantiated diagnoses of mental illness, and with the signature of only one psychiatrist, people disappeared into the bowels of these hospital hell holes.

Hell holes or snake pits became common vernacular, because that is exactly what conditions were like in these so-called *hospitals*. The outside or exterior of these places often looked like college campuses, but the insides were often dirty and drab. Patients were daily stripped naked and sprayed with hoses to clean them. Many patients were given daily *treatments* of electric shock, called ECT, or Electro Convulsive Shock Therapy, in order to subdue and control their behaviors. Insulin shock was also used, whereby a patient would be given a large dose of insulin, which would rapidly lower blood sugar levels, producing coma for a few hours, and thereby rendering the patient weak and listless for the rest of the day. It was well-known that these shock treatments produced irreversible brain damage, but the shrinks considered constraining or subduing behavior as beneficial treatments. Patients were also given large doses of drugs, including narcotics, in order to control their behaviors. State hospitals often housed twenty to forty thousand patients, and all of this was kept hidden from public view. (Breggin, 1991; Whitaker, 2002)

Sociologist Ernst Gruenberg (1966), in his exposé book, pointed out that patients became mindless, compliant robots with little or no will to live. Once their spirit was broken, patients could no longer survive in the outside world; he coined the term '*the social breakdown syndrome*' to describe human beings who spent their days listlessly sitting on a hallway bench, merely staring and smoking cigarettes.

Once these conditions became known, outrage ensued. Professors, students, physicians, psychologists, and the public all demanded major changes. The public stopped seeking the services of psychiatrists (Breggin, 1991), and an avalanche of lawsuits on behalf of patient's rights began. Psychiatrists were stripped, by the courts, of the power to commit patients, and physicians stopped referring patients to psychiatrists, which was not even necessary, since the public did not wish to go to psychiatrists anyway. Psychiatry almost disappeared. (Breggin, 1991; Whitaker, 2002)

While this was happening, coincidental events were unfolding within the field of psychology. Psychology, since its inception in the last quarter of the nineteenth century, had been content to remain an academic, scientific discipline. However, in the 1970s, it sought the right to treat patients and receive medical insurance reimbursements for services. State legislatures began granting these rights. Doctoral programs exploded across the nation (Stein, 2009). The American Psychological Association grew in size and power. Psychologists were highly trained in safer, non-medically-based and non-bodily-invasive treatments, especially behavior modification. Increasingly, the public sought treatment from them. Furthermore, psychologists were highly trained in scientifically-based research, which the psychiatrists were not. They did not like the use of a medically-based diagnostic system when there was mostly no scientific evidence for any known diseases causing abnormal behaviors. Psychologists believed more in the adjustment model, where diagnoses were viewed as labels for emotional, cognitive, and behavioral problems resulting from an inability to adapt to either early-life or immediate-life stresses.

Thus, during the 1970s, the American Psychiatric Association had grown weak, while the American Psychological Association had grown strong. The war was on!

Circumstances escalated when the psychologists confronted the psychiatrists that they either participate in the development of the next official diagnostic manual, the DSM-III, or else they would develop their own, separate system. Especially at issue were diagnoses that referred to, or inferred, the existence of underlying medical or disease causes for inappropriate behaviors, when, in most cases, no such evidence existed. Weak in strength and position, the psychiatrists capitulated. The DSM-III, published in 1994, was purged from most connotations or inferences of diseases (Seligman, 1994). Pejorative terms were changed or eliminated. Even such terms as 'neurosis' and 'psychosis', which were disease sounding, were stricken. Researcher Virginia Douglas changed the term hyperkinesis to Attention Deficit Disorder, ADD, and Attention Deficit Hyperactive Disorder, ADHD, viewing them as less disease connoting and less pejorative (Seligman, 1994), which ironically turned out to be a false assumption. The psychologists had won the day, or so they thought!

A statement from the DSM-IV (1994) Introduction Section is often overlooked:

> "In most situations, the clinical diagnosis of a DSM-IV mental disorder is not sufficient to establish the existence for legal purposes of a 'mental disorder', 'mental disability', 'mental disease', or 'mental defect'," (p. xxiii).

Thus, even the contributors to the DSM-IV admit that they cannot identify or separate diagnoses as diseases.

There are even more startling relations when the DSM is examined more closely.

The following statement, also in the Introduction, questions the term '*disorder*':

> "Moreover, although this manual provides a classification of mental disorders, it must be admitted that no definition adequately specifies precise boundaries for the concept of 'mental disorders'. The concept of mental disorder, like many other concepts in medicine and science, lacks a consistent operational definition that covers all situations," (p. xxi).

Thus, even the term '*disorder'* is rendered as not appropriate by the very people who composed the DSM!

The DSM-III and IV and the Issue of Accurate Diagnosis: A Secret History

Diagnoses in the DSM-IV are determined by vote and not by empirical research.

This is known as the consensus of committees (Robins and Helzer, 1986). Dilemmas confronting DSM committees were frequently resolved by majority vote (*Time* Magazine, December 2, 1985, p. 76). These circumstances encouraged various interest groups within the APA to campaign for outcomes consistent with their agenda, such as, homosexuality, women's rights, and theoretical beliefs. Diagnoses once considered as disorders can mysteriously disappear, or even vice versa. Oppositional defiant disorder, ODD, while listed as a disorder, evolved into a disease once the insurance companies agreed to pay for claims listing this as a diagnosis (Stein, 2004). This took years of behind the scenes haggling in order to make it happen. The insurance companies do not seem to offer explanations for why they are willing to suddenly allow a diagnosis to be considered a genuine medical problem after years of refusing to do so. This also opened the door to yet another diagnosis that became legitimate, once declared a disease, for prescribing psychiatric drugs. Why would they be willing to make payments for something they do not have to? This begs the questions of whether or not there are conflicting economic interests that are not being made public.

Klonsky (2000) makes the following statement, "The problem is that, as a rule, the DSM categories were not discovered through empirical research. Rather, they were hypothesized by psychiatrists and psychologists . . ." (p. 1616).

Validity and Reliability of Diagnoses

We previously discussed that psychological tests were not valid or reliable for predicting behavior. However, in this section, we explore whether or not these tests are valid and reliable for the purpose of diagnosis.

There are many types of validities within the world of psychological testing and diagnosis, and while they will shortly be discussed, it is important to highlight that the most important type of validity involves that diagnosis and testing actually predict observable behaviors (Mischel, 1996). In psychology and psychiatry, this does not happen (Haggen, 1997). In addition, validity cannot happen unless there is reliability (Mischel, 1996). Reliability can also have numerous meanings, but one of the most important forms involves observers, namely, the psychologists and psychiatrists agreeing upon that which they observe, and this includes agreement upon diagnoses. Reliable diagnosis is also known as inter-rater reliability (Anastasi, 1988). Do psychologists and psychiatrists agree on diagnosis? NO! Absolutely not! This is true even when psychological tests are administered (Mishcel, 1996). Oddly, this is yet another hidden mystery within the DSM's history.

The DSM-I and II had extremely low diagnostic reliability rates (Anastasi, 1988). Before its publication, there was a fervent belief that the DSM-III would resolve the problem, especially since it was based on observables behaviors known as symptoms (Lorandos and Campbell, 2005). Not only did this not happen, reliable diagnosis in the DSM-III (1980) was a dismal failure (Lorandos and Campbell, 2005). It was suggested that with the DSM-III that an inter-rater reliability be at .70 as its standard. No diagnosis met these levels, and the actual range was between .56 to .65, but for personality disorders, the average, or medium, was even lower and turned out to be .47. In order to better assist the reader in the meaning of these correlations, one may reinterpret them by converting them to a percentage of accuracy for prediction by using the *coefficient of determination*

(Ray, 1962), by squaring the validity and reliability figures. Thus, at its highest level of reliability, agreement would be 42%, and at the lower end, it would be 31% agreement rate. The means that inter-rater agreements never even reached 50% (Spitzer, Forman, and Nee, 1979; Lorandos and Cambell, 2005*). The solution was to remove any and all reports of inter-rater reliability from the DS- IV, which means removing all scientific evidence that was demonstrating the weaknesses of the diagnostic system.* APA's neglecting to report inter-rater reliability data for its diagnostic categories amounts to an egregious error (American Educational Research Association, American Psychological Association, National council on Measurement in Education in 1999, cited by Lorandoos and Campbell, 2005). This is unethical. Rather than trying to improve things, the course of action appears to be to hide it all. Ethics committees throughout the states and within the larger organizations of the American Psychological Association, the APA, and the American Association of Behavioral and Cognitive Therapies, ABCT, are remiss in their responsibilities because they refuse to take steps to stop practices such as this. They seem intent on only finding therapists who are having sex with patients, while they ignore the entire rape of the profession. Nothing is being done to make psychiatry and psychology more responsible and ethical professions. If anything, the trend is, and not just seems, to be going the other way.

Validity, or predicting actual behavior from diagnosis, is also equally poor.

Zeiler and Phillips (1961) state, "knowing what diagnostic category a patient falls into tells us little about their actual behavior," (p. 69). The most important forms of validity are:

1. *Predictive or Criterion Validity* – the extent to which a test or diagnosis can accurately predict behavior or performance, such as violence, homicide, or suicide, or any behavior for that matter. Once again, psychological tests do not do this with any accuracy (Lorandos and Campbell, 2005). All psychological tests and diagnoses are about as accurate as a Ouija Board, i.e., they do not predict behavior and they do not match with DSM-IV diagnoses. (Anastasi, 1988; Dineen, 2000; Hagen, 1997; Mischel, 1996;)
2. *Internal Validity* – relevant in studies attempting to demonstrate a causal relationship: The degree to which we can conclude the variables being observed caused the outcome, i.e., establishing a causal relationship between cause and event, i.e., C - E. Once again, psychological test and diagnoses are known to have almost no internal validity (Lorandos and Campbell, 2005). Only proper experimentation can do that, and proper experimentation is increasingly disappearing in clinical psychological and psychiatric research. (Dawes, 1994, Hagen, 1997)
3. *External Validity* – the certainty to which the results of a test or diagnosis can be generalized to specific persons, settings, and circumstances. Again, no psychological test and no diagnosis can do this (Mischel,

1996). In the arena of criminal behaviors, this lack of external validity was one of the reasons the FBI had to develop its own classification system, which now forms the foundation for criminal profiling, an area where there is little tolerance for extremely inaccurate predictions. (Doulas, Burgess, Burgess, and Ressler, 1982)

4. *Construct Validity* – the degree to which you can measure a hypothetical construct. Hypothetical constructs are giving names to things that cannot be observed, which is appropriate for philosophy but not for science. Psychology is loaded with hypothetical constructs, which are names of things no one can see, hear, or touch; they are made up (Lorandos and Campbell, 2005). Personality is a hypothetical construct. Unconscious is a hypothetical construct. Even God is a hypothetical construct. The existence of the things may be important but can only be the subject of conjecture, i.e., philosophy, and not appropriate for scientific study, which is based on observation.
5. *Concurrent Validity* – how well one test or diagnosis correlates with another test. This form of validity is relatively unimportant if two or more tests correlate well with each other but are measuring something that cannot be proven is consistently observable. An example would be two tests that correlate well for a hypothetical construct, which is useless in the sciences. If we test two Christians with different tests and find that both tests indicate they believe in God, this does not prove that God is there, i.e., observable and verifiable.

The Current War to Returns to the Mental Disease Era

In 'real medicine', diagnoses are centered on three basic forms of diseases:

1. infectious/contagious, 2. trauma, and 3. systemic. (Berkow, 1997)

1. *Infectious/contagious diseases* are caused by either bacterial of viral organisms. Infectious diseases involve the transmission of pathogenic organisms into the body through tissue damage or through injection of toxic substances. Contagious diseases involve transmission of the pathogen from person to person or animal to person, usually through the air or by direct contact.
2. *Trauma* involves a violent insult to the body that causes tissue damage.
3. *Systemic diseases* involve an automatic malfunctioning of bodily tissue, physiological functioning, or chemical imbalance, such as cancer or diabetes. Sometimes the *trigger* (Stein, 2009) for, or the beginning of, a systemic process may, at the current state of medicine, be unknown, for example, cancer or diabetes. However, the bodily malfunction can be clearly identified in most cases, with appropriate laboratory tests. For example, in cancer, the actual malfunctioning cells can be observed with

microscopes or CT scans, or in diabetes, the change in insulin production can be measured through testing of blood chemistries.

How Researchers Distort the Research

Thus, the currently popular movement in psychiatry/psychology is to classify clusters of misbehaviors as systemic diseases. In other words, there is a return to the disease error from the early 1900s. However, with the exception of the few diagnoses mentioned earlier, no laboratory tests exist to measure chemical imbalances in the nervous system, physiological damage, or tissue damage, which was pointed out earlier is actually stated in the introduction section of the DSM-IV (1994). There have been thousands of studies claiming to have found these anomalies in all sorts of psychiatric/psychological conditions, but, as yet, not one single study has been found to be credible. In other words, not one study has found a 'smoking gun' identifying anything really wrong that causes or produces most forms of abnormal behavior patterns (Baughman, 2006; Stein, 2009). It is because no test or measure has been found that the strategy of the current campaign is to inundate or flood the psychiatric/psychological journals, and lately the medical as well, with an overwhelming volume of bad research as a substitute for real data. Unfortunately, this strategy is working. Because of volume and the absence of real data, the professional communities and the public are being swayed into believing in nonexistent diseases. (Baughman, 2006)

Using Attention Deficit Disorders as an Example of the Misuse of Psychiatric Diagnosis

The trend is especially tragic when a child, and the parents of a child, is told that she/he has a disease, such as attention deficit disorder, ADD, when not a shred of actual proof exists (Stein, 2004). Think of the implications of this sham! That child's entire life will be affected by this piece of false information. All of his or her life decisions, such as education, marriage, choosing to have children, and choice of career, will be made, believing that she/he has a disease.

Trying to Make ADD/ADHD into Legitimate Diseases

In the late 1970s and early 1980s, Russell Barkley began a tireless campaign to convince the American public and the professional community that ADD/ADHD were diseases. At first he had no support and no evidence for his claim of disease. In 1993(a and b), as discussed earlier, very poor research was published by research physician Alan Zametkin, et al, claiming to have found the magic bullet by using PET scans to identify areas in the frontal part of the brain that appeared to emit unusual metabolic readings in adults who were formerly believed to be ADD or ADHD. This article has been completely discredited in scientific circles (Breggin, 1998). Nevertheless, it was this event that catapulted a number of researchers to begin using the cornucopia of new medical machines to similarly produce volumes of widely diverse claims.

In 1998, the National Institute of Health (NIH) held a consensus conference in an attempt to make sense from the overwhelming volume of material. The team of experts reviewed all the research and all presentations by the neuroimaging researchers. The following statement is in their summation report:

> "At this time, we do not have a diagnostic test for ADHD (Biochemical, physiological, anatomical, genetic, etc.). Therefore, the validity of the disorder continues to be a problem," (p. 3).

Russell Barkley, as a leader of the ADHD disease movement, makes the following statements, where he constantly contradicts himself. This is representative of the confusion, the contradictions, and the misleading statements and claims that represent the total lack of science which has created the quagmire in which we now find ourselves. Closely examine the following statements made by Dr. Barkley:

"ADD and ADHD are diseases . . ." (*ADHD-What can we do?* Video, 1992)

> "Children whose problems with attention, over-activity, and lack of inhibition reach a certain level have a developmental disability known as *attention-deficit/hyperactivity disorder,* or ADHD." (Barkley, 1995, p. vii)

> "We now understand that many children with ADHD have an inherited or genetic form of the disorder, that many do not outgrow their problems by adolescents..." (Barkley, 1995, p. viii)

> "ADHD children look normal. There is no outward sign that something is physically wrong within their central nervous system or brain. Yet I believe it is an imperfection in the brain that causes constant motion and other behavior that people find so intolerable in a child who has ADHD." (Barkley, 1995, p. 17)

> "I believe the disorder stems from under activity in an area of the brain . . ." (Barkley, 1995, p. 19)

> *"ADHD may simply represent a human trait and not a pathological condition in most cases.* As we just saw, which of us end up with ADHD seems to be determined much more by genetics than by environmental factors. In that sense, ADHD may be viewed as height, weight, intelligence, or reading ability, to name a few traits that are largely (but not wholly) genetically determined: . . . we differ in how much of it we inherit. . . . What is considered 'abnormal' for any trait is simply a reflection of where we draw a line on the

continuum for a trait, we label them as having a disorder. Such labels not only are based on a somewhat arbitrary measure but also obscure the fact that those with ADHD do fall along a dimension of normal abilities. *To put it another way, we all have a degree of this ADHD trait, and those with ADHD simply represent the extreme."* (Barkley, 1995, p. 65)

> "This means that ADHD should not be considered some grossly abnormal pathological condition-in fact it is a condition not qualitatively different from normal at all." (Barkley, 1995, p. 65)

His next statement is crucial for understanding the meaning of this paper:

> "As such, the *developmental disorder of self-control* may be the most accurate name for ADHD." (Barkley, 1995, p. 61)

Note the next piece of rhetoric:

> "Misled by research reports that lab measures have found differences between ADHD and non-ADHD children and by the fact that ADHD is a biologically-based disorder, many parents ask for medical tests to confirm the diagnosis of ADHD. At present, there are no lab tests or measures that are of value in making a diagnosis of ADHD, so blood work, urinalysis, chromosome studies, EEGs, averaged evoked responses, MRIs, and computed tomography (CT scans) should not be used routinely in the evaluation of ADHD children." (p. 122)

In this statement, and in a similar statement by Swanson at the 1998 Consensus Conference, Barkley apparently is stating that there are abnormalities that researchers can readily find in the recesses of their laboratories but cannot reproduce at the clinical level. In other words, the findings that he claims to be true are really fictitious and worthless. This is a theme of this current book, namely, that definitive claims are made of laboratory findings which cannot be replicated at a clinical level.

The Diagnostic and Statistical Manual-IV edition (DSM-IV) also states: "There are no laboratory tests that have been established as a diagnostic in the clinical assessment of Attention Deficit/Hyperactivity Disorder," (p. 81). When DuPaul debated Stein at the 1998 APA Conference, Dupaul fought for the disease of ADD/ADHD vehemently and then admitted that no cause had as yet been found, but he believed that one day it would be.

Perhaps Barkley is shifting away from his improvable disease claims, since hundreds of studies have been unable to validate the existence of any disease. What then is Barkley's purpose in redesignating ADD/ADHD as a "developmental disorder"? The answer may be unfolding with the recent publication of the DSM-IV, TR (2000). In the DSM-IV, the defining criteria for ADD/ADHD are introduced with the statement, "Six (or more) of the following symptoms of inattention . . . is maladaptive and inconsistent with developmental level:" (p. 83).

However, the latter part of the statement in the DSM-IV, TR (2001) now appears in bold type, "... is maladaptive and inconsistent with developmental level:" This heightened evidence may mean that Barkley is now beginning to maneuver to have ADD/ADHD declared as a developmental disorder and possibly as one of the forthcoming Pervasive Developmental Disorders, in the DSM-V. Pervasive Developmental Disorders include Autism, Asperberger's Disorder, and Rett's Disorder, which involve children who are seriously disturbed and often out of touch with reality. It is a sham to try to stretch the misbehaviors of ADD/ADHD into the very serious category of Pervasive Developmental Disorders. This has been taken to the limit by one of the scariest books to recently appear, *The ADHD-Autism Connection* by Diane Kennedy (2002). If this writer were the parent of an autistic child, I'd scream to the rooftops at the insensitive, appalling audacity to stretch the misbehaviors of ADD/ADHD into this category.

Since Barkley has not succeeded with reifying ADD/ADHD as a disease, he may succeed by calling it a *developmental disorder*. Is it only in the mental health literature that one can get away with ill-defined psychobabble and throw about terms that have no operational definitions?

Just when it seemed that psychology and psychiatry has stooped to its lowest, an even scarier book has appeared, *The Bipolar Child: The Definite and Reassuring Guide to Childhood's Most Misunderstood Disorder* (1999) by Dimitri and Janice Papolos. This book stretches the mood swings and sometimes annoying misbehaviors of normal kids into one of the most major diagnostic categories. And, guess what the solution is for this and the Kennedy books? Both books recommend giving children every known category of psychiatric drugs, including the antipsychotics, which are well known to produce irreversible brain damage. Worse, the Papolos couple even recommends using electric shock, known as ECT, or Electro Shock Therapy on children! Barlow and Durand (2008) clearly state that in order to make a bipolar diagnosis there must be clear evidence of prolonged cycles of depression, which, as Stein (2005) points out, are not present in children who have not undergone severe personal trauma, such as losing a parent. In other words, the precise symptoms labeled as bipolar are almost never seen in children (Stein, 2005). How do these writers sleep at night? (In a personal communication with Lloyd Ross, October 11, 2000)

This pattern of stretching words and distorting information can be documented for most diagnoses, but the lack of space and the risk of trying the attention of the reader does not permit an exhaustive review of these distortions which are now too frequently being made.

Adult Onset ADD/ADHD: A New Diagnostic Strategy to Open the Adult Market for Sales of Amphetamines

A new trend is emerging where adults are questioning whether or not they might have ADD, Attention Deficit disorder, or ADHD, Attention Deficit Hyperactive Disorder. Recently, a new diagnostic label has been suggested: Adult Onset of Attention Deficit Disorder.

The issue of adults in high-responsibility professions, which require serious and sometimes life and death decisions making, questioning whether or not they have a problems with attention and hyperactivity is a special problem necessitating that they, and therapists, be armed with appropriate information before allowing themselves to be labeled and placed on drugs for treatment, especially drugs which can impair judgment. Anyone in a high-responsibility profession encountering a critical incident, such as a police officer being involved in a shooting, can be subject to both criminal charges and civil liability for negligently and knowingly performing dangerous duties while having an impairment or disability of the mind, and, additionally, for performing their duties while ingesting judgment impairing drugs, such as Ritalin or any of the amphetamines commonly used to "treat" these disorders.

Imagine the following case scenario:

> Officer McDougal drives up to a burglary in progress. He draws his weapon and appropriately calls out, "Halt! Police. Drop everything and slowly raise your hands." The perpetrator suddenly turns and pulls a bologna sandwich, wrapped in aluminum foil, from his right pocket in order to offer it to the officer. Believing that it is a gun, Officer McDougal fires, resulting in the perpetrator being paralyzed from a bullet in the spine.
>
> One year later, Officer McDougal finds himself being cross-examined in civil court, facing a ten million dollar lawsuit for damages. The following dialogue between the plaintiff's attorney and McDougal takes place:
>
> Attorney: Officer, did you believe my client had a gun?
>
> McDougal: Yes.
>
> Attorney: Do you have any problems that impair your ability to pay attention?
>
> McDougal: Yes. I've been diagnosed as having Attention Deficit Disorder, or ADD.
>
> Attorney: Is it possible that your attention problem contributed to you mistaking a bologna sandwich for a gun?
>
> McDougal: Yes.
>
> Attorney: Do you believe that anyone with a problem with attention should be carrying a gun?
>
> Defendant Attorney: Objection! Calls for speculation.
>
> Attorney: I'll rephrase. Do you think, with your attention problem, that you should be carrying a gun?

McDougal: I don't know. I've never thought about it.

Attorney: Well, my paralyzed client has. Are you being treated for this disorder?

McDougal: Yes. I'm on medication.

Attorney: What is your medication?

McDougal: Adderall.

Attorney: What is Adderall?

McDougal: I don't know.

Attorney: Allow me to read into evidence the Physician's Desk Reference. It says here that Adderall contains four amphetamines, including Benzedrine and Dexedrine. Would you trust a gun in the hands of anyone who has taken four amphetamines?

McDougal: No.

Attorney: What would you do if you found a suspect who was holding four amphetamines in his pocket without a prescription?

McDougal: I'd arrest him for possession. Amphetamines are a controlled substances and potentially dangerous.

Attorney: But isn't that what you are consuming while carrying a gun?

The courtroom turns silent. This case is not going well for officer McDougal, is it?

In high-responsibility professions, where lives may be at stake, receiving such a label can jeopardize a career. Imagine a similar courtroom scene for the physician whose patient dies from a prescription, even if the prescription were correct; the surgeon whose patient dies; the firefighter who falls off a ladder with a victim in his or her arms; the engineer whose building collapses after an airplane crashes into it; the dentist whose patient develops a severe mouth infection following surgery, and on and on. Consider also, the construction worker who survives a fall while working on a building and then seeks disability only to find out that he or she knowingly contributed to the fall by working under dangerous conditions with an Attention Deficit Disorder. It is only a matter of time until the legal profession begins to have a field day, attacking those in high-responsibility professions who have these diagnoses and additionally take risks while high on stimulant drugs. It is therefore essential that all therapists and clients be armed with some important facts before seeking treatment for adult attention problems.

Fact 1: There is no medical test for Attention Deficit Disorders.

Fact 2: There is no psychological test for Attention Deficit Disorders. Therefore, there is no way to determine if anyone *has* such a thing called Attention

Deficit Disorder, ADD, or Attention Deficit Hyperactive disorder, ADHD. These are nothing more than subjective labels applied to someone by a psychologist, psychiatrist, or physician (Stein, 1999). Once diagnosed, it could cause legal problems to those in high-responsibility professions, especially if an accident, death, or disability results to a patient or client.

Fact 3: All diagnoses, when insurance claims are submitted, are housed in a computer in Washington, D.C., to which any attorney can gain access. This includes all so-called, confidential psychological or psychiatric diagnoses. Therefore, a label of ADD or ADHD becomes a matter of permanent record. Anyone who applies for a job in the law enforcement or intelligence communities will possibly find themselves denied employment when a psychiatric diagnosis is discovered during the mandatory background investigations. The FBI spends, at today's costs, $75,000 for a background check on each applicant. (Garner, Paul, former Virginia Bureau Chief in a personal communication, September, 13, 2009)

Fact 4: Once a diagnosis is discovered, it is relatively easy for an attorney to deduce possible medications and then obtain relative records.

Fact 5: The drugs used to treat Attention Deficit Disorders are stimulants, most of which are amphetamines (Breggin, 2002; Breggin and Cohen, 1999). Ritalin, the second most prescribed drug (Breggin, 2002), acts very much like cocaine in the body (DeGrandpre, 1999). Gradumet and Desoxyn are both methamphetamines. Adderall has four amphetamines in it. Benzedrine can no longer be prescribed, even for adults, and yet it is in Adderall (Breggin, 2002). Dexedrine and Dextrostat are both basic forms of amphetamines. Focalin is a stronger version of Ritalin. Concerta is long acting Ritalin. Should anyone in a life and death type of profession testify in court with these drugs on their record?

Fact 6: These drugs *do not* correct a chemical imbalance. All psychiatric drugs have one common property: They allay anxiety, and this includes the stimulants; stimulants also give a feeling of energy. (Breggin, 1998, 2002; Stein, 2002; Valenstein, 1998)

If someone believes that he *has* ADD/ADHD, because he or she is constantly misplacing or forgetting things, then the odds are that his or her real problem is anxiety or depression resulting from an overwhelming and hectic lifestyle. In fact, Breggin (1991) has pointed out that many psychological problems are the result of what he calls "*overwhelm*". Cognitive therapists, such as Meichenbaum (1977), Ellis and Harper (1961), or Beck (1961, 1979), point out that internal dialogue underlies anxieties and depression. When someone attends to this dialogue, he or she is distracted from attending to the environment (Ellis and Harper, 1961, 1975), which increases the likelihood of missing external cues or forgetting things. Those who claim that the drugs help are probably more accurately feeling anxiety relief with an increased sense of energy. However, make no mistake about it, that if anyone has an amphetamine in his or her system, she/he is *intoxicated* (Hanson and Venturelli, 1998), and his or her judgment *is* most likely impaired and can therefore easily be subject to liability in a court of law.

Stoned

Any adult taking stimulants for thought and emotional control because he or she is overwhelmed by our modern lifestyle must realize that he or she is choosing to stay *stoned* throughout the workday. Ritalin is synthetic cocaine (DeGrandpre, 1999), Adderall is a cocktail of four amphetamines, including Benzedrine, which has been removed from the market by the FDA as too addictive. Graduamet and Desoxin are methamphetamines (Breggin, 2002). Alcohol allays anxiety, but it does do not correct chemical imbalances, and the same applies to all stimulants. Adults are choosing to stay stoned or drunk in order to cope with life!

Alternative Solutions

There are healthy ways for therapists to help adults deal with attention problems. These are far less likely to cause unwanted scrutiny and embarrassment in a court of law.

1. If a patient is having problems with attention, let this serve as a warning that his or her life may have spiraled out of control. It may be that stress is contributing to feelings of anxiety or depression, which, in turn, is interfering with attending to everyday matters.
2. Check to see if a patient is overloaded with excessive responsibilities and/or commitments. Can she/he reduce church activities? Can she/he avoid going to every single game that his or her kid plays? Does she/he have to serve as a coach? Does she/he need more time for rest and relaxation? One solution to stress management is to cut out extraneous church and community activities when strong emotions and a problem paying attention may be indications of an overextended lifestyle.
3. Recommend more quiet reading time. DeGrandre (1999) points out that reading is far more relaxing than watching television.
4. Instruct patients to become more compulsive. Whether in the home or at the office, advise patients to rehearse by always putting things in the same place until a new habit is in place. Those who report attention problems frequently complain that they go back and forth to the car every morning because they keep forgetting one more item, or they run around searching for lost items.
5. Encourage patients to exercise. It is amazing how many people have allowed themselves to get out of shape. In addition, exercise helps with relaxation. When patients feel more fit and relaxed, attention and alertness improve.
6. Teach patients to write down to-do lists and reminders. Most professionals have to keep enormous amounts of information in their heads. Trying to remember everything causes an individual to pay attention to the dialogue that is going on in their head instead of paying attention to

their surroundings. Writing things down relieves the pressure of trying to remember and permits better focus on the environment.

7. Train patients to improve self-dialogue. Cognitive therapists, such as Ellis and Harper (1961), Meichenbaum (1977), or Beck (1979), have pointed out that our behaviors and emotions are responses to the sentences we tell ourselves. If someone is having trouble paying attention, then that can serve as a cue to begin self-talk for instructions to slow down, relax, and pay closer attention to what is going on in the environment. Cognitive therapists actually instruct patients to begin this practice by saying these self-instructions out loud, since cognitive therapy is a form of semantic therapy, until they become more automatic and habitual.
8. The use of relaxation techniques, such as yoga, meditation, progressive muscle relaxation, and biofeedback, are far more healthy alternatives than stimulant drugs.

Breggin (2002) points out that the public has a "right to know" of problems when enlisting the services of those in high responsibility and high-risk professions. He suggests that their licenses should clearly state:

> 'Warning: I have a special ADHD accommodation. I may be slower, more poorly focused, and more impulsive than most attorneys [or other high-responsibility professions], and you should take this into consideration when hiring me or when agreeing to an hourly fee schedule.' (p. 149)

This article further suggests that the warning should add: 'I may harm or kill you because of my condition and because I am taking drugs that make me intoxicated and can impair my judgment and ability to function.'

A Variety of Tricks for Distorting Research

How the research is being tainted is covered by a number of writers, such as Thomas Szasz (1961, 2008), Peter Breggin (1991, 2002), Elliot Valenstein (1998), Robert Whitaker (2002), and perhaps, most eloquently by Dr. Grace Jackson, a psychiatrist and one of the most outstanding authorities on psychopharmacology (2005). The following is a litany of the tricks of the drug-research trade on how the research is manipulated:

1. *Selection bias*: This was done repeatedly in the work of Castellanos (2008), who reported to the NIH, National Institute of Health, that his MRI studies indicated that the brains of ADHD children are smaller than normal children. He failed to report that the ADHD group children were one year younger than the normal group children.
2. *Failure to report manipulation of drug doses:* This is often done when introducing a new drug and touting it as better than another company's

drug or an old drug. This was one study (NDA, 1996, July 29) trying to introduce Zyprexa as a new and safer drug compared to the old drug Haldol. The old drug was given at very high doses and the new at very low doses, resulting in cases of the old drug developing movement spasms. If equivalent doses were given, then the drugs would be equal for the spasm problem.

3. *Placebo washout:* This is where participants, who are given a placebo instead of a drug, are either removed or left in the study depending on which direction the researchers want the placebo to react. If they do not want the placebo group to look too good, then the data of those who responded well to the placebo are removed, and if they want the placebo group to look good, then the data of those who reacted badly are removed. An example can be found in a study done by Faries, Helligenstein, Tollefson, and Potter (1997) on antidepressant drugs.
4. *Failure to report drug histories:* Hundreds upon hundreds of studies have been generated within each of the different psychiatric diagnoses claiming to find various disease causes. It was pointed out earlier how the different computerized neuroimaging medical machines have been used to make claims of different medical problems. For example, in ADD/ADHD, dozens of brain areas have been implicated as causing the attentional and behavioral problems. A CAT scan is used to indicate an anomaly in one part of the brain, while another implicates a different part, and on and on it goes. There is a similar pattern with PET scans, SPECT scans, MRIs, and other devices; the list is endless. One of the most glaring deficits in these studies is the failure to adequately, if at all, report the drug histories of the subjects. It is suggested that psychologists read these studies firsthand. They will notice that either no mention is made of drug histories or only one sentence is given, which is typically vague and inadequate for scientific research. It is already known that the long-term use of drugs produces the very anomalies they attribute as the causes of ADD/ADHD, and the same can be said for all the other diagnoses. How can scientists neglect to report in research papers proper documentation of subjects' drug histories? This is an especially unethical and glaring oversight when the effects of drugs are well-known and well documented. Only two studies, led by the same researcher (Castellanos, 2006; Castellanos, F. X., Giedd, J. N., Eckburg, P., Marsh, W. L., Vaituzis, C., Katson, D., et al., 1994) claiming that MRI measurements clearly show that ADHD children have smaller brains than non-ADHD children, was controlled for drug histories. In both studies, both the ADHD children group and the non-ADHD group clearly had not taken drugs. *However,* the ADHD group was significantly younger, by a year, which easily accounts for the differences in brain size. The researcher claimed to make a statistical adjustment for this difference, which is

another unethical research misstep. An adjustment such as this is really not permissible in solid research, because it may or may not adequately compensate for the difference. In addition, there was no mention of the drug histories for any of the children. These tricks of the trade seem to never stop, and worse, few seem to care. Castellanos (2006) presented this *junk science* as "factual research" before a hearing of the FDA, the Food and Drug Administration!

5. *The chemical imbalance scam:* Many, many studies on a wide range of disorders report all types of chemical imbalance etiologies. However, there is a built-in trick for the way these studies are being presented to the public and to the professional community.

   Nerve cells do not physically touch. Nerve impulses are transmitted from one nerve to the next by the micro-fraction of a second release of chemicals, known as 'neurotransmitters'. It is these neurotransmitters that certain researchers claim are out of balance and causing all types of psychiatric disorders, ergo, the chemical imbalance theories. Let's look at two neurotransmitters, norepinephrine and serotonin. We cannot measure the levels of these transmitters directly, because their amount is extremely slight, but their impact on behavior is extremely large. Researchers can, however, obtain collected samples that are radio activated for research purposes from the Center for Disease Control or other federal agencies. The transmitters can then be injected into research subjects and then can be traced with CAT scans or MRI scans to the exact nerve sites in the nervous system and brain, especially to neuron areas known as 'receptor sites'. Are you following this so far? The next step then involves injecting radioactive samples of a particular psychiatric drug, such as one of the amphetamines or an antidepressant. Viola! The drugs go to exactly the same receptor sites in the nervous system and brain as the drugs. Conclusion! The drugs are correcting the imbalance of these neurotransmitters. Right? Wrong! That is precisely what unethical researchers would like for professionals and the public to believe. We can take the research a step further, about which these researchers and writers do not seem inclined to inform us. We cannot measure the transmitters directly, but we can measure their metabolites, which are the chemicals left over and transmitted to the blood stream after they are used for transmission. This provides us with an indirect, albeit precise measure of the amounts of the transmitters (Barlow and Durand, 2008; Valenstein, 1998). When this is done, we find that those people with many types of psychiatric problems, and the subsequent diagnoses, such as depression, schizophrenia, and ADD/ADHD, do not have different levels of norepinephrine, serotonin, dopamine, or any other neurotransmitter, from that of other people! Therefore, failure to reveal this last research step appears to be a deliberate deception designed to convince everyone that different disorders are caused by chemical imbalances. Sadly, this campaign and other slight-of-hand tricks appears to be working in winning converts to disease theories.

6. *Falsifying genetic studies:* Many studies report specific gene factors that produce psychiatric diseases. Readers view these studies and are therefore convinced of their validity, but they fail to read careful critiques that dissect these studies and that indicate that no gene anomaly has yet been found. The reader is referred to the work in pscycho-genetic research of Joseph (2003) and psychiatrist Jackson (2005) that refutes all the studies on genetics thus far done.
7. *Omission of data:* One of the best ways to falsify studies is to merely omit any data that the researcher does not like, such as the suicide attempts on trials of Prozac. (Khan, Warner, and Brown, 2000)
8. *Dual appointments of researchers and reviewers:* Data is going to be made biased and become skewed when researchers and those who review the research have dual and lucrative appointments, such as academics serving on the boards of pharmaceutical companies, or those in trusted review position also serving on pharmaceutical company boards, such as nineteen of the thirty-three FDA reviewers serving on the panel of black box warning labels for stimulant drugs in 2008. If the reader wishes a thorough review of this practice, it can be found in the writings of Moncrieff (2003). Interest conflicts such as these are not in the interest of good science or the wellbeing of the public.
9. *Lack of replication:* One of the most important steps in the scientific research process is for other independent research to replicate the findings of particular studies. If research is replicated by other scientists who also have vested interests, such as making extra money from pharmaceutical companies, in a replication supporting the original study, then scientific integrity is compromised. Replication must be able to be done by neutral researchers who are interested in quality research rather than political or economic gain. Replication also means that the findings of disease etiologies must be sufficiently clear and precise enough to be done within clinical practices. Replication of drug safety studies, drug efficacy rates, and disease etiologies in the psychological/psychiatric arena seem to be fodder for some unsavory practices, especially when huge amounts of money are at stake.

Scientific research articles are written like a super precise recipe. Each step and measure is precisely documented in order to allow fellow scientists to redo, or replicate, the experiment. This is done to make certain that the initial findings were accurate and that the original claims had real merit. Replication, outside the pharmaceutical company researchers or the NIMH, National Institute of Health, which is committed to the idea of psychiatric diseases, has not as yet occurred. It is worth repeating for emphasis. No study reporting a disease finding in any of the psychiatric disorders, except the ones mentioned earlier, such as retardation, has as yet been replicated by neutral, independent researchers, and being independent means that they have no ties to pharmaceutical company monies. In other words, no support exists for all the claims made. It is just not there! It just does not exist! The question is, "Why is the public, and the psychological and educational communities, now siding with, and accepting, these disease theories?"

10. *Volume of supportive studies or the large scale misuse of replication:* An examination of the research indicates that only a few dozen researchers account for the hundreds and hundreds of studies. Replication by other researchers who also have conflicting ties to the pharmaceutical companies is a flip side or corollary built into the replication issue. The sheer volume of these studies (Stein, 2004) by a relatively small number of researchers is confusing to the public and the psychological community, and it is apparently succeeding as propaganda in winning an overwhelming number of converts. The disease point of view is now winning the day without a shred of substantive evidence or support from neutral scientists or practicing clinicians. All that needs to be done by any sincere practicing psychologist is to pinpoint studies that claim MRI findings to support an anomaly which is the cause of a disorder such as ADD or ADHD and request any practicing radiologist to conduct an MRI to confirm the diagnosis. It cannot be done, and not just for ADD/ADHD, but also for any other psychiatric disorder. Why is it that psychologists, once deeply opposed to disease notions, have said nothing? Why are they letting this happen? Why are they not reading the research carefully? Why are they accepting "bull" as gospel?

Why is this happening? There are two basic motivations, either greed or stupidity, and perhaps both. There is greed on the part of those pharmaceutical company executives and unethical pseudo-scientists who are growing rich off this propaganda campaign, and stupidity on the part of the large numbers within the professional community who are either buying into this propaganda or who are choosing to look the other way and allow this to go on. Too many psychologists, educators, and physicians are not examining the writings of the whistle blowers. If they would, it is highly likely they would become much more skeptical and reticent to accept that which is too readily being accepted and relied upon. There are huge amounts of money supplying this campaign.

Maybe psychiatric drugs have some legitimate uses, especially for stopping emotional pain. However, to convince so many people that they *need* to be on drugs in order to correct unproven chemical imbalances or unsubstantiated disease anomalies is downright unethical and sad for the damage that it is doing to psychiatry and clinical psychology.

An Alternate Model

Diagnoses in psychiatry/psychology can be looked at from a very different perspective, known as paradigms or models. Many disorders can be viewed as maladaptive reactions to stress, known as the adjustment model (Barlow and Durand, 2008). The stresses that precipitate maladaptive behaviors may occur in the present or they may occur during the early developmental years. Depression can serve as a good example. A person may experience severe depression as a result of a recent loss of a loved one. My hunch is that just about everyone reading this book has experienced this at some time or another in his or her life. However, there are people who have recurring depressions with no apparent immediate stress. Research by Lewinsohn and Talkington (1979) and Lewinsohn and Rosenbaum (1987) show that such individuals often have had bad early-life experiences, such as cold, distant, and aloof parents who rarely displayed love and affection, or highly punitive parents, who excessively rely on discipline. It appears that these patterns of poor parenting pave the way for developing thinking patterns, called 'cognitions' in psychology, which can precipitate frequent depression (Beck, 1961, 1979; Seligman, 1975). In fact, two researchers during the 1970s independently uncovered remarkably similarities about these thinking, or cognitive, patterns. Aaron Beck called these patterns 'Hopelessness', while Martin Seligman called them 'Learned Helplessness'. According to both researchers, consistently negative home environments early in life are conducive to viewing oneself as responsible whenever something negative happens as totally worthless, to viewing the world as a negative place, and finally, to viewing the future of their lives as hopeless, where nothing will get better. With such thinking patterns, is it any wonder that someone would self-precipitate recurring depressions? If this would be viewed from the medical model, then the recurring depressions would be the result of some disease in the brain or nervous system for which no clear evidence has, as yet, been uncovered. A comparison of these two very different models seems to indicate substantial support for the first and almost none for the latter. Most importantly, the two different paradigms direct treatment in two different directions. The disease model points to medicines as the treatment of choice. The adjustment model points to helping the patient change their faulty thinking and perceptions of themselves and the world, which is known as cognitive restructuring (Beck, 1979; Ellis and Harper, 1975). The use of drugs, in this case, antidepressants, is not ruled out and can be used as a brief adjunct to ease the pain of depression until the patient relearns new thinking patterns. The goal is personal change, with the use of drugs only being a temporary adjunct until the patient no longer needs them (Stein, 2004). In the medical model, the patient is viewed as having a permanent disease necessitating the permanent use of drugs (Beggin and Cohen, 1999). The main question is, "Which model is more healthy?"

This same argument can be made for most psychiatric/psychological conditions. The difference between the disease versus the adjustment perspective is most relevant for childhood problems. Childhood misbehaviors, if viewed as diseases, leads to children permanently being considered as incurably mentally ill (Stein, 2004), which then necessitates a lifelong regimen of toxic psychiatric drugs. If, on the other hand, they can be viewed as having behavior-thinking problems, then amelioration can be accomplished with proper behavioral/cognitive techniques (Stein, 2004). If behavioral treatments are correctly developed, then drugs may never be necessary (Stein, 2001), and children do not have to live believing that they *have* lifelong handicaps.

One final note: Every book used for teaching psychopharmacology, a course about psychiatric drugs, clearly points out that these drugs are *toxic* (Hanson and Venturelli, 2001). This is where the word in*toxic*ation comes from. When one is intoxicated, or drunk, she/he is actually in a state of being poisoned (Hanson and Venturelli, 2001, Valenstein, 1998). In fact, if the dosage of any psychiatric drug is sufficiently increased, one will go through the stages of drunkenness, then into coma, i.e., pass out, and subsequently, if increased further, even death (Hanson and Venturelli, 2001). It is, therefore, appropriate to view the taking of any psychiatric drug as producing a state of intoxication, or being drunk. Thus, a diagnosis viewed as a disease leads to prescribing that a child, or adult, remain in a state of intoxication, drunkenness, for the rest of his or her life. Psychiatric drugs do not correct chemical imbalances (Barlow and Durand, 2008; Valenstein, 1998); they sedate, just as alcohol does, producing a state of intoxication or drunkenness. This is yet another reason that if the disease model is to be applied, then there should be absolute and solid proof that there is, indeed, a disease present in the first place. As we delve further, we will see more and more evidence that the existence of disease, with the few exceptions mentioned, is both a myth and a lie.

Keeping Effective Behavioral Treatments Hidden

Stein (1998b, 2001a, 2001b, 2004) has developed cognitive/behavioral treatment methods that have received awards and are considered highly effective with children and teens no matter what is the presenting diagnosis. The author's treatment methods, based on parent training, have over a 98% effective rate. Shannon, one of the primary litigant attorneys at the 2001 Ritalin Litigation Conference, made the following statement directed at the pharmaceutical company attorneys:

> "You know that the behavioral treatments of Dr. Stein do work, and Lord help you if you fail to use his methods and one child case goes south [*develops a serious side reaction, including death*]* on the drugs." (March, 30)
> *Italics added.

In addition, his methods won an award for one of the top ten research projects at the 1998 Conference of the American Psychological Association in San

Francisco, California. His methods were also awarded at the 2005 Conference of the International Center for the Study of Psychiatry and Psychology, and there are still other awards. After successfully treating the child of an insurance company executive who had been on numerous medications but whose condition had progressively deteriorated to extremely severe levels, the executive campaigned for the insurance company to fund research on child treatment based on Stein's work. Higher executives continuously threw roadblocks in the path of any grants for research. Stein and the executive became suspicious that money was being exchanged into the hands of the highest levels of insurance company executives. Why did they not want effective treatments which would ultimately save the company billions of dollars? No answer has been forthcoming. This highlights the conflict of interests that seems to permeate research and treatments within psychiatry and psychology, helps explain why diagnoses are manipulated, and why ineffective behavioral treatments, i.e., both the drugs and the more publicized behavioral treatments, remain popular.

Prescription Privileges for Psychologists

Recently, Stein sent in a proposal to present his arguments, with pediatrician DuBose Ravenel, to the American Psychological Association 2003 Convention. No reply was ever made. Ravenel submitted a proposal to present with Stein at the 2003 American Association of Developmental and Behavioral Pediatrics. No reply was ever made. Scientific conventions are supposed to be the debate forum for different points of view. Both Stein and Ravenel are respected experts. Stein's research on cognitive/behavioral treatments for ADD/ADHD, called the 'Caregivers' Skills Program', CSP, had been recognized as one of the top ten research presentations at the 1998 American Psychological Association, APA, Convention. What changed? Why are they presently being ignored? Perhaps the answer lies in the current quest for psychologists to become licensed in all fifty states in order to write prescriptions for psychiatric drugs. Such privileges would make a huge difference in the incomes of psychologists, whose incomes do not nearly match those of "real doctors". Oddly enough, both Stein and Ravenel do not oppose psychologists writing prescriptions. They merely believe that psychiatric drugs should be used conservatively and avoided whenever well-designed behavioral treatment alternatives are available, and that patients should be made fully aware, in plain language, about the risks of these drugs. They counsel cautious and conservative use of such dangerous drugs. Apparently, such a moderate position is unacceptable when a huge hoard of psychologists are anxious to have nothing stand in their way for prescription writing privileges. Stein even served on the Virginia task force to lobby for this right, but he was excluded from meetings when he counseled that safeguards be set in place to prevent abuses of this privilege. No one seems to want sober moderation when, "There's gold in them thar hills!"

Summary

Recently, Stein (2003) was asked to testify when a bill was being considered banning school authorities from forcing parents to diagnose and drug their children. During three days of hearings, only Stein and the head of the Virginia State Police testified in favor of the bill. All the others who testified were hired guns, doctors and lawyers for the pharmaceutical company cartels. One of the Virginia State Senators asked Dr. Stein if he believed any children had the disease of ADD or ADHD. Stein replied as follows:

> "I am a scientist, a teacher, a writer, and a practitioner. I try to keep an open and objective mind. However, the research in psychology and psychiatry has been so compromised and abused by the pharmaceutical industry and by the ambitious researchers who do their dirty work that I can no longer tell fact from fiction. I can no longer trust what I read."

The bill passed unanimously!

A New Diagnostic System Based on Cognitive/Behavioral Patterns

In the next chapter, we will explore a newly proposed diagnostic system based on cognitive/behavioral concepts. This proposed system highlights a cognitive pattern which has thus far remained undetected. However, once understood, a clear connection between diagnostic categories becomes apparent and makes, perhaps, far more sense that the current loosely connected and chaotic diagnostic system.

CHAPTER FOUR

COGNITIVE DIVERSION: A HIDDEN PATTERN FOR DIAGNOSIS WITHIN THE DSM THAT CAN SERVE AS A FOUNDATION FOR A MORE CLEAR AND VALID DIAGNOSTIC SYSTEM BASED ON LEARNING AND COGNITIVE/BEHAVIORAL PRINCIPLES

We have reviewed that the current diagnostic system is deeply flawed. It is a chaotic cacophony of loosely knit diagnostic categories which seem to have little or no connection to each other and form a haphazard pattern. We have reviewed the inter-rater reliability, and the validity of diagnosis is unacceptably low. We have also reviewed the current campaign to reinstate the early 1900s campaign to declare more and more diagnoses as diseases, but when the evidence is carefully scrutinized by neutral researchers without ties to the pharmaceutical companies, the disease declaration does not seem to hold up. In this chapter, we will introduce the possibility that there is a hidden pattern to diagnoses which has thus far not been noticed or detected. This pattern suggests that diagnoses may be related to a phenomenon that shall be labeled for convenience as '*Cognitive Diversion*'. The concepts which underlie *Cognitive Diversion* lie in Behavioral/Cognitive and Learning theories which have an extensive and vast empirical history and are considerably more scientifically solid in clinical psychology than the current loose diagnostic system or especially the disease foundation which is extensively filled with loopholes. No claim is being made that this should absolutely be the foundation for a new diagnostic system, but it is hoped the soundness of the logic which underlies this proposed system will have heuristic value and help set the stage for psychology to take a new, and perhaps, more productive approach for developing a better diagnostic system. After all, the current system is not doing too well!

Why Learning Theory Makes Sense

Recall in our previous discussion, that following the 1952 revelations of H. J. Eysenck (1952), philosophically-based treatment modalities. i.e., Freudian, Rogerian, and other dynamic therapies, not only failed to work but actually made patients worse, and clinical psychology turned to learning theory in the name of behavior modification (Kanfer and Phillips, 1970) for a better way. The primary reason for this change lies in the belief that the dynamic therapies were not grounded in science, while scientific research had been going on for years in a few universities on learning theory and its applications to treatment, namely, behaviorism. In the late 1960s and throughout the 1970s, diagnosis became less important than applying learning principles to ameliorate *inappropriate and maladaptive behaviors* (Bandura, 1977) rather than the dynamic belief in mysterious unconscious forces deep inside the mind. As Stein (2004) points out, this led to a change from the medically-based diagnostic systems of the DSM-I and DSM-II to the more behaviorally-based DSM-III and IV (Seligman, 2004). However, the period of change only lasted briefly. The vast financial resources of the pharmaceutical companies paved the way backward toward a renewal of a medically-based diagnostic system. But, thus far, in most instances, as we discussed, earlier disease findings lack any real, substantial, and credible empirical support (Breggin and Cohen, 1999). In this chapter, the argument is made that learning theory may again have more to offer for a far more sensible and credible diagnostic system.

Early writers, such as Miller, Galanter, and Pribram (1960), Skinner (1953, 1963), and Kanfer and Phillips (1970) argue that cognitions or thoughts are nothing more than private internal language events and are, therefore, subject to the same rules of learning as external events, i.e., behaviors. Kanfer and Phillips (1970) state:

> "there is no reason to assume, however, that private behaviors are essentially different from public observable behaviors, or that their relationships to each other and to external events follow special laws." (p. 375)

There are eighteen main diagnostic categories within the DSM-IV, TR. However, there seems to be little connection between the categories. In fact, the DSM is and always has been a hodgepodge of disconnected, seemingly randomly thrown together groups of symptoms. In addition, matters are further obfuscated with biological issues. Slowly, because of pharmaceutical company pressure and financial power, and in order to justify more sales of pills, the pendulum is swinging back to the medical camp, only more for the politics of money rather than for the sanctity of good science (Breggin 1991). Thus, we now have a diagnostic system, the DSM-IV, TR (2000). It is a system that is illogical, makes little sense, and is grounded in very little science, and often bad science at that.

It is in the effort to bring some sanity and order to diagnosing that this chapter is intended. Five broad categories of disorders are proposed, not for all diagnoses but for most: 1. *Pain experiential disorders:* those where painful feelings (affect) break through as anxiety and/or depression and other emotions; 2. *Pain escape-avoidance disorder*: those where inappropriate behaviors and cognitive patterns serve as attempts to escape and/or avoid painful feelings (affect), i.e., anxiety and/or depression and other emotions; 3. *Child and adolescent misbehaviors and struggles with schoolwork;* 4. *Criminal behaviors;* and 5. *Identified disease disorders.* There is, or at least, should be a fourth category, namely, a diagnostic system for criminal behaviors. Thus, an argument will be made for four main categories, with most of the specific diagnoses clustering within each of the main categories. The categories included are:

Category I – Pain Experiential Disorders:

1. Anxiety Disorders
2. Depressive Disorders

Category II – Cognitive Diversion Disorders, also Known as Pain Avoidance Disorders

1. Obsessive – compulsive disorder
2. Substance related disorders
3. Mood disorders
4. Somatoform disorders
5. Dissociative disorders
6. The paraphilias – sexual and gender identity disorders are not included
7. Eating disorders
8. Delusional disorder
9. ADD – attention deficit and hyperactive disorders overlaps considerably with Category III
10. Arguments for the Schizophrenias are less robust, but some consideration will nevertheless be made. A brief discussion will be made toward the end of the essay on the remaining categories.

Category III – Childhood and Adolescent Misbehaviors and Schoolwork Disorders.

1. ADD – attention deficit disorder
2. ADHD – attention deficit hyperactive disorder
3. ODD – oppositional defiant disorder
4. CD – conduct disorders

Category IV – Criminal Disorders

1. All of the categories of the FBI's criminal classification system:

Included in Category IV are certain types of criminal patterns, which, curiously, have been sorely neglected by psychology. This is a tragic oversight. Instead, sociology adopted criminal justice as a discipline. However, it is noted that specific diagnostic categories of criminal behavior have been neglected by both psychology and criminal justice, and, instead, diagnosis had to be developed by those outside psychology, sociology, and criminal justice, namely, police officers, especially the FBI (Douglas, Burgess, Burgess, and Ressler, 1992). If one places the FBI's *Crime Classification Manual* alongside the DSM-IV, TR, then a more complete and comprehensive diagnostic system emerges. Interestingly, neither sociology, criminal justice, nor the FBI considers criminal behaviors as diseases, even though the behaviors are often severe, dangerous, and sometimes horribly heinous. Is this because the pharmaceutical companies lack drugs to curtail criminal behaviors and therefore have had no interest in a campaign to convince anyone that many of society's most severe behavior disorders are diseases? Politics and economics did not enter into the development of this system; instead, its goal was to identify specific patterns of behavior in order to solve crimes. More discussion about some forms of criminal behaviors and their relationship to Cognitive *Diversion* will be made later in this chapter.

Category V – Identified Disease Disorders

1. Retardations – most forms
2. Substance induced iatrogenic brain damage disorders
3. Brain trauma disorders
4. Dementia and Alzheimer's disorders
5. Amnestic disorders due to a medical condition, such as a tumor

What is a Disorder?

Unfortunately, the term *disorder* has evolved to connote disease. This is far from realistic. The DSMs are nothing more than a cluster of behaviors to which a label has been given, and the label becomes official when it is voted on by a majority of the committee assigned to develop the checklist of criteria needed to receive the label (Breggin, 2002). Unfortunately, the label has been called a diagnosis, and the mere use of the term 'diagnosis' reifies the label to be something medical, i.e., a disease, even in the absence of supportive empirical evidence. The use of the term 'diagnosis' is one of the most misleading blunders in the history of psychology and psychiatry, because the mere use of the term is medical. Thus, a voted upon label equals a disorder, which, in turn, in the minds of too many non-critical thinkers, equates to disease. This is known as *'reification'*, where a label is declared and the label takes on a life of its own, and in the minds of many, it becomes real (Stein, 2004). However, in the interest of reducing obfuscation, the term 'disorder' will be used, but only to mean label, and it will only be used to mean disease when clear, irrefutable evidence exists, and this will be pointed out when necessary.

The following cautionary statements are actually made in the DSM-IV desk reference:

> "The diagnostic criteria and the DSM-IV Classification of mental disorders reflect a consensus of current formulations. . . . (p. xi). It is to be understood that inclusion here, for clinical and research purposes . . . does not imply that the condition meets legal or other non-medical criteria for what constitutes mental disease, mental disorder, or mental disability." (p. xi)

It is unfortunate that perhaps too few people are careful enough to read the preface of the manual.

Cognitive Diversion Based on Basic Operant Principles

One of the most important principles in learning theory is that *any behavior or cognition that is being maintained or increased is in some way being reinforced* (Kanfer and Phillips, 1970). In operant theory, there are two types of reinforcement:

1. *Positive Reinforcement* – is defined as a procedure where a behavior leads to the presentation of positive stimulation. (Kanfer and Phillips, 1970)

Negative Reinforcement – is defined as a procedure where the behavior leads to the removal of aversive [painful, author's term] stimulation. (Kanfer and Phillips, 1970) The following Figure 4.1, from Kanfer and Phillips (1970) is helpful, but for expository purposes is made more concise here:

Figure 4.1 Consequent Stimuli

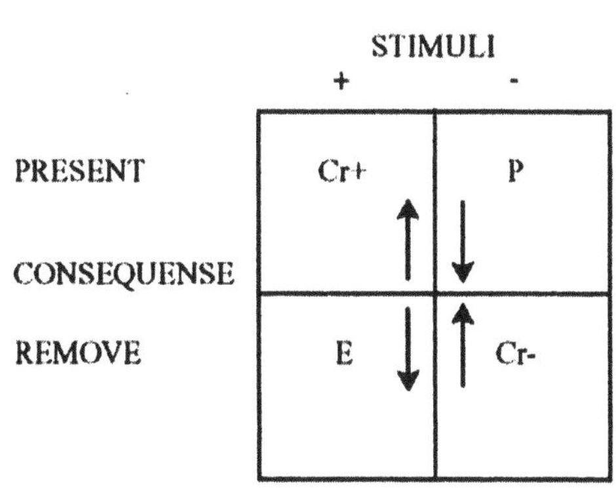

Learning theorists readily accept these principles as guidelines for behaviors, but it has been applied to private events, namely, thoughts or cognitions. The reader is reminded of the classic text by Dollard and Miller (1950), *Personality and Psychotherapy,* where they indeed support the idea that thoughts are shaped just as are behaviors. More will be said on this matter shortly. Osgood (1953) views thoughts as private meditational events that result from the initial effects of learning verbal behavior. Thus, private events, or thoughts, are viewed as being subject to the same forces that effect overt behaviors. Therefore, Figure 4.1 applies to both overt behaviors *and* internal verbal processes, i.e., thoughts.

Cognitive Diversion

Stein (1977) demonstrated that people do not think two thoughts at the same time. The speed of thought creates the illusion of simultaneous thought. Furthermore, any thought that produces pleasure is being *positively reinforced* and will therefore increase the probability that it will be repeated, and, any thought that helps escape or avoid feelings of pain will also have an increased probability of being repeated. This is the *Negative Reinforcement* effect from Figure 4.1. There are individuals where the thought patterns help escape a life that is painful, and, for them, the likelihood of an intrusive thought being repeated is particularly strong, i.e., increase in negatively reinforced thoughts. This principle of a thought helping to escape painful feelings and therefore becoming habitual is defined here as *Cognitive Diversion.* Another way of stating this principle is that certain thoughts may provide a means of *escape and/or avoidance* from life stresses or from thoughts that bring pain, such as depression and anxiety.

When viewed in this way, a relationship emerges where obsessions, fantasies, dissociations, paraphilias, addictions, eating disorders, and delusions may, in fact, be variations of repetitive and ruminating thought patterns that fulfill the role of cognitive diversion. The differences in thought patterns across diagnoses are considered in the DSM as completely separate and with no connection. However, cognitions across diagnoses may not be as disparate as psychology has traditionally believed. These cognitive patterns may be considered as intense obsessions where the individual unknowingly develops these cognitive diversions as intense habits to escape from the pain enshrouded in their lives. Thus, the cognitive escape and avoidance tends to negatively reinforce the obsession, i.e., it eases pain. In addition, the content of the obsession may, in some instances, contain elements which tend to cause heightened physiological arousal, such as obsessing about behaving in a forbidden or taboo manner, which can add to the element of positive reinforcement. Heightened arousal can be positively reinforcing and, therefore, may add a second source of reinforcement, thus strengthening the thought diversion pattern even more.

The combined effect of a thought being both positively and negatively reinforced, therefore, increases the likelihood that the thought will escalate. Over time, the new thoughts will become habits, and very tenacious habits at that.

Category I: Experiential Pain Disorders

There several conditions, or disorders, where psychogenic pain is experienced. It was pointed out in a previous chapter that there is a relationship between experiential pain and stress, i.e., where stress serves as the trigger. In certain disorders, the stress may be current, while in others, it can be traced to early childhood stresses.

Immediate Stress related Experiential Pain Disorders:

1. post traumatic stress disorder – triggered by life-threatening stress
2. major depressive disorder – triggered by a recent major loss (Beck, 1961; 1979) or difficult early-life experiences (Lewinsohn and Rosenbaum, 1987; Lewinsohn and Talkington, 1979)
3. dysthymic disorder (single episode, which curiously is absent as a category in the DSM-IV) also triggered by a recent loss (Beck, 1961; 1979) or difficult early-life experiences (Lewinsohn and Rosenbaum, 1987; Lewinsohn and Talkington, 1979)
4. adjustment disorder with anxiety and/or depressed mood

Early-life Stress Experiential Pain Disorders

While the apparent stress trigger may in some instances seem immediate, the origination of the disorder can often be traced to early-life stresses, such as poor parenting practices or other continuous early-life stresses. However, when early-life stresses are involved in the history of persons manifesting the symptoms, the argument can be made that a pattern of cognitions develop early in life, become habitual, or, to use Gordon Allport's term, become '*functionally autonomous*' (1937; Beck, 1979; Seligman, 1975). It is not the purpose here to engage in a moot argument about origination, but, instead, to highlight that for each disorder Experiential Pain occurs. Cognitions serve, at the very least, to perpetuate the pain. (Barlow, 1988)

Depression Related Disorder: Martin Seligman (1975) and Aaron Beck (1961) developed remarkably similar cognitive patterns for people with recurring depressions. It does not matter whether or not the level of the depressions are dysthymic, i.e., mild to moderate or major. Both believed that negative early-life experiences served as the launching point to develop these thought patterns, and once well learned, the patterns can last a lifetime and are highly resistant to psychotherapy. Seligman called his pattern '*Learned Helplessness*', and Beck called his '*Hopelessness*'. Three major components of the underlying cognitions are:

Dimension 1:

Seligman – used the terms '*internal*' as opposed to '*external*', which means that when the person experiences a negative life-event, such as failing a math exam, the depressed person blames himself completely, i.e., an internal pattern of thought.

Beck – called his a '*negative view of the self*', which means about the same thing as Seligman's term, i.e., blaming oneself for a failure.

Dimension 2

Seligman – termed this dimension to mean *global* versus *specific*, which means that the depressed person not only blames himself for a negative event, but he damns himself completely, i.e., he sees himself as a total screwup. Specific would mean that the person sees himself as failing only in the specific event, which the person does not do.

Beck – differs a bit on this dimension, where he found that the person develops a *negative view of the world*, which means that after a failure, he sees the world as an evil, dark, and bad place.

It seems that both writers may be correct, where the person does view himself as a total failure and also sees the world as a nasty and harsh place.

Dimension 3

Seligman – termed this as '*stable*' versus '*unstable*', with stable meaning that the depressed person views himself as a worthless failure, and this is the way it has always been and will never change, i.e., stable.

Beck – seems to concur, and views the depressed person as having a *negative view of the future*, which is quite similar and means that things have been bad in the past, bad in the present, and will never get better in the future.

Thus, the depressed person develops an early-life cognitive pattern, which eventually becomes *functionally autonomous* (Allport, 1937). Unfortunately, the biomedical viewpoint has replaced these concepts in modern psychology, and yet not one shred of evidence truly exists to substantiate this model which persists stubbornly within the professional community (Barlow and Durand, 2008). This presents a number of questions. Is the psychosocial model too complex for professionals to grasp? Is the medical disease concept of depression more attractive because it is simplistic, neat, and tidy with a simplistic solution—drugs? Has the pharmaceutical companies' propaganda campaign succeeded because of the vast volume of junk science (Stein, 2004)? There is solid research to support the

Seligman and Beck concepts, which, at one time, were highly accepted but sadly now appear to be waning.

1. major depression, single episode and recurring (Beck, 1979; Lewinsohn and Rosenbaum, 1987)
2. dysthymic disorder, single episode *and* recurring [terms added by author] (Beck, 1979; Lewinsohn and Rosenbaum (1987)
   Ongoing, lifelong problems with anxiety can also be traced to familial and childhood environmental problems (Barlow, 1988). Resulting disorders can include the following:
3. panic disorder (Barlow, 1988)
4. phobias (Wolpe, 1958)
5. generalized anxiety disorder (Barlow, 1988)

Category II: Cognitive Diversion Disorders

Earlier, it was discussed how ruminating or obsessive cognitions can be reinforced. Dollard and Miller (1950) long ago stated, "As soon as the soldier stops thinking about his experience in combat, the cues eliciting the fear are removed and the fear is reduced," (p. 201). The authors further state that such diverting thought, ". . . motivates certain thoughts so strongly that they occur in inappropriate situations. They produce preoccupation that distracts him from thinking about other matters," (p. 224). Thus, thought diversion, or *cognitive diversion,* may become affixed as an obsession because of its reinforcing value to escape thoughts on things which might be noxious or highly disturbing to the individual, such as the problems in their lives or external stresses. It is also probable that the habituation of these cognitions may for some individuals begin in early life, which for some may be quite stressful.

Are their differences between obsessions, disassociations, fantasies, and delusions? Arnold Buss (1966) pointed out that they may be on a continuum where only the intensity of the content may differ. Why is the belief that one must count every crack on the sidewalk and/or not step on them any less bizarre than the belief that one is being followed? Boyle (2002) and Buss (1966) argue that they may not be all that different, but the main argument here is that the cognitions become compelling ruminations that escape or avoid dealing with life stresses, either current or early. Barlow and Durand (2008) state, "The 'deluded' individuals expressed a much stronger sense of purpose and meaning in life *and less depression,*" (p. 409). In addition, Hazelwood and Michaud (2001) point out that the fantasies of a serial killer require that he spends enormous amounts of time in fantasy, carefully working out the details before acting out the mechanics of his ritualized offense. Are fantasies helping to escape the horrors of reality for serial killers? Athens (1992, 1997), Holmes and Holmes (2002), and Dietz (1986) point out that between 90% to 100% of serial killers had horrible childhoods, most often involving sever abuse by their parents. Fantasies are both positively reinforcing, i.e., the excitement that comes with obsessing, planning, and preparing for a kill, i.e., a rush, if you will, and negatively reinforcing, i.e., escaping thinking about how loathsome they see themselves and the world around them (Hazelwood and Michaud, 2001). Skinner (1953, 1963) has proposed that private events, i.e., thoughts, including language behaviors, be treated within the framework of the same experimental analysis developed for animal behaviors and the over-human responses. It was pointed out in an earlier chapter about so-called psychological diseases that evidence for a genetic and/or biological cause, or predisposition, as in Zubin and Spring's (1977) stress/diathesis model, is lacking. So compromised is the research in the biological arena that ferreting out support for it is almost impossible. The avalanche of poor research is actually backfiring because of the loss of credibility. In the zeal to prove biological cause or predisposition, volumes of bad research is actually working against its supporters. Therefore, the model presented here focuses on the more plausible, better documented, and more strongly supported psychogenic etiology.

When we look at different specific diagnoses, a pattern emerges about the similarities between them. It may be that the only differences between them are the *content* of the obsessive thoughts and the variations of the manifested, ritualized, and *compulsive behaviors*. The diagnoses involved in this pattern include:

1. obsessive-compulsive disorder
5. somatoform disorders, including:
    a. somatization disorder
    b. undifferentiated somatoform disorder
    b. conversion disorder
    c. hypochodriasis
    d. body dysmorphic disorder
    e. pain disorder
6. dissociative disorders, including:
    a. dissociative amnesia
    b. dissociative fugue
    c. dissociative identity disorder
    d. depersonalization disorder
    e. body dysmorphic disorder
7. eating disorders, including:
    a. anorexia nervosa
    b. bulimia nervosa
8. paraphilic disorders
    a. exhibitionism

b. fetishism
c. froteurism
d. pedophilia
e. sexual masochism
f. sexual sadism
g. voyeurism
h. transvestistic fetishism

9. attention deficit, and hyperactive, disorders
10. delusional disorder
11. addictions or dependencies
    a. gambling
    b. sexualand,

    not included in the DSM would be many repetitive criminal behaviors where the incessant and continuous embellishment of fantasies serves as cognitive diversion (Douglas, Burgess, Burgess, and Ressler, 1992), such as:
12. serial killers
13. serial arsonists
14. serial rapists

Let us examine the specific changes in focus or content of the obsessions and the subsequent compulsive behaviors which result from each.

Each of the twenty-one diagnoses, with the exception of major depression, recurring, before the DSM-III, were previously subsumed under the generic category of neuroses. Now, in this essay, they are reunited under two overall categories as *Category I, experiential pain disorders* and *Category II, cognitive diversion disorders*. However, instead of clustering them around the ill-defined term of 'neurosis', they are defined in learning/cognitive theory, where in Category I, the individual's cognitions perpetuate and maintain the pain, while in Category II, the individual's cognitions serve as attempts to escape and/or avoid pain, and/or provide, in some cases, the additional reinforcing property of focusing on something that adds a sense of thrill or excitement.

The arguments for the diagnostic categories, formally known as psychoses, are that the bipolar disorders and the schizophrenias are in a far greater state of confusion. Volumes have been written supporting the cognitive/stress relationship as etiological, and even more has been written supporting the disease or mental illness position. These diagnoses will be discussed shortly but with considerably more caution, and hopefully, considerable open-mindedness for both sides, since definitive empirical evidence is lacking for either side. At present, the arguments for both sides are viewed as resting on emotional favoritism with a lack of clear empirical support.

The Obsessive-Compulsive Connection

It is argued here that all of the Cognitive Diversion diagnoses are variations of the obsessive compulsive diagnosis, with only the content of the obsession changing along with the concomitant compulsive behaviors. Thus, obsession, disassociation, fantasy, and delusion are all viewed as forms of obsession, each requiring intense focus that redirects attention away from troubling thoughts, i.e., cognitions, toward the obsession; subsequently, emotional pain associated with stress is avoided or escaped.

How It Works; a Brief Experiment

The reader is asked to do an exercise. This exercise was formally conducted by Stein (2006). The reader is asked to recall, as vividly as possible, a painful experience in his or her life which was caused by another person. The reader will write on a blank piece of paper a letter about his or her pain and resentment. However, when the command is given to write, the reader will begin writing while simultaneously repeating out loud a ritual that was actually performed by a previous obsessive compulsive patient, which involves saying as loudly as possible, "The light is off one. The light is off two," on and on, until told to stop.

Get pen and paper ready. Focus on what you wish to say, and begin to write and speak NOW.

Within a few seconds you will probably begin to laugh, because you will discover that it is impossible to focus on the letter content and the ritual at the same time. Thus, focusing on the ritual helps to escape and avoid thinking painful thoughts.

Depressive patients (Beck, 1961) and anxious patients (Barlow, 1988) report that their pain begins when waking in the morning but subsides once they get to work and begin to get busy. Their focus is diverted from the pain-evoking cognitions to the work at hand. However, once the day's work ends, the focus shifts back to the painful thoughts and the pain resurges. One cannot usually go back to the worksite, but the convenience of focusing on a ritual is always readily at hand and can be summoned at any time, and for some people this becomes a habit, better known as obsession and compulsion.

Barlow and Durand (1999) miss the essence of this point when they point out that the obsession itself can be frightening, and that the compulsion is a ritual that helps escape these thoughts. They state, "Individuals with this severe anxiety disorder suffer from intrusive, frightening thoughts—for example, that they might have become contaminated with the poison and will poison their loved ones if they touch them. To prevent this drastic consequence, they engage in compulsive rituals such as very frequent washing to try to scrub off the imagined poison," (p. 45). First, the idea of poisoning may be itself frightening, but at the same time it is exciting, because it is taboo and therefore provides a degree of excitement, i.e., positively reinforcing. Thus, this part of the obsession may be less frightening than real life itself. Secondly, the thoughts must change away from the initiating one to the ritual of washing. Behavior requires thought (Beck, 1968; Ellis, 1969). It is the thought of continuing to wash and wash and wash that ultimately diverts attention away from reality, which consists of cognitions about the pain in the person's life, i.e., stresses. This same concept can be applied to other events, such as wrist cutting. Although physically painful, it can be exciting to the individual as a forbidden behavior, i.e., positively reinforcing, and it can serve as an obsession that diverts the individual from his or her painful life, i.e., negatively reinforcing.

Diagnostic Implications; Changes in Content

Let us examine each of the different diagnostic categories and examine the changes in cognitive content and the concomitant compulsive behaviors.

1. Obsessive compulsive disorder:

   The cognitive or obsessive component in the obsessive compulsive disorder is usually on the ritualistic behaviors. This is the *mother* of all cognitive diversion disorders, because in the diagnostic system suggested here, all of the diagnoses are subcategories of the obsessive compulsive pattern. It takes considerable and singular focus on the ritual itself in order to continue a prolonged ritual. The patient will continue the ritual until there is an improvement or relief in feelings, which involves an escape from painful cognitions in the person's life, whether the pain is caused by current-life stresses or, perhaps, by early-life stresses. The initial part of the cognition may involve some sort of dreadful, repetitive thought, which can provide a so-called adrenalin rush. The focus then shifts to the ritual itself, which then provides escape from reality or the initiating cognitions, which is negative reinforcement. Barlow and Durand (2008) point out that obsessive compulsive thoughts are reinforced by avoiding or shutting out other thoughts which to the patient may be considered dangerous and/or unacceptable.

   Viewing obsessive compulsive rituals as reinforcing is consistent with cognitive/behavioral theory. It is clear, straight forward, and, more importantly, devoid of any magical or mystical interpretations. Thus, both cognitions and behaviors are reinforced, just as Dollard and Miller (1950) pointed out.

2. Somatoform disorders:

   The somatoform disorders involve patients focusing on health issues. The literature is replete with their typical patterns:

They doctor shop, which means focusing on the making and keeping of doctors appointments, which requires focus diverted from whatever stresses are or have occurred in their lives.

a. They read health and medical literature, which one can readily ascertain switches focus away from everyday or early-life issues.

b. They must remember the schedule for taking medications.

c. They must keep multiple doctors' appointments, which requires focusing on the schedule, and playing the sick role is one of the most convenient ways to receive attention from doctors, nurses, and even from personal friends, i.e., positive reinforcement.

d. They talk incessantly about their health problems, which requires focusing on these issues, i.e., negative reinforcement, and also gets attention from others, i.e., positive reinforcement.

Each of the different somatoform disorders involves a mere shift in content: 1. For the somatization disorder, the focus is on specific imagined medical symptoms; 2. For the undifferentiated disorder, the focus is on vague medical problems; 3. For the conversion disorder, the focus is on imagined handicaps; 4. For the pain disorder, the focus is on imagined pain at a specific body site; 5. For the body dysmorphic body disorder, the focus or preoccupation is on the supposed need to change a specific body part; and 6. For hypochondriasis, the focus is on the possibility of getting a certain disease. It is unnecessary to make too much of the content of the different somatoform disorders, because the main issue is that they serve as cognitive diversions necessitating focus on medical issues as a cognitive diversion from real-life issues, and secondly playing the role of being a sick patient engenders lots of interpersonal attention. Thus, the behaviors are compulsive, highly inappropriate, and maladaptive, but again, mystery and mystique need not be part of a diagnostic system.

3. Dissociative disorders:

a. dissociative amnesia and fugue disorders: A one time popular form of behavioral treatment was called "thought stoppage" (Wolpe, 1958; Wolpe and Lazarus, 1966) or "thought interference" (Barlow, 1988), which is part of the cognitive pattern for two of the dissociative disorders, i.e., dissociative fugue and dissociative amnesia. The reinforcing element is to stop thinking about or to forget some disturbing and highly stressful event. These processes appear to be triggered by a heightened stressful event and appear to block out intrusive memories of a stressful event (Barlow and Durand, 2002). "Dissociative amnesia and fugue states are clearly reactions to severe life stress," (Barlow and Durrand,

2002, p. 174). Sackeim and Devanand (1991) point out that amnesia and fugue can be triggered by such stresses as severe problems at home or work. Much of the time, the amnesia and fugue states are temporary and memory may return when the patient is better able to cope with the stress. Thus, these two disorders are immediately reinforcing but seem to be difficult to maintain. There are some who believe that prolonged amnesia and fugue may actually involve malingering (Glasser, 1998; Hagen, 1997). Nevertheless, long-term or short-term amnesia and fugue still follow the pattern of cognitive diversion. Perhaps the terms 'psychogenic amnesia' and 'fugue', used in the DSM-III (1980), may actually be better descriptors than the current terms.

b. dissociative identity disorder: Dissociative identity disorder (DID), previously known as the multiple personality disorder (DSM-IV, 1994), has been the subject of numerous books and movies, such as *The Three Faces of Eve* (Thigpen and Cleckley, 1957) and Sybil (Schreiber, 1989). It is not argued here as to whether or not the disorder exists; it is accepted that some people do engage in this strange form of inappropriate behavior. However, the DSM-I (1957) and II (1968) treated the disorder as a form of neurosis (Martin, 1983), and even though the term 'neurosis' has been expunged from the DSM-III and IV, and TR, it is presented more closely within the texts with anxiety type disorders, therefore connoting a non-psychotic connection. The argument presented here is not whether or not it is neurotic or psychotic behavior, which is a moot argument, but that it is an inappropriate behavior whose mystery is removed once it is understood within the framework of cognitive diversion as a behavior that requires intense thought and focus, i.e., obsession, which redirects thought away from life stresses and is therefore reinforcing to the person manifesting the so-called symptoms.
It is well documented that individuals manifesting dissociative identity disorders have almost universal histories of being severely abused as children (Barlow and Durand, 2002). Thus, certain behaviors may become associated with the abuse, i.e., conditioned association, and are therefore considered by the individual as taboo or forbidden behaviors.

In order to engage in any of these behaviors, the individual avoids feeling of guilt and/or responsibility by *intensely pretending* to be someone else. Pretending requires great concentration and may become extremely absorbing as the person gets deeper and deeper into the role. One can view this as an extreme form of obsession with each different personality requiring a different form of compulsive behavior, i.e., a different personality. One can imagine young children at some form of imaginary play. The child can become so absorbed in his or her role playing that he or she can cut out extraneous stimuli, such as hearing Mother call for lunch. One can multiply the intensity of focus for the adult multiple personality by a factor of one hundred or even one thousand. Is this a form of malingering? The answer is yes and no. Does the individual at some level know that he/she is behaving inappropriately? Yes. In Sybil's story, at around the seventh year of therapy, she tried to tell her therapist that she knew about all of her personalities and could switch at will, but the therapist rejected the admission as some form of defense mechanism. Indeed, the real mystery is why some therapists choose to reject obvious answers and explanations? Chris Sizemore, the real *Three Faces of Eve,* admitted before her death that she had made up her multiple personalities and that she was pretending (1989). However, this does not detract from the functionality of the pretending. Intense role playing is a strong obsession that diverts thought away from reality, a reality that may have been extremely harsh for the multiple, while at the same time providing a secondary form of reinforcement by absolving the individual from responsibility for engaging in a behavior that to him may be frightening.

Kluft (1984) makes the claim, "Such observations have led to wide-ranging agreement that DID [dissociative identity disorder] is rooted in a natural tendency to escape or 'dissociate' from the unremitting negative affect associated with severe abuse. A lack of social support during or after the abuse also seems implicated," (p. 25). Thus, DID is associated with early-life stress. A study by Putnam (1989) found that 95% of DID patients reported early-life physical and/or sexual abuse, and 68% reported incest. Often the abuse was extremely severe with torture being used, such as burnings with matches, scalding with steam irons, or cuttings with knives, razor blades, or glass.

Thus, dissociative amnesia and fugue appear to be escape or avoidance reactions to immediate or current-life stress, while DID appears to be associated with escape and avoidance of memories of early-life stress.

c. depersonalization: Depersonalization is a feeling as if one is elsewhere, out of body, if you will, and looking at reality as if it were not real or as if it were distant. Unlike amnesia, fugue, and DID, where one escapes reality fairly effectively, depersonalization is less successful. It seems to be a way of distancing one's self from stress, which helps reduce the immediate impact from the stress. This cognitive diversion method is perhaps less effective, because the pain from the event still "breaks through" but is reduced by focusing on being at a distance. It involves a cognitive *attempt* to escape, avoid, or distance one's self from the pain of the stress, whether it is current or early life, but, again, this appears to be less successful. Therefore, depersonalization does not fully qualify as a good fit for the spectrum of cognitive diversion disorders; instead, it is considered as a state of emotional shock, not unlike the early impact period for post traumatic stress disorder, PTSD. It is only after the depersonalization wears off that one of three things will occur: emotional pain breaks through, which then takes the course of one of the experiential pain disorders; one of the cognitive diversion disorders emerges; or the individual returns to normalcy.

d. body dysmorphic disorder: Body dysmorphic disorder involves a deep obsession with a false belief that a part of the body is ugly or unsightly, with the concomitant compulsion to repeatedly fix the problem, possibly by surgical means. The choice, like most cognitive diversion disorders to subsume this inappropriate obsessive compulsive behavior in the category of dissociative disorders, is arbitrary, since it is also similar to the somatoform disorders. It is merely another preoccupation, or obsession, that diverts one's attention from the reality of life stresses.

4. Eating disorders:

a. anorexia nervosa: Anorexia nervosa involves an obsession with weight, calorie counting, food choices, exercise or calorie expenditure, with an intense focus on heart rate, time spent exercising, the number of calories burned, and a body dysmorphic component where the individual is obsessed with the appearance of thinness. The concomitant compulsive behavior involves food avoidance, picking at food, and exercise. Once again, only the focus and content of the cognition is different. This inappropriate behavioral pattern serves to divert attention from life stresses, whether current or early-life. There are several reinforcing properties for this obsessive compulsive pattern. There is considerable positive reinforcement in the early stages, where the individual may receive considerable attention and compliments from others when she reaches a desirable weight level, and, secondly, there is a period of feeling healthy and fit, with an abundance of energy. The additional negative reinforcement occurs when the individual diverts attention away from life stresses onto body and food preoccupations. As the obsessive compulsive behavior progresses, positive reinforcement from others escalates when they pay considerable attention and express ever-growing concerns about her appearance, ergo, she receives more and more time and attention from others.

b. bulimia nervosa: Bulimia nervous often overlaps as a co-occurring behavior to anorexia, with the intense obsession with body image, food, calories, exercise, and so forth. However, even as a separate behavioral pattern, considerable attention is diverted toward food, weight, exercise, body image, with additional attention on binging and purging. The obsession seems to be an escalating focus on food, especially when stress increases, culminating in an orgy of eating followed by an intense obsession to eliminate consumed calories. Thus, there is the obsession with consuming food, followed by a compulsion to eat, and then followed by an obsession to eliminate, followed still further by compulsive eliminating behaviors, such as regurgitation and/or consuming laxatives and diuretics. Once again, attention is diverted, i.e., escape and avoidance, from a reality that to the individual seems overwhelming and painful.

Obesity is not included in the context of cognitive diversion, even though, at times, it may have similar characteristics for some people, especially when their eating escalates during stressful times. The problem is that obesity may involves a behavior that is, for some people, extremely positively reinforcing and, over time, may become functionally autonomous, i.e., an out of control habit. Therefore, the negative reinforcing properties of overeating may be absent much of the time, while the positive reinforcing properties may be overwhelming, ergo, cognitive diversion is considered not to be a core element for this behavioral pattern.

5. Paraphilic disorders:

Perhaps the most pervasive of the cognitive diversion disorders are the paraphilias. Sexual obsessions, i.e., fantasies, universally begin, or at least strongly escalate, in adolescence, often consuming enormous amounts of waking and even sleeping hours. Many of the institutions of society, especially religion, are aimed at controlling the expression of sexual obsessions, i.e., the compulsive element. However, an ever-growing number of institutions, especially the media and advertising, are in opposition where they are aimed at bombarding society with myriads of sexual stimuli, culminating in more and more youth acting out their sexual fantasies.

Many adult problems center on sexually compulsive behaviors, such as affairs, sexual harassments, and addiction to computer porn, videos, and magazines. The war between restraint and expression is never-ending, well into the senior years. Sexual issues are enshrouded with secrecy, guilt, shame, lying, deceit, and on and on. However, the issue in this essay is the cognitive diversion that sexuality can play.

We need not review the litany of paraphilias; it is assumed that the reader is well familiar with all of them. Shortly, we shall discuss the elements that lead to the variations of not only sexual obsession and compulsion, but all of the other disorders as well. One well-recognized police psych profiler (Perry, 2005, in a personal communication, October 21, 2006) believes that all serial killings are based on some form of sexual obsession. The cognitive diversion properties of sexuality are quite powerful. Certainly, they provide for powerful positive reinforcement with, call it whatever, euphoria, ecstasy, lust, or hormonal pleasure. The important point is that sexual thought and preoccupation is one of the most overwhelming positive reinforcing forces for the human race. However, it is also one of the most powerful negative reinforcing forces. Indeed, few thoughts help to escape reality and stress as much as obsessing about something sexual. In fact, this assumption is axiomatic to this essay, needing little in the way of evidentiary proof. It is there, and it is powerful. All that changes for the different sub-paraphilic disorders is the content and the compulsive acting out. As stated, more will be said about content shortly.

6. Attention deficit (hyperactive) disorders:

   Few disorders have been enshrouded in as much controversy as the attention deficit disorder, ADD, and the attention deficit hyperactive disorder, ADHD. This may be because these disorders are proving to be among the most profitable to both the pharmaceutical company industry (Breggin, 2002) and the psychology industry (Dawes, 1994; Hagen, 1997). About two thousand studies appear yearly attempting to *prove* that these disorders are caused by biological triggers, but there is not one single study claiming to have discovered the chemical or biological etiological anomaly as stated by Stein at the 2006 FDA, Food and Drug Administration, hearings.

   The author, having published five books and numerous papers on this topic, has observed in over thirty years of practice an obvious underlying cause. Long ago, while asking children who were manifesting inattentiveness at school and a broad spectrum of school misbehaviors whether or not they liked school, I found that about fifty percent said they liked school, and, of course, the other fifty percent responding that they hated it. However, when the question was changed to whether or not they liked schoolwork, the response rate was that one hundred percent simply stated that they hated it! The process of education is arduous and noxious (Stein, 2004); in other words, it is stressful. What better way to deal with this stress for those youngsters who hate schoolwork than, as Kendall (1998) points out, to *not think*, which he calls the hallmark of these children. *Cognitive diversion is best severed by both not thinking and daydreaming.* One wonders why this obvious observation seems to elude the professional community. In addition, the positively reinforcing elements are intrinsically built into the currently popular, and ineffective (Stein, 1998, 2001a, 2001b, and 2004), behavioral treatments, where the child is considered handicapped and, therefore, in need of lots and lots of individual attention in the form of constant assistance, which provides an abundance of positively reinforcing attention for the very behaviors which are trying to be extinguished.

Of course, there are other cognitive elements of ADD and ADHD, such as not respecting authority, disliking reading (for most, but not all), parental neglect, and a horrible educational system. But the main focus here is cognitive diversion, which, as stated, is so obvious that it is being overlooked by the many. Not thinking and much daydreaming is the stuff that ADD and ADHD is made of! Ockman's Razor is thus vilified.

There are often interesting connections between ADD, ADHD, ODD, and CDs. A child teen who hates school and conveys his boredom by impatiently tapping his pencil, wiggling his foot, staring at the ceiling, and frequently looking at the clock, will probably be labeled ADD. The child or teenager who misbehaves at home and at school by talking back to his parents and teachers, being sarcastic and disrespectful, cursing at adults, locking his room door, and blasting his Hard Rock music, will probably be labeled as ODD. If he's rude both at home and at school, then he'll probably be labeled as having the co-morbid conditions of ADD/ADHD and ODD. That's all there really is to it. If he doesn't pay attention and is rude only at home, he's labeled as ODD. If he doesn't pay attention and is rude only at school, he's labeled ADD/ADHD. If he is a pain at home and at school, then he is labeled as having the co-morbid conditions of ADD/ADHD and ODD. The CD, or conduct disorder child and teen, hates school, misbehaves in a wide variety of ways, talks back to his parents and teachers, and breaks the law by either being truant, the ultimate escape and avoidance, or engaging in defiant crimes such as vandalism and even worse crimes. In summary, then the relationship of the disorders as child and teen disorders looks like the following:

ADD – hates schoolwork

ADHD – hates schoolwork and misbehaves

ODD – hates schoolwork, misbehaves, and talks back disrespectfully

CD – hates schoolwork, misbehaves, talks back disrespectfully, and breaks the law

Thus, each diagnosis is not a reflection of co-morbidity but merely reflects a broader and broader pattern of misbehaviors.

7. Delusional disorder:

Perhaps the most confusing, convoluted, and misunderstood cognitive patterns are the delusions. No one seems to know where they should be placed, or, for that matter, what they are. Well known attorney Allen Dershowitz (1994) maligns all of the environmental stresses of abuse as causing preoccupations, i.e., delusions, that are used all too frequently in the courts as excuses for committing crimes that exonerate the offender from responsibility. Delusions are often viewed as the hallmark of psychosis writes Barlow and Durand, 2002, but as the same authors point out, no one seems to be able to distinguish between a delusion and an obsession, as with body dysmorphic disorder. They (2002) state, "This brings up the very major issue of what is 'delusional' and what isn't . . ." Mary Boyle (2002) eloquently states that ". . . a 'delusion' only officially comes into being when a speaker and a more powerful hearer disagree about a belief claim." Buss (1966) long ago indicated that the difference between an obsession and a delusion may only be a difference in degree, as on a continuum, and not a real difference at all. No one has satisfactorily differentiated a delusion from an obsession. Why is an obsession, such as the belief that one must touch every parking meter in order to avoid something bad happening, considered a neurosis, while a belief that one is being followed by the FBI is considered a mark of insanity or psychosis, especially during the Nixon and Bush presidencies?

Dietz (1986) indicates that more than ninety percent of delusional killers were abused as children, while Athens (1992, 1997) places the figures at one hundred percent. What role do delusions play? Could it be that delusions are merely mental fodder that are exciting and positively reinforcing on the one hand, and on the other, a way to escape thinking about themselves as miserable human beings who have been taught to see themselves as worthless, a negative reinforcement or cognitive diversion? Did Andrea Yates kill her five children in an extremely organized fashion because she had postpartum depression with delusional features, that is, she was mad as in insane, or did she kill them because she was a nonassertive mouse who was seeking revenge on an obnoxious and controlling husband, that is, she was mad as in pissed? Was it delusion or obsession? Kanfer and Phillips (1970) call this a private event because it cannot be verified, which is supported more recently by Boyle (2002). The position taken here is that there is no difference between an obsession and a delusion. Both are intense. Both are private internal self-talking or language. Both lead to a compulsive act. Both provide a degree of excitement. And, both are cognitive diversion, where they help escape a dismal reality, i.e., negative reinforcement. The arguable differences are moot, while the reinforcing effects are real. It is interesting to note that the delusional person is often less obvious and more able to function well in society (Barlow and Durand, 2002), while the obsessive compulsive behaves in a more obvious and disabling way (Barlow, 1988). If the delusional person is worthy of the defense of not guilty by reason of insanity, NGBI, then so too is the neurotic who touches parking meters.

Delusions require intense focus requiring elaboration and additions of increasing detail. They are an obsession that is refined. Sometimes the refinements are extremely refined and may be called crystallized delusions, and sometimes the refinement is poor producing more scattered and illogical content. But in the context of this essay, it does not matter. The important aspect is that the evolution of delusions draws attention away from the person having to attend to his own life, his own lack of self-worth, his own personal miseries, i.e., cognitive diversion, which reflects the power of negative reinforcement. The more miserable the individual sees himself or his life, the more drawn he is to focusing on his delusions. Does he fully escape reality? No. It is made clear that these individuals function fairly well in society, and to do so requires attention to everyday life and to themselves (Davison and Neale, 1994). However, the more painful one's life is or the more he distains himself, the more drawn he will be to focus attention on his delusion, *but* only when he can sneak it in during his daily routine.

Acting on delusions is no different than acting on any obsession. The action is no different than the hypochondriac who must purchase medicines, or the body dysmorphic who must undergo corrective surgery, or the obsessive-compulsive who must step on every sidewalk crack, and so forth. However compelling any of these acts might be, they are controllable. The reinforcement of the thought and the act are powerful, but not mystical. The individual does have the power to control himself. Control is especially vital if the content of the obsession or the delusion is violent. The individual may feel drawn to act, but he still has the choice to act or not to act. William Glasser (1998) emphasizes this point in his text *Choice Theory.* If we deny this axiom, then every serial killer and every serial rapist has the right to be found NGBRI, because all of them are delusional (Holmes and Holmes, 2002). Our entire legal system is predicated on free will (Schmallager, 2006). It is only the psychologists who appear in our courts providing excuses for these *poor unfortunate souls* who had terrible lives and who could not help themselves from behaving on their misguided delusions (Dershowitz, 1994; Hagen, 1997). This topic, about allowing psychologists to testify in the courts as expert witnesses will be elaborated upon in a later chapter.

8. Bipolar disorders and the schizophrenias:

Thomas Szasz (1961), Peter Breggin (1991), and William Glasser (1965) have devoted their careers toward dispelling the notion that mental disorders, especially the bipolar disorders and the schizophrenias, have medical etiologies. This essay does not take, at this time, an extreme position on this issue for the bipolar disorders and the schizophrenias. It does for the disorders previously covered. The position taken here is simply that no medical evidence, at the time of this writing, exists for underlying physiological etiology. Not one study can be verified. Not one anomaly can be proven to exist. The argument is considered moot, i.e., nothing more than based on opinion, and any position, strongly taken, is presently without empirical support or evidence.

The extreme behaviors present in both disorders makes it compelling to accept the disease theories, but to do so would violate the tenants of good science. In addition, there are good arguments that require the open-minded thinker to look at alternatives, at least until proper empirical evidence is produced.

Ty Colbert (1995) argues well the cognitive theory of etiology for the bipolar disorders, viewing mania as a cognitive attempt to excessively focus on extremely happy things as an effort to ward off and impending depression. He argues, in a similar fashion to Beck (1961), that childhood stresses can generate depressive cognitions that trigger depressive experiential pain episodes, but with the additional argument that the patient is aware of an impending episode and indulges in euphoric thoughts as a last ditch effort to escape or avoid an inevitable painful depression, i.e., a failed attempt at cognitive diversion (author's remark). However, it is again stressed that this argument is at present moot.

It is easy for most to agree that the schizophrenias are diseases, but consensus does not equate to accuracy. The majority opinion in even the basic sciences has often been disproved as new evidences emerge, such as quantum mechanics superseding relativity when new discoveries of the very small emerged. However, worse is psychology, because good science is today absent (DeGrandpre, 1999). If a disease etiology for schizophrenia does exist, then the finding of it may not emerge from the rubble of shabby research. It may be in there but may be unrecognizable because too much has been compromised for profit. Lucy Johnstone (1995) and Mary Boyle (2002) present an intriguing argument that schizophrenia may be a psychosocial phenomenon and not medical. They point out that the rate of acute schizophrenia episodes are fairly uniform throughout he world, but that chronic schizophrenias occur rarely in Third World corners of the Earth where access to so-called *antipsychotic drugs* is absent. This poses the question about the possibility that chronic schizophrenia may not exist and that the brain damage done by the drugs may be an iatrogenic condition produced by the drugs themselves. Indeed, patients who have taken the drugs for long time periods do appear quite similar, if not indistinguishable, as those who suffer from dementias caused by many other reasons, such as strokes, head trauma, or edemas. The original term for schizophrenia, prior to Bleuler, was dementia praecox. The term dementia may have indeed been accurate, with only the attribution of the praecox bacteria being incorrect.

The temporary view taken in this essay is that acute and chronic schizophrenias are separate, discrete, and distinct phenomena. Acute schizophrenia is viewed as emotional shock reactions to the perception of overwhelming stresses, with the brain reacting in a state of disarray or what has been called an adrenergic storm. And, with time, rest, and nurturance, most people will recover. Chronic schizophrenia is viewed in this essay mostly as a long-term side effect of the very drugs used to subdue short-term symptoms. However, it is advised that all disciplined minds remain open while awaiting the arrival of good, decent, and ethical research.

9. Addictions – dependencies:

When the term 'addiction' is used, most people think of addiction to substances, i.e., alcohol and drugs (Peele, 1995). However, there exists another form of addiction, one frequently not recognized as addiction (Peele, 1995), namely, addiction to behaviors, also known as process addictions, which include gambling, sex, exhilarating thrills, such as skydiving, bungee jumping, car and motorcycle racing, and so forth. The DSM categorizes some of these behaviors as impulse control disorders.

The concepts of learning theory used here aptly apply to addictive behaviors just as much as the ones previously covered. Drugs and alcohol are highly positively reinforcing when they produce feelings of being high, which is sometimes called 'euphoria' (Barlow and Durand, 2002). However, alcohol and drugs have powerfully negative reinforcing properties, i.e., a characteristic of the five categories of all psychoactive drugs, including alcohol, is that they allay anxiety (Hanson and Venturelli, 1998). Furthermore, alcohol and drugs reduce intrusive thoughts (Kanfer and Phillips, 1970), and therefore fit the model here suggested for thought diversion. However, certain thrill behaviors do the very same things. Gambling produces a euphoric rush, known in gambling circles as 'juice' (Peele, 1995). Gambling requires considerable thought. It requires focusing on strategies, on odds, on reading other player's *tells,* which are behavioral mannerism suggesting the possession of a good hand, and on calculating bets. Thus, gambling is highly cognitively diverting. It is strongly positively and negatively reinforcing.

Equally reinforced are sexual and thrill addictions, which provide hormonal highs and obsessions that help escape early-life and current stresses. Books have been written about sexual addicts, such as Peter Trachtenberg's *The Casanova Complex: Compulsive Lovers and Their Women* (1989). Unfortunately, ever since the 1930s, attempts to impose the disease model on both substance and process addictions have been frenetic (Peele, 1995), but just as with most DSM disorders, not one shred of corroborative scientific evidence exists. The disease concept was deliberately orchestrated beginning in the 1930s and '40s by Yale researchers forming a public relations company and by the two men who founded AA, Alcoholics Anonymous, one of whom was a physician who merely viewed alcoholism as a disease. Propaganda seems to have succeeded in the absence of science (Peele, 1995). Twelve step programs have proven to be popular, and since their basic philosophy is the disease model, it remains popular, not true or accurate, just popular.

Criminology

Psychology has been remiss in the study of criminal behavior. Few doctoral programs offer any courses on criminal behaviors, and those that do seem to focus on criminal evaluations using psychometric devices that are invalid, unreliable, and never specifically designed for the myriad of criminal behaviors (Dawes, 1994; Hagen, 1997). In fact, the DSM has *no* diagnoses that accurately describe criminality; instead, psychology mostly relies on antisocial personality as its panacea for the wide variety of criminal behaviors. The FBI, Federal Bureau of Investigation, had to utilize the experience and expertise of its own police personnel to develop a diagnostic manual known as the *Crime Classification Manual: A Standard System for Investigating and Classifying Violent Crimes* (Douglas, Burgess, Burgess, and Ressler, (1992).

This writer had been formulating the ideas for this chapter, and book, for that matter, for many years, but it was through his affiliation of the Virginia State Police, Bureau of Criminal Investigations Behavioral Science Unit, now retired, and as a sworn police officer with the Prince Edward Sheriffs Department, that led to affirmation of the concepts herein presented. Furthermore, he considers it a blessing that Sociology adopted the Criminal Justice Sciences, because had Psychology done so, then there is a strong possibility that criminal behaviors would have been viewed as being diseases instead of as products of social and familial etiologies.

Insights into the Complexities Cognitive Diversion from Criminality

There are two critical elements necessary in order to understand and profile serial criminals: 1. narcissism, and 2. fantasy. Both elements are connected.

1. *Narcissism*: Serial criminals are often found to be narcissistic, where they have a need to prove they are clever, powerful, and superior over their victims and

over the police. They may *stage* a crime, where they may deliberately manipulate the crime scene, leaving clues or evidence in order to taunt the investigators, thus sending a message that they are more clever or smarter than the police. Narcissism is the criminal's way of demonstrating power over the victim, power over the police, power over the public, and even power over the media. He has a basic attitude of exaggerated self-importance (Holmes and Holmes, 2002), which includes:

1. Being self-centered and loving to talk about himself.
2. Impressing others with his prowess, his cunning, and his skills.
3. Being smarter and more clever than law enforcement.
4. Demanding admiration from the police and the public.
5. Being unable to accept criticism and blaming others for their criminal behaviors.
6. Showing off, such as serving as his own attorney.
7. Torturing his victims in order to demonstrate his power over their life and death.
8. Courting the media in order to get his crimes noticed.

Hazelwood and Michaud (2001) emphasize narcissism as the most common personality disorder among serial killers and sexual offenders. The key to understanding such pervasive narcissism may have first been hinted at by Alfred Adler (1870-1937) when he indicated that a false sense of superiority over others was the product of unhealthy feelings of inferiority which are exacerbated by an unhealthy childhood environment. Adler (1927) emphasized *aggression* as the main form of inappropriate striving for superiority. Holmes and Holmes (2002) state that, "They [serial killers] almost always have feelings of inadequacy." (p. 126)

Support for feelings of inadequacy comes from research indicating bad family backgrounds (Holmes and Holmes, 2002), where 47% came from homes with parental infidelity, where 23% were physically abused by their parents, where 20% were sexual abused, while Lonnie Athens (1992, 1997) reports that 100% of the cases of serial killers that he investigated (N=100) were severely abused, physically and mentally. The main point is that life for these criminals has been hellish, and their self-image is beneath low or poor, i.e., they see themselves as worthless.

Once the degree to which these criminals loath their lives and themselves is understood, then it becomes easier to understand the negative reinforcing, or cognitive diversion, role of fantasy. Indeed, Hazelwood and Michaud (2001) make it clear when they state, "He [the serial killer and rapist] spends enormous amounts of time in fantasy, carefully working out the details before acting out the mechanics of his ritualized offense," (p. 42). In this essay, fantasy, just like any obsession, is viewed as a means of escape and avoidance, i.e., negatively reinforcing, from dealing with thoughts about one's life or one's self-image, and the more impaired they see both, the more they need to obsess, i.e., cognitively diverge. The fantasy is also highly positively reinforcing, because focusing on it and preparing for it provides an adrenaline rush, an excitement, or a thrill. It is rehearsed and refined until it is finally acted upon.

The Composition of Fantasy

Cognitive diversion is made confusing largely because different writers call it different things (Barlow and Durand, 2002), Dollard and Miller (1950) call it 'suppression' and/or 'repression', Hazelwood and Michaud (2001) call it 'fantasy', Boyle (2002) calls it 'delusion', and Stein (2004) calls it 'obsession'. The important point is that whatever it is called, it requires ruminating thought which over time is refined, elaborated upon, and honed to a sharp edge upon which the thinker will possibly act, i.e., called a 'compulsion', and the act may be stepping on every crack, walking in hidden alleys to avoid the FBI, visiting doctors, and taking unnecessary drugs, and for the criminal—murder or rape.

Why do fantasy, obsession, and delusion develop into a specific content, which differs from individual to individual? Insight is gained when examining the content of the fantasy of the serial killer. The elements that influence content can indeed be complex. Holmes and Holmes (2002) state:

> "The content and character of the fantasy will change from one person to another and from one serial killer to another. The fantasy of the visionary serial killer may center on a voice from God or a vision from hell. The sexual fantasy of the lust or thrill hedonistic serial killer may focus on a victim who is faceless." (p. 126)

The things that influence this content may include:

1. culture
2. early-life environment, such as parental abuse or merely the type of relationship with the parents
3. media, where the authors note that serial killings have increased since the advent of mass media
4. pornography, especially the kind that has violent content
5. detective magazines and books, which serial killers usually collect and read voluminously
6. current stressors, which the authors note often triggers the onset of focusing on the fantasy
7. unique experiences, which can vary infinitely from one person to another
8. decay of society and social norms, which provides an increasing number of persons with low values and attitudes which the serial killer may encounter during his cognitive development

9. reading magazines and viewing video games that have pagan themes and rituals
10. and, numerous other influences which can be extremely extensive.

This partial list provides a clue about what may influence the content of, not only fantasies, but obsessions, delusions, and possibly even hallucinations. Mary Boyle (2002) points out that all of us, meaning so-called normal people, have delusions and hallucinations all the time. We constantly listen to our thoughts, but the disturbed person seems to listen more intensely, which we call an obsession or a delusion. We often act on our thoughts, and so does the disturbed person, except that his behavior is judged to be bizarre and inappropriate. In addition, we fantasize much of the time. A fantasy, however, contains more than an auditory component; it also contains a visual component, and so does a hallucination. But once again, the normal person's behavior that results from a fantasy is judged to be appropriate, while the compulsive concomitant behavior of the disturbed person is judged to be bizarre and inappropriate. Fantasy and hallucination involve more perceptual cognitive modalities than do obsession and delusion.

Engaging in inappropriate behaviors can be highly reinforcing. It gains lots of attention from others. It can be exhilarating, taboo, forbidden, and possibly even dangerous. Recall, if you will, the behavioral axiom: that any behaviors which are maintained or are increased, are in some way getting reinforced. More empirical work is needed to answer the age-old question of why certain people act on their obsessions while others can control themselves. The elements of the complexities of personal experiences that separate the actors from the non-actors needs much more research.

Why do some people obsess about things that are scary and painful?

1. It is alluring to the individual.
2. It is exciting and exhilarating.
3. It is, to the individual, less painful than focusing on his own self and his own life.
4. It is fundamental in the argument presented here, that people who engage in past and perhaps current-life obsessions are more negatively reinforced than so-called normal people.

Conclusion: Why We Should Have a Diagnostic System Centered on Cognitive Diversion?

It is recognized that each separate diagnosis discussed here has many other influential elements, but the concept of cognitive diversion contributes a meaningful core that creates a hitherto unrecognized pattern within the diagnostic system. It makes diagnosis simpler for the student of not only abnormal behaviors, but of normal behaviors as well, i.e., the KISS principle. It is based on the most well researched arm of human behavior, i.e., learning, behavioral, and cognitive theories. It helps, by highlighting a connecting pattern, to remove some of the mystery surrounding diagnosis. And, hopefully, it establishes a pattern which may very well pave a more clear and focused heuristic path for abnormal behaviors than the confusing, unconnected, and chaotic system that currently exists.

In the next chapter, we will explore a visual model, known as *The Pyramid,* that will hopeful prove fruitful for integrating and explaining how to better formulate strategies for psychosocial interventions or treatments.

CHAPTER FIVE

THE PYRAMID: A UNIFIED MODEL OF PSYCHOLOGY

What is the mind? It was pointed earlier in the book but perhaps needs a bit of reminding here that philosophical speculation to the question can be traced to ancient Greece. Plato (427-347 B.C.E.) began the long chain of debate emphatically believing that only logic could be applied to this question. Aristotle (384-322 B.C.E.), on the other hand, argued that the question could be answered by applying the same standards for understanding any natural phenomena, i.e., observation. The former can be said to have begun the philosophical arm of psychology, while the latter can be said to have begun the scientific arm of psychology (Lefton, 2000). Only until modern times has the question remained exclusively within the speculative domain of philosophy (Durant, 1961). However, with the beginning of psychology as a formal science being one hundred and twenty five years ago, both science and philosophy have attempted to answer the mystery.

Many introductory psychology textbooks define psychology as, "The science of human behavior." (Morgan and King, 1966; Zimbardo, Weber, and Johnson, 2000). However, Stein (2000) argues that this definition is extremely inaccurate. A more accurate definition might be, "Psychology is the science, art, and philosophy of human behavior." One need only leaf through the pages of any introductory psychology text to become aware of a dramatic switch in content and prose. Chapters on learning, memory, sensation, and perception, etc., appear to be written with extensive scientific support, but suddenly the switch occurs in those chapters that focus issues of theories of personality, assessment, and therapies. It is in these chapters that explanations of human conduct shift from science to mostly philosophical speculation. Discussions surround the speculations, or philosophies, of Freud (1856-1939), Jung (1875-1961), Adler (1870-1937), Rogers (1902-1987), Maslow (1908-1970), and others (Zimbardo, et al., 2000). In reality, therefore, an overview of psychology represents a loose web of concepts, where some are scientifically based, and some are philosophical based. Which concepts are right, and which concepts are wrong? Instead of religions, we may think of these concepts as diverse schools of thought. Is it possible to integrate these perspectives in to a meaningful Gestalt? Can an overall unifying and interconnecting model be developed that would clarify the overall picture. This chapter is devoted to the goal of a unified model of psychology and psychiatry that helps to clarify the understanding of the human mind, and the mind is what defines man.

The Riddle of the Sphinx

Why were the Sphinx built? The myth states that the solution to the riddle was made by Oedipus, who, ironically, was also the focal character for the first proposed method of psychopathology and personality. (Freud, 1915)

> "It was said in late lore that Hera or Ares sent the Sphinx from her Ethiopian homeland (the Greeks always remembered the foreign origin of the Sphinx) to Thebes in Greece where she asks all passersby the most famous riddle in history: 'Which creature in the morning goes on four legs, at mid-day on two, and in the evening upon three, and the more legs it has, the weaker it be?' She strangled and devoured anyone unable to answer. Oedipus solved the riddle by answering: Man—who crawls on all fours as a baby, then walks on two feet as an adult, and then walks with a cane in old age. Bested at last, the tale continues, the Sphinx then threw herself from her high rock and died. Thus, Oedipus can be recognized as a 'liminal' or threshold figure, helping effect the transition between the old religious practices, represented by the death of the Sphinx, and the rise of the new, Olympian gods." (http://en.wikipedia.org/wiki/Riddle_of_the_Sphinx#The_Riddle_of_the_Sphinx)

The Pyramid itself has also been a puzzle. However, for brevity's sake, we may deduce that the pyramid is, at times, a symbol for knowledge, and, at other times, a symbol for the resurrection of man on his journey toward Heaven. (author unknown, 2005)

Are the Sphinx guarding knowledge of man, or, if put together, are they guarding the Pyramid as the symbol for knowing what is man, i.e., his mind or his soul. In order to avoid an academic war or epistemological argument over this issue, it is merely used here as a light-hearted introduction to model The Pyramid. The Pyramid is used here as A Unified Model of Psychology: Based Upon a Trigger -Reciprocity Theory of the Normal and Abnormal Mind/Brain. Now, one hundred and twenty-five years after Freud's use of the myth of Oedipus Rex for his Oedipus Complex, a new solution is proposed.

The Sphinx guard the pyramids. It is the pyramid, or rather its shape, that serves as the model for the currently proposed paradigm to unify many diverse concepts in psychopathology. This paper is intended to get past the guardian, the Sphinx, in order to reveal the secrets of the pyramid, the mind. Each of the four corners and the convergent peak at the top are used to describe how the mind functions.

The Evolution of the Pyramid as a Model: Cognition as a Trigger

Ellis and Harper (1975) introduced a two-dimensional model, or paradigm, for what was called Rational Emotive Therapy (RET). This paradigm attempts to integrate the four basic responses studied by psychologists (Hull, 1943; Lefton, 2000), i.e., behavior, physiology, cognition, and affect. The model explains how external events are filtered through the belief, or cognitive system, producing the consequences of behavior, affect, and physiology. The model is unidirectional and linear. It fails to adequately account for the separate and reciprocal effects of behavior, affect, and physiology on either cognitions or the environment.

Figure 5.1 Ellis' RET Model

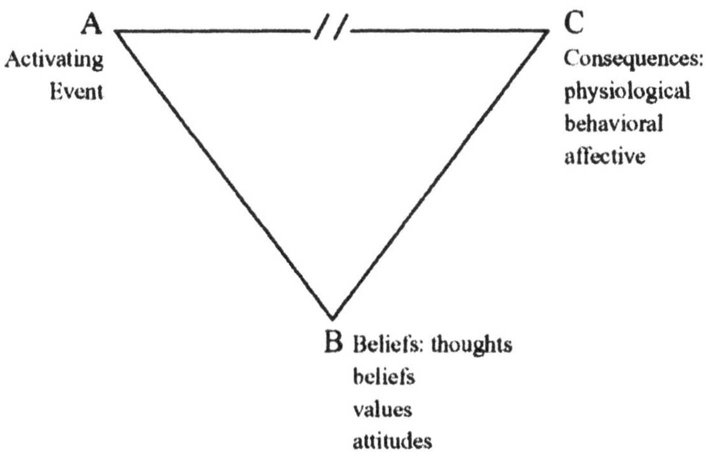

Bandura (1969, 1977) attempted an improvement on Ellis' model, calling it 'reciprocal determinism'. This paradigm reflected how cognition, behaviors, and the environment mutually influence each other. In particular, Bandura (1997) elaborated on the cognitive set he terms 'self-efficacy', a cognitive concept that helped explain how people develop a sense of mastery over the environment. This model, while a step forward, does not adequately account for the roles played by physiology, behavior, and affect as initiators or triggers of an overall response pattern.

Spiritualist and endocrinologist Deepak Chopra (1989) posses an interesting point. Thought can occur spontaneously, i.e., in the absence of any external stimulation. In turn, thought can then be made into a neuropeptide, which can then initiate all the other response modalities, e.g., physiology, behavior, and affect. We now know that receptor sites for neuropeptides exist in all cells of the body (Valenstein, 1998), which helps explain the mechanisms for thought independently initiating, or triggering, a global response. Thus, pure thought, without any external stimulation, can trigger all the other responses. Chopra (1989) calls this, 'creating stuff, from non-stuff'.

The cognitive perspective focuses predominantly on faulty thinking, beliefs, or perceptions as the cause, or trigger, for pathological conduct (Ellis and Harper, 1975; Beck, 1979). Again, such a singular-linear model fails to adequately take into consideration that abnormal behavior can have other triggers, such as abnormalities in physiology, or inappropriate behaviors, or inappropriate affect. (Barlow & Durand, 2008)

Physiology, Disease or the Medical Model as a Trigger

Another model is the disease or medical model (Glasser, 1998), where brain and nervous system anomalies, chemical imbalances, or genetic make-up serve as triggers for the functioning of the mind. Here, the focus is the brain, which is the physiological house of the human spirit that we call the mind. Since the advent of advanced, computerized medical machines, such as CT Scans (Computerized Axial Tomography), MRI Scans (Magnetic Response Imagery), PET Scans (Positron Emission Tomography), and electron microscopes, different aspects of suspected abnormalities of physiology and anatomy are being implied as the causes, or etiologies, of all behavioral and cognitive pathologies (Stein, D. B., and Baldwin, S., 2000). The validity of this model for some abnormal behavior patterns, such as retardation or dementia, cannot be denied. However, viewing faulty physiology as the sole trigger for all disorders, under all circumstances, fails to recognize the role of cognition, as previously discussed, the role of behavior, and the role of affect, and most essentially, the role of the environment or stimuli or activating events. (Barlow & Durand, 2008; Stein & Baldwin, 2000; Valenstein, 1998). Unfortunately, fanatical devotion to this model appears to be undermining the ethics and credibility of good psychological/psychiatric research (De Grandpre, 1999; Stein, 1999). Much of the physiological disease research is contaminated by minimizing, or even failing to mention, the impact of medication on physiological measures (Breggin, P., 1991, 1998; Stein & Baldwin, 1999; Valenstein, 1998), and, equally, the impact of stress and environmental events on physiological measures (Breggin, 1998; Valenstein, 1998). It also fails to account for the role cognition plays on behavior and physiology. (Beck, 1967; Ellis, A. and Harper, 1975; Stein, D. B. and Baldwin, S., 2000)

The shortcomings of the Disease Model have been discussed at length throughout this book and need not be repeated here. The main point here is that on the Pyramid, the physiological corner may serve as a trigger for behaviors and mental functioning, but for most disorders, the evidence is scant. Perhaps, in the future, better research and more solid evidence may be developed, but for now, it only serves as a possible trigger for initiating a global reaction of the human response. More will be said shortly.

Affect as a Trigger

Several theories have been attempted to explain emotions and their interconnection with the four response modalities:

1. The James/Lange Theory: Developed separately, but quite similar, are the theories of William James (1884) and Carl Lange (1885), collectively called the James/Lange Theory. This unidirectional model proposes that environmental stimuli arouse physiological changes, and then the brain, or cortex, cognitively interprets the bodily feedback as an emotional state or affect. In this theory, affect is apparently not considered as a primary trigger.

2. The Cannon/Bard Theory: Walter Cannon (1927) and his colleague, Phillip Bard, noted that physiological arousal for different emotions, especially fight or flight, were identified. They argued that physiological arousal and cognitive appraisal occur simultaneously. Interpretation of emotion occurs separately from physiological arousal, since immediate physiological arousal was essential for the automatic functional reactions of fight or flight. This theory does not adequately explain how cognitive appraisal further impacts on physiological arousal, and vice versa.

3. The Schacter/Singer Theory, Two-Factor Theory of Evolution: Schacter and Singer (1962) argue that environment stimulates physiological arousal. Cognitive appraisal is then made of both the physiological arousal and the environment, and then an interpretation, or label, called an 'emotion', is made. But, why does emotion change? What causes differentiated behavioral responses? Why can physiological arousal be altered? This theory fails to explain much of this.

4. The LeDoux Emotional Brain Theory: Joseph LeDoux (1996) claims that emotions can occur as automatic reactions to stimuli, without thought. The physiological changes occur while first producing a behavioral reaction, and then cognitive appraisal is made and can determine subsequent reactions. The brain does not have to cognitively appraise the environment or the physiological arousal to label an emotion. Instead, the emotion occurs when the brain experiences a physiological arousal at a spontaneous or subcortical level, but, nevertheless, the brain is still part of the equation. The immediacy of the fight or flight response does not rule out the reciprocity between response modalities. This theory rests on a timing concept and on a hypothetical subcortical mechanism. Some very rudimentary emotions may occur as an immediate reaction to stimuli without any cognitive interpretation.

For each of these emotional theories, external stimuli initiate the responses. Whereas, cognitive theorists claim that the initiation of a response sequence can originate with, or be triggered by, thought in the absence of any external stimulation. Beck (1967), Ellis and Harper (1961), and Seligman (1975) have argued, and substantially demonstrated, that thought can trigger emotional, behavioral, and physiological responses. Apparently, theorists do not consider emotion as an initial, self-generated response that can trigger a response sequence, but in the pyramid model, it still functions reciprocally with other response modalities to modify the pattern of behavior. Indeed, emotions play a crucial role in abnormal behavior patterns.

Behaviors as a Trigger

Barlow and Durand (1999) state that behaviors can serve as triggers, but their argument is flawed. In their model, which will be discussed at more length later, they discuss how behaviors are learned via classical conditioning, operant conditioning, and modeling. However, this does not clearly explain how behaviors can trigger a global response sequence. In addition, their explanation may be more applicable for animal research, since human learning, as with the affective models discussed earlier, involves cognitive appraisal and cognitive mediation. Behaviors, nevertheless, can serve as an initiating trigger, but for different reasons. As cited in Lefton (2000), kinesthetic, or proprioceptive, feedback can serve as information that can initiate or trigger a response sequence. Behaviors can also become habitual, or, as Allport (1937) and the late Clark Hull (1943) called it, 'functionally autonomous'. Thus, behaviors, once learned and once becoming habitual, can serve to trigger abnormal behaviors.

With this in mind, a more elegant and accurate model is needed, one that encompasses all existing empirical evidence.

The Barlow and Durand Model: A Multidimensional Integrative Approach

A major step forward for integrating the massive, and often confusing, information about psychopathology has been made by Barlow and Durand (1999). Their model is called the Multidimensional Integrative Approach. The model represents that different "triggers" can initiate behaviors. Then, a system, or feedback loop, maintains the behaviors. Triggers include biological, social, behavioral, and emotional/cognitive influences. While this is an elegant model, it has numerous flaws, including the following:

1. The visual representation of the model (Barlow & Durand, 1999, p. 28) is unclear and confusing. In fact, it is so confusing, although

comprehensive in its scope, it cannot even be depicted here. Nay (in a personal communication, 1973) claimed that in order for a paradigm to be useful and meaningful, it should be represented as simply as being possible. He stated, "The rule for rules, is simplicity." Some of the most basic paradigms in psychology are represented in precisely this manner, e.g., classical conditioning, operant conditioning, and rational emotive therapy.

2. The model lacks clarity about which trigger(s) can initiate a response sequence and under what circumstances. For example, it does not make clear that depression can be initiated by loss (Beck, 1967), by cognition (Seligman, 1975), or by early-childhood trauma. (Lewinsohn and Talkington, 1979)

3. The model does not separate cognition from emotion, and from the earlier discussion, there has been controversy on this very issue. The separation of cognition from emotion should be represented within an integrative model. Affect has a separate and distinct role from cognitive appraisal.

4. While the model does emphasize the importance of development in psychopathology, it lacks clarity about what factors alter, or impact on, development.

5. The model excludes the crucial issue of stress, an issue that is central to the DSM-III and IV. In addition, the model does not represent the influences of early-life stresses, current-life stresses, or immediate-life stresses. It also fails to relate the impact of early-life stresses and current-life stresses on development.

6. Of primary concern is the lack of clarity on biological influences. Under what conditions do biological influences initiate a response sequence, and in precisely what manner can biological influences be considered a psychiatric disease. An operational definition of disease is essential to any integrative model of psychopathology. This issue is currently at the pinnacle of controversy in psychology and psychiatry (Breggin, 1998; DeGrandpre, 1999; Stein & Baldwin, 2000; Stein, 1999) and must no longer be ignored. (Stein & Baldwin, 2000)

The Pyramid Model: A Representation of the Functioning of the Mind

The proposed model, in the shape of a pyramid, is shown in Figure 5.2.

Figure 5.2 The Stein and Baldwin Model

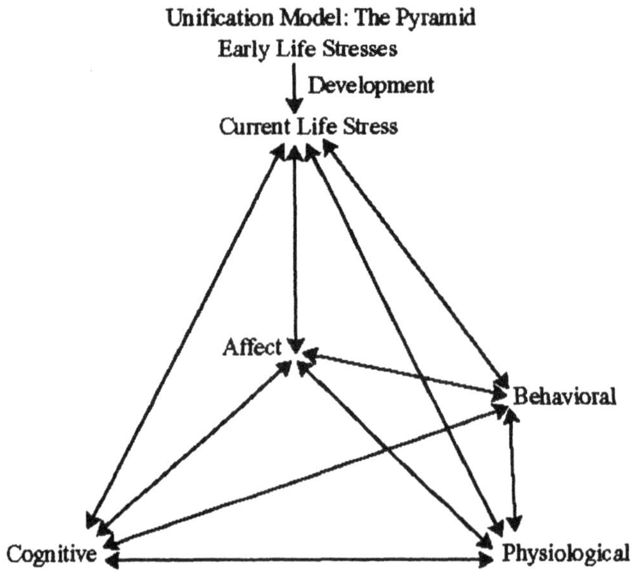

Triggers or Etiologies

The points, or corners, on the pyramid represent those things that can initiate any, or all, human responses. The crest point represents environmental stimuli or stresses. In Ellis' and Banduras' schema, these may be called 'Activating Events'. However, it is important to note that stressors may be categorized as: 1. current-life or immediate-life stressors, or 2. early-life stressors. The space between early-life stressors and current-life stressors represents developmental influences (Barlow and Durand, 1999). The difference between current-life and early-life stresses is time. With the progression of time, i.e., ageing, the response sequence or pattern changes, which is, therefore, development. The remaining four points of the pyramid represent the four basic responses studied in psychology/psychiatry, i.e., behavior, cognition, physiology, and affect.

In this paradigm, the points are conceptualized as both responses and triggers, except stressors, which serve as environmental triggers. This means that any of the triggers may initiate the totality of a global human responses pattern. Any trigger, then, can initiate a global reciprocal relationship between each of the responses and also with the environment. Each point interacts with all other points for any and every conceivable life circumstance. Nothing can occur in isolation.

Collectively, the Pyramid therefore equals the Mind. This is how the Mind functions in its totality.

Triggers

Triggers are classified as four types:

1. Stresses are activating events, or environmental factors, that occur from external sources, i.e., other people or the surrounding environment. Stresses may be classified as immediate, such as the death of a loved one, or early-life stresses, such as growing up with selfish and unloving parents. The space between current stressors and early-life stressors is represented here to incorporate *developmental factors*.
2. An *initiating trigger* is any point, one of the four responses or stresses, on the pyramid that can initiate a response sequence. Cognition can serve as an initiating trigger. For example, Barlow (1988) and Ellis (1961) represent ruminating thoughts about future catastrophes, i.e., worry, as underlying many anxiety and panic disorders. The initiating trigger, as stated in the previous item, may be a stressor, such as loss (Beck, 1967), that can start an episode of depression. If physiology serves an initiating trigger, then the concept of disease is at issue. However, few diagnoses are classifiable clearly as diseases. Retardation can serve as a clear example of a disease, but for many other diagnoses, this issue is mired in controversy. This issue will be addressed in more depth later.
3. A *dominant trigger* is any of the four responses that become temporarily prominent during the unfolding of a response sequence. For example, the primary trigger of a loss, such as a divorce, can initiate depression. Immediately following the revelation of a failing marriage, cognition may become the dominant trigger, such as worry over finances or how one would care for the heavy responsibilities of caring for the children. Soon, affect may become dominant with overpowering feelings of depression and anxiety. Dominance is not stagnant. It can reverberate back and forth, and through any and all of the response modalities.
4. *Recessive triggers* are the other responses that may momentarily fade into the background but nevertheless remain active and function within a *reciprocal feedback loop* (Barlow and Durand, 1999; 2008) during a response sequence. Each response reacts to the other responses but also serves as a trigger for the continuation of the response sequence. How long, or what timeframe, a response sequence lasts will vary from person to person and depend on environmental circumstances. If, for example, a depression is initiated by a divorce and affect becomes dominant, then the physiological changes and the cognitions may wane in the background for a while, but they never disappear. They continue to reinforce and cue the continuation of the depression. For some individuals the depression, or response, may last weeks, but for others it may last years.

As long as the depression continues, a dance, or exchange of dominance and recessiveness, continuously unfolds. One moment physiology is dominant, with symptoms such as loss of appetite or inability to sleep. Then, cognition waxes, with worry about being alone dominating. Then, affect again takes over, and on and on the sequence continues.
Response patterns may involve an ongoing variation between dominance and recessiveness, i.e., some responses when dominant appear to be of particular importance, while recessive responses, still occurring, appear for a time to be less intrusive. Nevertheless, each response is affecting the others. Ergo, all the points can initiate, react, and interact continuously within a *reciprocal feedback loop*.

5. The developmental issue, as discussed in Barlow and Durand's (1999) model, is equally viewed as important in the current model. All triggers change in form and content over time, i.e., development. Development is represented in the Pyramid Model as a widening space between early-life stressors and the way an individual alters his or her response patterns to current-life stressors. This visual representation is clearer than Barlow and Durand's.

Meaning:

The most crucial part of this debate focuses on the disease issue. Disease proponents demand that we accept the idea that all human behavior is triggered physiologically, i.e., a molecular viewpoint of causality. In some instances this may be right, but in others it may be totally wrong. Clearly, many forms of mental retardation are triggered physiologically, e.g., hydrocephaly, microcephaly, or phenylketonuria (PKU). But it is also well accepted that retarded I.Q. measures may be environmentally caused, i.e., early childhood stressors of impoverishment. Disease theories require empirical proof according to the operational guidelines established by Stein and Baldwin (2000), but rarely is this available.

The study of depression can further elucidate the pyramid model. Can an immediate stressor, such as when a primary trigger of loss occurs, i.e., death of a loved one, trigger depression? Yes, according to Aaron Beck (1967). Once triggered, can affect become dominant? Often, the answer may be yes. Can other recessive triggers, such as behavior, be affected? Consider, sluggishness of movement, or the sad facial expression, or hiding under the covers, in bed, or tearfulness. Is physiology affected? Consider, loss of appetite, loss of energy, or inability to sleep. Can the stressor be altered? Consider, the act of burying the dead as a dramatic alteration of the environment.

Can the very same response pattern, known as depression, have a completely different trigger? According to Lewinsohn and Talkington (1979) the answer would have to be yes. Individuals, with dysthymic patterns seem to have early-life experiences that involve high rates of punishments or painful experiences, and/or low rates of reinforcements in the form of few parental expressions of love, tenderness, or nurturance (Lewinsohn and Rosenbaum, 1987). Thus, early-life stressors can trigger ongoing, lifelong battles with depression. However, the symptoms of depression are identical. The interplay of all the other responses and the reciprocal feedback loop are the same, even though the initiating triggers differ. Cognitive patterns can also serve as an initiating trigger for lifelong bouts with depression. Consider Seligmans's (1975) theory of Learned Helplessness and the cognitive pattern of blaming the self, global damnation, and the belief that things will never change, i.e., remain stable. The remarkably similar cognitive theory of Hopelessness by Aaron Beck (1967) also supports cognition as a possible initiating trigger for some people. Thus, depression can have a third initiating trigger. Are physiology, affect, and the environment affected as recessive triggers? Again, the accepted DSM-IV (1994) symptoms criteria would insinuate yes as an answer.

However, the most germane question today is whether or not depression is initially triggered physiologically, i.e., the disease theory of depression. Disease theories abound, e.g., the catecholamine hypothesis (Schildkraut, 1965), or the serotonin hypothesis (Carlson and Kashani, 1988). In mainstream medicine, what is a disease is fairly clear. In infectious or contagious diseases, laboratory findings give objective measures for the presence or absence of a disease. Physiological abnormalities are measured and quantified. Symptoms are also measured and quantified. Sometimes the causative agent is identified.

For traumatic diseases, the insult to the body is clear, and the resulting damage is evident. For systemic diseases, again, causative anatomical, chemical, and physiological measures are usually clearly identifiable. However, when medicine crosses the boundary into so-called psychiatric diseases, the picture dramatically changes. Definitions become obscure and vague, since identifiable physiological causative abnormalities are absent, and symptoms do not correlate with any known systemic etiology (Breggin, 1990; DeGrandpre, 1999; Baldwin and Stein, 2000; Stein and Baldwin, 2000). Can there be such a thing as disease etiology in the pyramid model? Perhaps, but the state of psychological and psychiatric research has to be considerably improved. Stein and Baldwin (2000) have taken the first step by offering a clear and precise operational definition of disease in psychology/psychiatry. To qualify as a disease, the following criteria must be satisfied:

1. Molar Level: At the molar level of observations, descriptions of behaviors and cognitions can qualify clusters of symptoms as abnormal, as disorders, as syndromes, or as addictions. However, at this level, the term '*disease*' is not justified. Inclusion of a response pattern in the DSM-IV, therefore, does not qualify for the use of the term 'disease'. Moot arguments have been ongoing for thousands of years, and it must be acknowledged that at this level the argument can never be satisfied. The severity of disorders at this level cannot justify the use of the term 'disease'. Addictive behaviors, also, at this level do not justify the use of the term 'disease'.

2. Molecular Level: The presence of systemic, physiological, or biochemical abnormalities should be established and is essential for the proper use of the term '*disease' in psychology and psychiatry* BUT only if each of the following criteria are satisfied:

   a. Causative and Not Resultant: It should be clearly established that the systemic pathology causes the molar pattern of behavior. Detection of the systemic pattern should clearly predict the onset of the disorder, as shown in numerous and well-conducted studies. Prediction is a basic part of the definition of causation in the deterministic philosophy of science and should be satisfied in this definition.

   b. Systemic patterns resulting from the environment, use of drugs or medications, and cognitive patterns should rule out the use of the term 'disease'. They may qualify as resultant medical diseases but should not qualify as causative diseases in a psychological/psychiatric diagnostic system. If any of these entities precedes the onset of the systemic pattern, then the term 'disease' should not be permitted.

   c. Clear Non-contaminated Research: The establishment of a causative systemic etiology should be made in the context of well-designed and well-conducted research. Contaminations of medications, drugs, environment, and cognitive patterns should be well accounted for.

   d. Replicability: The term 'disease' should not be used until well-conducted studies have replicated the causative systemic etiology for an abnormal pattern of behavior. The replication should be so evident that the detection methods can be used for routine outpatient office visits. If such a routine level of clinical identification is not possible at the present stage of technology, the term 'disease' should not yet be used.
   Inference from Drug Research: Inference of a disease from the effects of drugs is unacceptable. Eminent researchers Balderessarini (1985), and Valenstein (1998) respectively called this invalid and dangerous form of research, "allopathic logic" or "*ex juvantibus*" reasoning. While receptor sites have been found for numerous neurotransmitters, and drugs gravitate to these same sites, abnormal levels of the neurotransmitters themselves have never been proven. (Valenstein, 1998)

Therefore, this route of logic cannot make the argument that drugs are correcting a neurochemical imbalance. The fact is, we do not, as yet, understand what it is that any of the psychiatric drugs are doing. (Valenstein, 1998)

The influence of the pharmaceutical companies must be controlled or, if uncontrollable in psychiatric/psychological research, then erased. Research standards must return to ethical quality. Psychology and psychiatry journals must adhere to more rigorous standards for publication and not permit pharmaceutical advertising to dictate their standards. Universities and medical schools must monitor more closely the standards of grant-funded psychological and psychiatric research. The absence of ethical research is actually retarding discoveries of psychiatric diseases, because credibility of findings is increasingly being questioned and unaccepted (NIH Consensus Conference on ADHD, 1998). The overwhelming volume of poor research, called "junk science" by DeGrandpre (1999), or "unethical science", by Stein and Baldwin (2000), will only lead to a possible rejection of psychiatry and psychology by both the medical and scientific communities.

3. Genetic Level: Twin and familial studies should not be used to justify the term '*disease*'. These are only correlational studies and contain numerous contaminations (Joseph, 2003). Use of them to justify disease is unethical. DNA findings must be well established as related directly to the systemic pathology as defined in criteria two. Connection to a molar behavior pattern, as outlined in criteria one, does not justify the use of the term 'disease'.

Genetic research, in psychiatry and psychology, is currently being conducted in the same fashion as disease research. Again, a large volume of junk/unethical research is undermining the credibility of all research. (Stein & Baldwin, 2000)

Implications of the Pyramid Model for Diagnosis

It is evident that the same disorder, i.e., diagnosis, or presenting symptoms, may have different causes or etiologies. As pointed out earlier, a good example is depression, which can be triggered by events at different levels. Excellent research supports a wide range of primary triggers as initiating episodes of depression. Five types of initiating triggers may be classified as separate sub-diagnoses or sub-categories within the broad diagnostic category of depression, ranging from a molar level to a molecular level. Examples are:

1. Environmental, or immediate stress, depression

2. Environmental, or early-life stress, depression
3. Cognitive depression
4. Systemic depression, i.e., organic, biological, disease, or mental illness (all synonymous terms)
5. Behavioral depression

Supportive Research for Each Initiating Trigger and Changes for Diagnostic Labeling

1. Environmental, or immediate stress, depression: Beck (1967) has repeatedly demonstrated that a major loss in life, e.g., death of a loved one, divorce, or loss of a job, can trigger a major depressive episode. Fisher (1992) points out that this form of depression can last from several months to as long as three years.
2. Environmental, or early-life stress, depression: Lewinsohn and Rosenbaum (1987) have clearly demonstrated that a consistently negative childhood with a high frequency of punishment or a low frequency of positive reinforcement, e.g., no love, can trigger a lifetime of recurring dysthymic episodes.
3. Cognitive Depression: Seligman (1975), Beck (1967), Ellis (1961), and many others, have repeatedly demonstrated that ongoing cognitive patterns can trigger recurring depressive episodes. They have also demonstrated that therapies focusing on the restructuring of the dominant cognitive and behavioral components can significantly reduce the intensity and frequency of depressive episodes.
4. Systemic or Disease Depression: The initiating or disease trigger of depression, and of most other disorders in the DSM-IV, is at present only hypothetical and unproven. The pharmaceutical companies would probably like nothing better than for all disorders to be classified as diseases, for this would considerably heighten the sales of their drugs (Breggin, 1998; DeGrandpre, 1999; Stein & Baldwin, 2000; Valenstein, 1998). In fact, the sale of psychiatric drugs has elevated drug companies from millions of dollars of profits to billions of dollars of profits (Valenstein, 1998). Sadly, too many drug company executives and psychiatric and psychological researchers have compromised their morals and ethics for financial interests. Recent lawsuits may prove tremendously embarrassing, and expensive, to those who think they are currently basking in glory. Who are those most at fault? Are the unethical researchers and writers at fault, or are the large numbers of blind sheep at fault who are failing to scrutinize the research more closely before accepting it at face value?

Drug therapy does have a place in treating psychiatric disorders. However, the use of drugs brings with it many dangers (Valenstein, 1998) and should be utilized very conservatively. Drugs may be the quickest way to alleviate symptoms, but they are also the least healthy. Even if disease etiology is proven for any disorder, it is evident from the previous discussion that other primary triggers can produce the same symptoms and that disease findings should not be interpreted globally. In addition, a disease finding does not necessarily mean that drugs are the only treatment course. Other forms of treatment may, even in the disease case, prove to be highly effective. This is an important empirical question which remains to be solved.

5. Behavioral Depression: Can depression be initially triggered by behavior?

   Schnert (1984) points out that continuous work, without adequate rest, can trigger depression, sometimes also called 'burnout'. Excessive exercise can also trigger depressed feelings. Hanson and Venturelli (1998) point out that excessive drinking and drugging can often trigger bouts with depression. By modifying, any of these behavior's episodes of depression can be ameliorated.
6. Affective Depression: The evidence is lacking to support the idea that affect can occur spontaneously, i.e., can be functionally autonomous (Allport, 1937). While it is possible, empirical evidence is needed. The case for affect, therefore, acting as an initiating trigger, is lacking. It cannot be justified as one of the diagnostic sub-categories. However, in depression, affect becomes the primary dominant trigger within the feedback loop.

It is not only depression that requires a more sophisticated breakdown, or sub-diagnosing, into several primary triggers. Probably, most disorders can be divided into sub-categories of different primary triggers. Current research may also support this approach for other disorders, such as the anxiety related disorders (Barlow, 1989; Barlow & Durand, 2000). It is possible that the primary trigger may be quite different for chronic versus acute onset of schizophrenia. If chronic schizophrenia is to be classified as a primary systemically triggered disorder, then the operational requirements will have to be empirically met, as outlined earlier for the operational definition of disease. It is also possible that acute schizophrenia is primarily triggered by stress, but, again, more accurate empirical evidence is needed.

The Pyramid Model: Implications for Treatment

As can be seen by the previous discussion, identifying the correct initiating triggers *within* different disorders, or diagnoses, can more clearly have implications for better selection of treatment modalities.

Trigger – Early-Life Stresses

If the initiating trigger involves early-life stresses, then, perhaps more dynamically-based treatments may be most effective. This is not meant as an endorsement of the content of dynamic therapies, but, as Brehm (1966) has pointed out, people seem to need attributions or explanations for why they behave as they do. Merely finding an explanation for behaviors, even if it is not necessarily accurate, may aid patients in finding purpose and meaning to help in overcoming crippling emotional problems or maladjusted behaviors.

Trigger – Current-Life Stresses

If the initiating trigger involves a current severe stress, then, perhaps, Rogerian methods may prove useful, where the therapist provides a safe, warm, and caring environment for the patient to ventilate powerful emotions. The content of the therapy may not necessarily be responsible for any therapeutic effects, as might be the methods of warmth, caring, sharing, acceptance, and positive regard (Fisher, 1992). Reactions to severe stress may include PTSP, post traumatic stress disorder, which can be *triggered* by exposure to combat, surviving a severe accent or crash, being the victim of a life-threatening crime, such as rape, being robbed at gunpoint, or even going through a divorce. It should be noted that even though the trigger is current stress, the emphasis is actually on *affective therapies*, where the patient can express his or her feelings over and over again until their system is cleared from the pressures which such emotions can exert when kept inside. Group therapy, or support groups, often serve as an excellent milieu for the patient to feel understood more fully by others who have experienced similar circumstances and who do not judge the patient for having such strong feelings. (Yalom and Lesczc, 2005)

Beck (1967) has repeatedly demonstrated the effectiveness of cognitive therapy for current severe stresses, such as loss. In addition, it is perhaps in circumstances of severe stress, such as loss, that a cognitive/spiritual approach may be most beneficial. Spirituality may offer answers to important existential questions during periods of overwhelming stresses. (Kushner, 2004)

Trigger – Erroneous Cognitions

If the initiating trigger involves faulty cognitions, then cognitively-based therapies may be the best treatment of choice. Cognitive therapies are offering some of the most promising therapy modalities, and it is important to understand the writings of Beck (1976), Ellis (1962), Meichenbaum (1977), and all the research and writings of others who have since followed. However, considerably more research is needed to understand those cognitions which result for the variety of both immediate and early-life stressors. In other words, the therapist must be familiar with all *specific human problems*. Different life-stress triggers dictate specific patterns of cognitions. Furthermore, therapists must remain current on such issues. For example, if a woman is raped, then a therapist working with her must be familiar with the patterns of cognitions associated with such an ordeal. What runs through her mind? She may believe she caused the rape, that she is dirty and tainted, that she is pregnant, or that she has contracted a disease. It may be equally as important to understand the cognitions of other family members, such as, her spouse or her children. How do they view her as a result of her being a rape victim? Her husband may blame her or see her as dirty or tainted. An effective cognitive therapist must, therefore, be well-read in many specific topics on life stressors.

Cognitive therapy could prove to be more useful if it would expand its repertoire to include spiritual issues. When loss occurs, people often find comfort from spirituality (Chopra, 1989; Fisher, 1992). When the presenting problem involves existential meaning in life, again, cognitive therapy may need to incorporate spiritual approaches (Fisher, 1992). Unfortunately, mainstream psychology has been reluctant to adopt spiritual approaches as an important cognitive milieu, and yet, as Fisher (1997) points out, eighty percent of the world's population has some form of a spiritual belief system. If it works, should we not use it?

Trigger – Behavior Problems

If the initiating trigger appears to be behavioral, then the treatment of choice may be various forms of behavioral treatment modalities. Stein (2001a, 2001b, 2005) has repeatedly demonstrated the effectiveness of properly designed parent training based upon sound behavioral principles for dealing with difficult children, no matter what the presenting diagnosis may be. He also cautions about how poorly designed too many behavioral programs may be and that it takes a well-trained eye to discern the differences.

Trigger – Biological Abnormalities

If the initiating trigger is systemic, assuming the operational criteria for systemic etiologies have been met, then medication may be a treatment consideration. However, the research on biological, i.e., systemic, problems has been severely comprised by pharmaceutical company greed (Breggin, 1991; Stein, 2001a, 2001b, 2005). Over a thousand studies seem to be appearing each year for each of many disorders which use modern medical machines, such as CT scans and MRIs, claiming to find biological etiologies, but not one single piece of research can be replicated (Stein, 2005). Thus, one can safely say that no biological etiology has ever been found for almost all mental disorders, with a few exceptions such as retardation.

Trigger – Affect

As previously discussed, current-life stresses can precipitate severe episodes of grief, depression, anxiety, and post traumatic stress disorder. As Fisher (1992, 1997) points out, the most productive form of therapy involves discussing feelings or ventilating feelings, i.e., affect, in a safe, supportive therapy setting, especially in a group setting with other individuals who have experienced the same forms of stress.

Discussing feelings, or ventilation, may equally be useful for early-life stresses, and as stated previously, dynamic forms of therapy may be useful. (Rogers, 2004)

Addressing the Reciprocity Issue in Treatment

In selecting treatment modalities, the reciprocity of other recessive triggers needs consideration when formulating treatment plans. For example, the initiating trigger for depression may be an immediate loss, such as a divorce. Recessive and reciprocal triggers obviously involve affect, e.g., depression, cognition, and physiological changes. Therefore, a comprehensive choice of treatments may involve a combination of a brief regimen of an antidepressant, participation in a supportive group setting, prevention of inappropriate behaviors, such as frantic dating, and help with irrational thinking, such as believing that one cannot have a good life without a partner. Thus, a thorough treatment program may need to be customized encompassing several of the primary and secondary triggers.

The pyramid model can help clarify issues of diagnosis and treatment. The model also elucidates the complex reciprocal interaction of triggers within psychopathological disorders. Hopefully, this model will serve to clarify concepts, have heuristic value, aid in improved diagnosis and treatment strategies, and help in the teaching of psychopathology.

The next chapter focuses on the physiological trigger, i.e., the disease model, and whether or not there is substantial proof to support it.

CHAPTER SIX

Toward an Operational Definition Of Disease in Psychiatry and Psychology

The introduction of new medical technologies has improved observation and measurement of chemical changes and physiological variances within the medical sciences. Nonetheless, the apparent 'face validity' of these medical machines and associated technologies being marketed and sold to the general public, when used in psychiatric research, has been extremely problematic, with unwarranted images of precision, accuracy, and reliability (Mayberg, 1998; Sedvall, 1997). Moreover, revival of the 'disease concept' by bio-psychiatrists has also been falsely linked to supposed 'discoveries' in biochemistry and physiology (Degrandpre, 1999). In addition, investment in research programs, such as the human genome project, has added more complexity to the mired disease campaign by the recent supposed 'discoveries' of genes for 'schizophrenia', depression, handedness, hyperactivity, substance misuse, aggression, and gambling. Currently, there is an ongoing debate about whether or not such supposed changes in biochemical, physiological, genetic, or metabolic functions constitute a true *disease process* or not. The committee that reformulated the DSM-IV (APA, 1994) had never defined "mental disease" (p. xxxi). Scientific challenges to the disease concept in the mental health industry (DeGrandpre, 1999; Stein, 1999), however, necessitate and require the establishment of a widely accepted operational definition.

Many times in this book we have highlighted the misuse of science to establish mental diseases in psychiatry and psychology. Most of this has been done in the interest of selling pills. Now it is time to make an attempt at leveling the playing field by concretizing what is a disease in this nebulous industry.

When Using the Term 'Disease'

Accuracy, validity, reliability, and utility of operational definitions should be at the foundation of both psychology (Skinner, 1957) and psychiatry (Clare, 1976).

The term 'disease' sets the occasion for particular physical treatment modalities, i.e., medicines, surgery, hospitalization, electroshock, and drugs. The legal profession has only partly resolved this dilemma. It is well-known that in the USA during the 1970s and 1980s, lawsuits helped to reduce hospital populations to 10% of their previous size (Bachrach, 1984). Civil commitments were removed from the responsibilities of psychiatrists. Counter controls were established on many psychiatric treatments. In the 1990s, however, there was a revival of many physical treatments, including more use of drugs (Breggin, 1998) and the use of shock on minors (Baldwin & Oxlad, 2000; Baldwin & Jones, 1996) and elderly people. (Oxlad & Baldwin, 1996)

In the 2000s, use of the disease concept has been associated with purposes of corporate and personal gain. Political agendas, special interest groups, e.g., Alcoholics Anonymous, Narcotics Anonymous, global economic industries, e.g., pharmaceuticals, all threaten to further erode scientific standards. The term 'disease' has been manipulated, marketed, and retailed to the public as a product base for pharmaceutical drug sales (Breggin, 1998). The incorporation of the disease concept into the professional territories of clinical psychology and psychiatry has been a useful platform to launch pharmaceutical products for supposed pathophysiological states such as 'depression' and 'schizophrenia'. Unfortunately, however, the scientific evidence for these conditions as 'illnesses' or 'diseases' does not exist. Since 1990, overwhelming volumes of poorly-designed and flawed studies have been published that claimed to have found the 'disease' which causes attention deficit disorder (ADD) and attention deficit hyperactivity disorder (ADHD), depression, and schizophrenia. These studies, however, have been a camouflage of 'junk science' (DeGrandpre, 1999; Schlesinger, 1998) many of which are *unethical* (Stein, 1998) (see Tables 6.2, 6.3, and 6.4), and none of which has been accepted as valid. For example, the following statement was made in the summation about ADHD at the NIH Consensus Conference, 1998:

> "At this time, we do not have a diagnostic test for ADHD (biochemical, physiological, anatomical, genetic, etc.). Therefore, the validity of the disorder continues to be a problem," (p. 3).

The same may be said for depression, schizophrenia, obsessive-compulsive disorder, and so forth. Many may wholeheartedly "believe" that some of these disorders are diseases, but belief should not overzealously replace the validity of real scientific findings, which, at present, do not exist. As will be discussed later, if such findings were to be made, several potential contaminations must be cleared up to make the claim of disease. These clarifications will later be made clear in the development of a definition of disease in psychiatry and psychology.

What Underlies Premature Disease Claims

Pharmaceutical companies have financed large research grants to generate findings that promote disease discoveries as well as the positive qualities of their drug products. Pharmaceutical products have both positive and negative effects. The ingestion of drugs, especially by minors, is a serious activity. Formal drug prescription should be predicated on rigorous scientific analysis of risks and benefits, i.e., monitoring of side effects and collection of follow-up data. Scientific, not economic, interests should underpin prescription drug use. As many modern drugs are marketed, targeted, and directed toward children and teenagers, this is especially salient (Baldwin & Anderson, 2000; Stein, 1999). The 'money trail' unfortunately has unduly influenced researchers doing so-called 'scientific investigation'. Negative results or findings by drug-company researchers are ignored, suppressed, and are never submitted to the pharmaceutical-sponsored psychiatric journals (Valenstein, 1998; Jackson, 2005). Hundreds of flawed research articles about 'disease findings' and studies only espousing the positive qualities of drugs have been published in psychiatric journals funded mostly by drug companies. The sheer volume of these papers that promote disease and the virtues of pharmacotherapy contribute directly to the promotion and sales of drug products (Baldwin & Anderson, 2000; Breggin, 1998; DeGrandpre, 1999; Glasser, 2003; Stein, 1999; Valenstein, 1998). Has volume replaced quality and integrity?

The Impact of the Disease Concept on Science

At the interface of psychiatry and clinical psychology, several related concepts intersect. There are two major components to the disease concept. First, there have been several previous unsuccessful attempts to define 'disease'. Second, there is also a low-level and poor-quality research campaign to find "magic bullets" that supposedly cause and explain these psychiatric conditions. In the field of problem drinking, for example, the search for a biochemical marker, specific gene, or metabolic trigger has remained elusive for more than fifty years. As yet, no conclusive scientific evidence for a 'biochemical trigger' has been established (Miller & Heather, 1999). The same is true for other behavioral disorders. Especially during the 1990s, bio-economic interests prevailed, with the generally fruitless search for the supposed 'underlying pathological conditions' of thought disorder (aka, 'schizophrenia'), bipolar disorders, drug and alcohol problems, and ADD/ADHD research.

Multiple Definitions

A literature search for a definition of so-called 'mental disease' has yielded multiple definitions (see Table 6.1). None of these conditions, however, fulfill the scientific conditions of clarity and precision required for an empirically anchored, operational definition for 'psychiatric disease'.

Table 6.1 Attempts at Operationally Defining Disease in Psychology and Psychiatry

1. Peele, S (1989)
"Disease might be defined as an abnormality of bodily form or function that causes an adverse or unfavorable effect." (pp. 5-7)

2. Kaplan, H. I. and Sandock, B. J. (1995)
"The social construction, or illness, involves a series of intersecting or nested explanatory models for the diseases, held or promulgated variously by the patient, the family, the physician, other health-care personnel, and the larger culture as represented, for example, by religious authority or the law." (pp. 351-352)

3. Lavin, M. (1985)
"Disease is at once a biological event, a generation-specific repertoire of verbal constructs reflecting medicine's intellectual and institutional history, an aspect of an potential legitimization for public policy, a potentially defining element of social role, a sanction for cultural norms, and a structuring element in doctor/patient interactions." (pp. 535-543)

4. Rosenberg, K. E. (1989)
"Many words have been used to refer to conditions whose definitions to date have been generally unsatisfactory; among them are *abnormality, affliction, condition, defect, deviation, disability, disfigurement, disorder, disturbance, dysfunction, impediment, illness, injury, lesion, reaction, variant, wound.* In medical anthropology, disease refers to whatever biological reality underlies the disorder in question; illness refers to the social construction of the disease (e.g., the explanatory model that is favored by the culture)," (pp. 1-15).

5. Damjanov, I. (1995)
"The psychological and social aspects of disease are as important as their biological basis. As a result, a person does not have to be physically ill to feel sick." (pp. 167-168)

Magic Bullets

Tables 6.2, 6.3, and 6.4 list samples from many studies whose authors have claimed to have found the magical medically-based etiology, or "magic bullets", of ADD and ADHD, depression, and 'schizophrenia'. Examination of these studies, however, has revealed a sideshow of inadequate research. No study has yet received overall recognition within the scientific community, because *every study has been seriously flawed.* In many studies, participants were taking psychotropic medications, either during the study or in the preceding years (Breggin, 1998). These psychotropic drugs can typically produce identical effects improperly attributed to a supposed disease state. They can cause the chemical and physiological changes that are touted as disease etiologies. Often, the Discussion section in these studies has marginalized the significance of such drug contaminations and confounds.

Table 6.2 Representative studies of Brain and Nervous System Dysfunction in ADD/ADH

Area of the Brain or Chemical Imbalance Implicated	Date of Study	Author(s) of Study
1. brain stem,	1995,	Lahat, et al.
2. caudate nucleus,	1994,	Castellanos, et al.
3. corpus callosum,	1994,	Giedd, et al.
4. dopamine,	1991,	Levy
5. folic acid,	1994,	Greenblatt, et al.
6. frontal lobe,	1991,	Heilman, et al.
7. brain metabolism,	1993,	Zametkin, Nordahl, et al.
8. prefrontal cortex,	1993,	Amen, et al.
9. serum lipid,	1994,	Arnold, et al.
10. serotonin,	1997,	Halperin, et al.

Table 6.3 Representative studies of Brain and Nervous System Dysfunction in Depression

Area of the Brain or Chemical Imbalance Implicated	Date of Study	Author(s) of Study
1. serotonin,	1990,	Goodwin and Jamison
2. dopamine,	1989,	Depue & Iacono
3. dopamine agonists,	1985,	Silverstone
4. norepinephine,	1992,	Samson, et al.
5. dexamethasone,	1964,	Gibbons
6. catecholamines,	1965,	Schildkraut
7. cortisol,	1964,	Gibbons, et al.
8. melatonin,	1998,	Shafii and Shafii

Table 6.4 Representative Studies of Brain and Nervous System Dysfunction in Schizophrenia

Area of the Brain or Chemical Imbalance Implicated	Date of Study	Author(s) of Study
1. dopamine,	1995,	Carlsson
2. serotonin,	1992,	Meltzer
3. smaller frontal lobe,	1993,	Gur, et al.
4. smaller cortial gray matter,	1997,	Buchanan. et al.
5. reduced blood flow,	1996,	Zemishlany, et al.
6. viral infections before birth,	1988,	Torrey
7. deficient activity in the dorsolateral prefrontal cortex (DLPFC),	1990,	Berman and Weinburger
8. lack of migration of nicotinamide adenide dinucleotide phosphate-diaphorase (NADPH-d),	1993,	Akbarian, Bunney, et al.

Pharmaceutical companies have developed an almost unlimited power to fund psychiatric research to produces outcomes consistent with their own drug product marketing needs. Researchers in universities frequently have collapsed their ethical principles to secure and win large drug research grants. Universities generally do not discriminate about the source of funding, and their administrators may perceive such large grants as prestigious. Researchers who accept this money may be seduced into making untrue statements about their work, e.g., "methylphenidate is not addictive," in order to appease powerful pharmaceutical company sponsors. In general medical research, drugs control, or do not control, an identifiable disease entity. Only in psychiatric research, however, vagueness and confusion often obscures conceptual clarity. Although behavioral control can be achieved with psychiatric drugs, this is not de facto evidence for the presence of a disease state (Baldessarini, 1985; Valenstein, 1998). It has already been established that the sedative, tranquilizing-effects properties of anti-psychotic drugs (Julien, 1998) are the characteristics most valued by psychiatrists and family members. There is, however, no clear scientific evidence that specific receptor site action influences neurotransmitter levels to directly modify abnormal individual thought patterns. Rather, it can also be interpreted that the celebrated effects of anti-psychotic (more properly called *anti-behavioral*) medications (Julien, 1998) may be based on their ability to *exert restraint* and *to establish akinesis*.

Scientists should protect the general public by adhering to excellent standards. When scientific standards are compromised, the general public can suffer severe and sometimes irreversible consequences (e.g., when a dangerous drug such as Thalidomide is licensed). The nature of human service provision and honest science means that corruption is *eventually* exposed, although this may take time. Tobacco industry-type investigations are now being applied to psychiatry, psychology, and pharmaceutical companies to determine 'conflicts of interest' and 'insider trading'. As self-regulation by psychiatrists within psychiatry seems impossible, stronger counter-controls clearly are required from independent, external monitoring agencies.

Lack of Replicability Adds Another Contamination

This flawed research based on volumes of weak non-scientific reports has unduly influenced the uncritical psychiatric community. The issue of the nonreplicability of the huge volume of disease-claiming research was discussed earlier. The general public and professional community has been duped about the non-existent disease validity of concepts such as hyperactivity, depression, obsessive-compulsive disorder, and schizophrenia. The external monitoring of journals, university research, and professional organizations should be more rigorous to prevent the hijacking of science to achieve other goals.

DNA Research Is Also Being Compromised

The substitution of volume at the expense of quality has also occurred in the DNA field. In Table 6.5, many different genes supposedly 'cause' ADHD. The identification of multiple genes to 'explain' behavior wholly undermines the scientific enterprise. Genetic research has proven to be an ideal arena for unethical researchers to identify 'disease states' in both psychiatry and clinical psychology. In the ADD and ADHD fields, for example, diagnosis has increased at a yearly rate of 400% to 500% (Stein, 1999). Genetic disease, however, does not increase at such rates. Only a major environmental event (e.g., a massive radiation leak) could account for such an increase. In the absence of such an event, only politics and economic interests can explain this explosion of 'ADHD diagnoses'. (Stein, 1999)

Table 6.5 Gene and Chromosome Theories of ADD/ADHD

Name of Gene	Author	Date of Article
Fragile X	Samango-Sprouse	1999
Dopamine Transporter	Comings, D. E., et. al.	1996
Dopamine 4-D Receptor		
Dopamine B – Hydroxylase		
Dopamine D2 Receptor		
Serotonin 1A Receptor		
Tryptophane 2, 3 – dioxygenase		
Monomine Oxygenase A & B		
C 4B	Odell, J. D., et. al.	1997
DAT 1	Cook, E. H., et. al.	1995
Monosomy AX	Samango-Sprouse, C.	1999

The Stress/Diathesis Issue

The Stress/Diathesis model (Zubin & Spring, 1979) presents still another problem. In this model, it is assumed that there exists a 'genetic predisposition' to develop a disorder in the presence of sufficient stress levels. This model is now being expanded to include many types of disorders and lends to the reification of these disorders into diseases. No proof of diathesis exists, and yet it seems to have taken on a life of its own because it seems to be appearing in more and more abnormal psychology textbooks. There is no available evidence for the existence of any DNA, or gene, or chromosome that produces a state of diathesis. There is no evidence of an anatomical, chemical, or physiological 'thing' called diathesis. It is a name, a hypothesis, that is taking on an unfounded and unsubstantiated reality.

Triggers: Same Disorder – Different Causes

The 'disease business' has involved a quest to discover and name the 'biological triggers' that 'cause' each of the disorders, i.e., conditions categorized in DSM-IV. A 'trigger' is that which initiates or causes a behavioral disorder to occur. This quest involves the traditional deterministic search for the discovery of cause/effect relationships. The establishment of such a relationship implies that prediction and control, i.e., treatment, is possible. The quest for disease states is to find a reductionistic trigger. This requires a shift in the level of explanation of causation, from the molar (environmental) level, to the molecular (biological) level. Even if the *cause* of the cause/effect relationship is molecular or biological, then control or treatment does not necessarily have to be biological (i.e., medical). For example, behavioral interventions can be highly effective to modify action repertoires with biological conditions such as Down's syndrome and autism. (Kazdin, 1994; Lovaas, 1987)

There is much literature about the supposed cause of many of these disorders. Different authors have viewed causes, or triggers, at different physical levels. Some authors have argued for molar or environmental causes. These include Seligman's (1975) theory of 'Learned Helplessness' underlying depression. Others have argued solely for molecular or biological causes. These authors include Schildkraut's (1965) 'Theory of Catecholamine Imbalance' that supposedly causes depression. Arguments about biological or environmental causes often have become quite impassioned. There is abundant evidence that disorders can be triggered or caused by events at different physical levels.

Depression, i.e., affective disorder, can be triggered by events at several different levels. Research studies have been presented which support the hypothesis for different triggers or causes of depression. Types of triggers (from molar to molecular) include:

1. Environmental depression
2. Cognitive or behavioral depression
3. Systemic depression (i.e., biological, disease, organic illness).

Viable Research for Each of the Triggers

1. *Environmental Depression*: There are two time periods for environmental depression.
   a) Immediate stressors
   b) Early-life stressors

   The primary working model for the DSM-III was based on stressors or environmental causes (Seligman, 1994). Beck's (1967) contention was that severe and immediate environmental stressors , e.g., loss, could trigger depression. Most people have experienced depression triggered by a loss. Such events are an inevitable, painful part of life. However, early-life environmental stressors may also trigger depression. Lewinsohn and Rosenbaum (1987) demonstrated that an ongoing negative family environment could contribute to depression. This depression is produced by a high frequency of punishment, or by a low frequency of positive reinforcement ('love') that can trigger a lifetime of recurring depressive episodes. Thus, both immediate loss and early-life stressors can be environmental triggers for depression.
2. *Cognitive or Behavioral Depression*: Seligman (1975), Beck (1967), Ellis (1961), and many others have demonstrated that ongoing cognitive or behavioral patterns could trigger recurrent depressive episodes. They have also demonstrated that by altering behaviors and restructuring cognitions, the frequency, duration, and severity of depressive episodes can be reduced. The development of maladaptive cognitive or behavioral patterns can be attributed to environmental problems, e.g., early-life stressor events. If faulty cognitive or behavioral patterns have been established, they can trigger *recurrent* depressive episodes.
3. *Systemic Depression:* Research at this level has become muddied and unclear. Depue and Spoont (1986) have argued that depression can be triggered systemically. To confirm or refute this hypothesis, research methods will need to be improved, using: a) improved technology, b) improved integrity in research, and c) elimination of arguments with the development of a solid, operational definition of the term 'disease'. The argument about a variety of triggers for depression can also be made for other psychosocial problems, e.g., 'hyperarousal' disorders, 'schizophrenia', attention disorders, alcohol problems, and addictive disorders. All three types of triggers are potentially valid explanations. However, an operational definition of 'disease' is required for the third trigger to be valid, i.e., systemic disease, in the psychiatric nosology.

Identification of correct triggers for these disorders will require more sophisticated levels of analysis, diagnosis, and treatment for psychiatric and psychological conditions. The training and detection skills of practitioners should be improved.

Practitioner analytic skills to detect triggers should be more sophisticated. Correct identification of a trigger helps a more appropriate choice between treatments. If the trigger is a stressor (e.g., a loss which triggers depression) the therapy could be focused on the stressor. If the trigger is cognitive or behavioral, therapy should focus on rational restructuring. If the trigger is systemic (i.e., where a biochemical imbalance has been clearly and accurately identified) a pharmacologic treatment may be indicated. Nonetheless, even when systemic etiology exists, behavioral and cognitive treatments may still be preferred.

Reciprocity between Triggers

Neuropeptides can be stored as memory or may migrate to receptor sites to trigger cellular activity. This activity occurs in the central nervous system (CNS) and throughout all cells creating global bodily responses. Such responses translate into a range of cellular activity, e.g., mobilizing the immune system, excitation of neurotransmitters, or initiating behavioral responses. Brasfield (1999) noted that either repeated experiences, repetitive cognitions, or repeated use of psychotropic drugs can reorganize the molecular configuration of receptor sites. This can alter the type of neuropeptides that adhere to the CNS or body cells. There are interesting implications for treatment, as the use of a drug is the *least healthy form of intervention.* (Breggin, 1991; Jackson, 2005)

Any of the triggering mechanisms can initiate this global bodily response pattern, i.e., there is reciprocity interaction between triggers. Any trigger can start events, but a systemic trigger requires special consideration. Disease theorists (incorrectly) believe that systemic triggers initiate all behavioral occurrences. This claim is false, although *sometimes* there may be a causal sequence from cellular to behavioral levels. The poor quality of existing research is hampering the search for systemic causality, or trigger, and this research is hampered even further by the absence of a precise definition of 'disease'. The interpretation of most systemic 'causality studies' is therefore virtually meaningless. Hence, an operational definition of the term 'disease' is required.

The Need for an Operational Definition of Disease in Psychiatry and Clinical Psychology

In contrast to psychiatry, clear definitions of disease entities have anchored most pathological conditions in mainstream medicine. Clinical research has focused on the presence of identifiable germ organisms, observable trauma, or systemic cellular damage. In medicine, a disease is believed to exist when there is identifiable and observable physical, i.e., cellular/organic, damage and etiology, i.e., pathological *process[es].* In psychiatry and clinical psychology, however, different standards have been applied. There has been a lack of conceptual clarity about what is observed and measured in psychiatry and in clinical psychology.

This has promoted incorrect statements about non-existent processes and false declarations about so-called 'diseases' or 'illnesses' in the absence of any real evidence. So-called 'personality theories', psychological testing, and theories about psychological abnormality have been littered with claims based on nebulous, dubious, obscure, and often fatuous postulations about human behavior. In the 1950s, Eysenck (1952) had revealed how therapies based on such theories, e.g., psychoanalysis or humanism, did not work. Many clients treated with psychoanalytic methods and humanistic interventions failed to improve, and some people deteriorated.

As previously stated, in the 1990s, scientific standards and principles in psychiatry and clinical psychology were abused to make false claims about 'diseases' and 'illnesses'. These claims were made in the absence of valid and reliable data. Moreover, operational definitions of 'disease' and 'illness' have not been developed which has paved the way for such poor quality research. To reduce the problems and abuses inherent in psychiatric 'disease research', an operational definition is now required.

The Criteria for Defining Disease in Psychiatry/Psychology

Attempts to define disease have been made at different physical levels, none of which have, to date, been satisfactory.

Levels

Attempts to define 'disease' in psychiatry and clinical psychology have been made at three different levels:

1) *Molar* – patterns of behaviors and cognitions
2) *Molecular* – etiology, or presence of cellular, chemical, genetic, pathologic, metabolic, or physiological abnormalities
3) *Genetic* – DNA identifiers and histories of disorders in family and twin studies.

To operationally define the term 'disease', the themes and consequences involved in each of these levels should be resolved.

1. Molar: DSM-IV listed the presence or absence of abnormal patterns of diagnostic symptoms, or symptom clusters, at the molar level. Diagnosis is based on recorded behaviors or cognitions, which are based on observable self-reports. By general consent in the psychiatric community, these conditions in the DSM-IV are accepted as 'abnormal'. Attempts to define what is considered 'abnormal and unacceptable' versus 'normal and acceptable' however have produced considerable controversy. Therefore, the DSM is a 'manual of consensus' within psychiatry and psychology about what has been agreed as 'abnormal behavior'.

Nonetheless, inclusion of a disorder, syndrome, or cluster of behaviors or cognitions in the DSM-IV *does not confirm a disease state or pathology*. The recent controversy (Seligman, 1994) has been focused on which of the DSM-IV diagnoses are real diseases rather than socially constructed labels. Moreover, the most recent informal discussions about what should be included in the proposed forthcoming DSM-V have featured debates about whether 'road rage' and smoking behavior should be included in the revised manual. Such bio-psychiatric excesses have fuelled speculation that pharmaceutical company hidden agendas seek to identify and label up to 50% of U.S. citizens with a psychiatric diagnosis in the 2000s

This debate about 'disease states' cannot however be resolved at the molar level. For thousands of years, there has been debate about which molar processes can be legitimately considered a 'disease'. The definition of 'disease' at this level is frequently a matter of nothing more than opinion rather than established fact. Even the oddest patterns of behaviors and cognitions (e.g., autism and schizophrenia) cannot be operationally defined and classified as diseases at this level. Disputation about disease for conditions listed in the DSM-IV cannot be resolved at the molar level. People do show the most bizarre behaviors without being 'diseased', 'sick', or even 'ill'. Dollard and Miller (1950) identified numerous disordered acts as 'stupid behaviors'. Some people will show very bizarre behaviors to benefit from immediate reinforcement, i.e., social gratification or escape from interpersonal discomfort. There have been many attempts to operationalize the definition of disease at the molar level. Trying to resolve the definition at this level cannot be achieved. By restricting the debate to this level, the definition of 'psychiatric disease' will never be achieved. *To behave abnormally does not indicate the presence of a disease state.*

2. Molecular: The controversy about 'disease' should be settled at this level. The proliferation of new medical technologies is at the core of the current disease controversy. The identification and discovery of systemic pathology is a *necessary but not sufficient condition* for an operational definition of 'disease'. For the term 'disease' to be applied, several preconditions should be established.

Potential Contaminations

If anatomical, physiological, or chemical anomalies are found, it may be that they did not trigger, or cause, the disorder, but they were instead the result of potential contaminants that must be ruled out before making claims of systemic disease. These include:

1. *External Events Causing Systemic Changes*: Systemic pathology should be clearly established to *precede and cause, i.e., to trigger,* a pattern of abnormal behavior. The mere *detection* of a pathological process is

insufficient to establish the presence of a disease or a biologically-based psychiatric condition. Systemic pathology can be a resultant, which means that pathology can be produced by external events (Brasfield, 1999; Breggin, 1998; DeGrandpre, 1999; Stein, 1999). These external events may include early childhood stressors (e.g., a dysfunctional family). Alternatively, they may include severe current stressors (e.g., repeated setbacks, losses, and failures). Early-life or even recent stressors can change body functions (Brasfield, 1999; Breggin, 1998). The person may react to these molar life problems, with possibly depression, hyperarousal, or even schizophrenia. Simultaneously, subtle bodily changes occur. Detection of these co-occurring bodily changes does not however support the proposition that they *cause* the psychological problems of depression, hyperarousal, or schizophrenia. Thus, detection of a systemic pathological process is insufficient by itself to establish the presence of a psychiatric disease state.

a) Resultant Diseases: Many diagnoses in the DSM-IV qualify as *resultant diseases*. In these examples, there is clear evidence of *cellular or other structural damage resulting from the environment or the behaviors inherent in the psychological disorder.* An example of this disorder type is Wernicke-Korsakoff syndrome. This syndrome is a *resultant disease pathology* but *not a psychiatric disease*. The excessive alcohol intake that produces the massive irreversible cellular damage *does not qualify as a psychiatric disease*. Instead, alcohol problems and problem drinking can be argued to be a *potentially reversible behavioral disorder* (Baldwin, 1990,1991; Heather and Robertson, 1983; Peele, 1989). Again, systemic disease has not been proven to *cause* the abuse of substances. Rather, there *is an association between events.*

   Some medication-induced movement disorders, e.g., akinesias, are also resultant diseases. One example is the Parkinsonism caused by neuroleptic medication (Breggin, 1991, 1998). Such movement disorders include tardive dyskinesia and kinesthesias. An operational definition should be applied to separate *causative from resultant diseases*. To qualify as psychiatric disease (i.e., causative disease) the operational requirement is to establish whether an abnormal pattern of behavior is *caused* by systemic pathology.

2. *Medication Caused Systemic Changes*: It is well established that a prolonged intake of medications , psychotropic and non-psychotropic, can produce iatrogenic bodily changes. This is, in fact, one of the main contaminations in most disease studies. For example, almost every study about ADHD that claims to have discovered the *systemic cause* of the condition has been contaminated by the ongoing medication of the children. These medications can produce the systemic readings, i.e., elevated

arousal levels, attributed as causative of ADHD. Systemic studies should be designed to isolate the medications that can produce pathological processes. Therefore, the biopsychiatric claims that *systemic pathology causes the behavioral or cognitive diagnosis* have been premature. Professional journals should not accept research articles when the medication histories of participants have not been properly documented, are unclear, or have been dismissed as irrelevant.

3. *Environmental Caused Systemic Changes*: Prolonged environmental stresses, whether current or early childhood, can produce systemic changes and should be ruled out before making the assumption that the systemic changes were there first and were responsible for the behavioral problems.
4. *Cognitive Caused Systemic Changes*: Cognitive patterns can cause systemic changes and must be ruled out before making the assumption that the systemic anomalies have produced the behavioral problems.
5. *Contaminated Studies*: The training of psychologists includes experimental research design and applications of sophisticated statistical techniques and methods to reduce the risk of random error and contamination. Yet many studies of systemic diseases or the biological basis of behaviors have been deeply flawed by weak experimental design, poor methodology, or inadequate statistical analysis. These studies have been used to bolster the persistent biopsychiatric claims about supposed disease states. There has been too much appeasement amongst psychiatric researchers of pharmaceutical companies for financial gain. The quest to 'discover' disease etiology in psychiatry and clinical psychology has promoted flagrant irresponsibility and a total disregard of ethics. Examples of poor science have included: a) insufficient information about medication histories, b) selection of research participants from biased population samples, where selected participants have been from lower socio-economic strata or where early environmental stressors can produce systemic changes, i.e., known as statistical confounding, c) failure to separate diagnostic disorders within the studies, e.g., not studying ADD separately from ADHD, and d) failure to include properly controlled participant groups. With such poor-quality research methodologies, a proper discovery of disease entities can never be made. Ironically, the continued use of poor methods selected by disease researchers to search for diseases means they are unlikely to ever be found.
6. *Lack of Replicability*: Premature declarations have been made about diseases and about the supposed 'biological basis' of psychiatric conditions. In science, new findings should be subject to replication, *without undue influence from external vested interests* , e.g., from pharmaceutical companies. Interpretations from these contaminated studies, however, are meaningless until responsible, independent scientists, i.e.,

those who are not funded by the drug companies, have completed successful replications. As indicated earlier, the modern-day revivalist of ADD and ADHD disease theories, Barkley (1995), readily admits that these studies cannot be replicated on a clinical level. In fact, close examination of the literature indicates that Barkley has backed off from using the term 'disease' and instead has been substituting 'biologically-based disorder' or, more recently, 'developmental disorder' (Barkley, 1995). However, it is proposed that neither the public nor the professional community fully understands the different meanings of the terms and tend to interpret them all as some type of systemic disease.

Replication should be of sufficient quality that subsequent measurement could be conducted at the standard beyond the research level, i.e., in the clinic. When clinical measurement is sufficiently reliable that it can be used as a diagnostic tool, then it may be possible to specify a disease or biological disorder. The term 'biologically-based disorder' should not be used as a clever substitute for the term 'disease'. Again, both Swanson (1998) and Barkley (1995) have made claims of finding biological causes of ADHD/ADD in their research that even they admit cannot be repeated under everyday clinical conditions.

7. *Genetics:* In psychiatry and psychology, there has been an ongoing quest for the genetic base of behavior as proof of the existence of a disease. Two types of studies have been included: a) Twin studies, and b) DNA 'discoveries'.
    1. Twin Studies: These studies have been used to attempt to 'prove' a genetic basis in disorders such as 'schizophrenia', depression, problem drinking, and more recently, ADD and ADHD. Twin studies, however, have not been widely accepted as proof of a disease entity. The extensive review of twin studies by Joseph (1999 2003) showed the overwhelming contamination and flawed methodologies embedded in these reports. All twin studies, moreover, are *correlational*; such research *proves nothing*. Correlational evidence, even at best, is merely *suggestive* and cannot support definitive claims about *causal evidence of diseases*.
    2. DNA "discoveries": Many ADHD studies have been used to make claims about the discovery of the genetic basis for abnormal conditions, e.g., 'schizophrenia', depression, problem drinking, and ADD/ADHD (see Table 6.5). Close examination of these studies has revealed a slew of findings which have the same problems as the previously mentioned disease studies: they are not replicable, with poor methodologies and unsubstantiated, premature claims; there is a mass production of numerous unsubstantiated claims of finding *the* gene, and volume has replaced quality. However, in DNA research, any findings associated with an unproven systemic

etiology are meaningless (Joseph, 1999, 2003). Again, the lack of an operational definition of 'disease' prevents real understanding. DNA findings may *be associated with a molar behavior pattern* represented as abnormal in the DSM-IV. These findings, however, do not prove the existence of a 'disease'. For a DNA finding to be meaningful and valid, *it should predict an identifiable systemic disease* (i.e., fulfilling criterion two), which is clearly causative of a behavioral abnormality. *It is incorrect to jump from a DNA finding to a behavioral abnormality that has not been proven to be a disease.*

Again, attempts to convince practitioners in the psychiatric and psychological community about 'disease' states based on DNA findings may be strongly motivated by economic interests and political agendas. If a disease entity has not been established, scientists cannot claim that a 'DNA finding' proves the existence of a disease or the 'biological basis of behavior'. The conceptual shift from 'DNA findings' to molar (or overt) behavior is *implausible*. Even if a DNA finding has a 100% (1.00) correlational relationship with a behavioral disorder, this finding is not evidence of a 'disease'. As noted in Criterion One, no such disease can be established at the molar level. Therefore, jumping from DNA to molar is insufficient. It is the elements in Criterion Two (i.e., at the molecular level) that should be satisfied as evidence for a real systemic basis for a disease. Then, accurate DNA findings can lend powerful support to the statement of a disease finding.

Operationally Defining the Disease Concept

In order to develop an operational definition of disease in psychiatry and psychology, the three previously discussed issues must be addressed:

1. *Molar Level*: A molar description of behaviors and cognitions can signify clusters of symptoms as pathology, abnormality, or as a syndrome. At this level, however, these behavioral or cognitive patterns cannot qualify for the use of the term 'disease' or 'biologically-based disorder'. Inclusion of a symptom pattern in the DSM-IV does not qualify for the use of the term 'disease'. *Severity* of the behavioral or cognitive pattern, i.e., schizophrenia, autism, or major depression, does not qualify for the use of the term 'disease'.
2. *Molecular Level*: The *presence of systemic, physiological, or biochemical abnormalities* should be present to qualify the condition as a 'disease', with the establishment of the following *necessary and sufficient conditions*:
   a) Causative and Not Resultant: It should be established that the *systemic pathology causes* the molar pattern of behavior. Detection of the systemic pattern should predict the onset of the condition, as shown in several well-conducted studies, *before any molar symptoms have appeared.* Prediction is a basic aspect of the definition of

causation in the deterministic philosophy of science and should be fully satisfied in this definition. Systemic patterns resulting from the environment, drug use or medications, and cognitive or behavioral patterns, do not qualify a condition for the use of the term 'disease'. If any of these entities *precedes* the onset of the systemic pattern, then the term 'disease' is inappropriate.

b) Clear Non-Contaminated Research: Establishment of a systemic causation etiology should be made in the context of well-designed and well-conducted research. The criteria for publishing in refereed psychiatry/psychology journals should be much improved (i.e., more scientific rigor). Ethical policies should determine the publishing of scientific papers, not pressure from pharmaceutical companies.

c) Replication: The term 'disease' should not be used until well-conducted studies have replicated the causative systemic etiology with an abnormal behavior pattern. Replication studies should be completed independently of pharmaceutical company financial support. The level of replication should be available at the clinical level, and detection should be so evident that measures of systemic pathology can be used on routine, outpatient, office, and clinic visits. If such a routine level of clinical identification is not possible at that stage of development of technology, the term 'disease' should not be used. Without clearly well-established causative systemic pathology, the term 'disease' should not be used.

Genetic Level: Twin and familial studies should not be used to justify the use of the term 'disease'. They are only *correlational studies* and have many contaminations. DNA findings strongly support a disease concept if they are clearly related to a well-established systemic pathology (outlined in the molecular level, criteria two). If criteria two has not been satisfied, then DNA findings are insufficient for the use of the term 'disease'.

Qualifying Diseases

Few diagnoses would fulfill the requirements for the proposed operational definition of 'disease'. With such diagnoses: systemic damage has been clearly established; the damage is clearly causative of the molar behavior patterns; neither medications, environmental stressors, nor cognitive or behavioral patterns clearly have produced the systemic damage; the research has a sufficient history of uncontaminated inquiry, and there is sufficient replication of findings. These 'diseases' include:

1. Some forms of mental retardation, e.g., Down's syndrome, hydrocephalus

2. Certain forms of dementia, e.g., Alzheimer's, Pick's, and dementia due to other general medical conditions, i.e., GPI
3. Amnestic Disorders due to general medical conditions
4. Certain forms of Sleep Disorders, e.g., sleep apneas, where criterion two has been met
5. Certain forms of Communication Disorders , e.g., some aphasias, where criterion two has been met
6. Certain forms of Perceptual and Sensory Disorders ,e.g., alexias, proposagnosia, where criterion two has been met

It can be tempting to claim that some severe behavioral disorders have causative diseases. Current research findings, however, are presently inadequate to make that judgement. The severities of the behavioral and cognitive abnormalities are insufficient to be identified as psychiatric diseases, i.e., if clear evidence for criterion two has not been fulfilled. These disorders include 'schizophrenia', pervasive developmental disorders, and bipolar disorders.

Attentional disorders, learning disorders, and depressive disorders are even less established. The molar and behavioral patterns of the attentional disorders are more subtle and even more disputed. Addictive disorders are also not supported for systemic causation. Historically, the use of the term 'disease' for addictions is based on molar behavioral patterns. The term 'disease' has been used metaphorically and politically for addictive behaviors. Even Jellinek's (1960) gamma alcoholic does not qualify in this scientific context. The designation of any of the above disorders as causative diseases will depend on whether future research findings fulfill the requirements of the operational definition of 'disease'.

Proposed Revision of Diagnosis Based on Triggers or Causes

The discovery of any causative disease will not be a panacea for a specific diagnosis. Even with the establishment of a true systemic etiology, almost any diagnosis will require further sub-diagnosis, according to the trigger. For example, a systemic cause for 'depression' may be discovered. This does not, however, mean that all depression is a 'disease'. There is still 'environmental depression', 'cognitive or behavioral depression', and then, possibly, 'systemic depression'. The same is true for numerous other diagnoses. This will require realignment, or even abandonment, of DSM. A formal scientific system will reduce confusion about which diagnosis is or is not considered a disease. With an accurate diagnostic system, directions for intervention will be clearer. Incorrect treatment prescriptions will be reduced, resulting in improved treatment.

Closing Comments

Use of the term 'disease' in psychology and psychiatry sets the conditions for the use of medications. This is especially crucial when the psychological and physical health of children is involved. Vague use of the term 'disease' and the poor quality of disease research have justified the epidemic use of drug treatments. An operational definition of disease is required for professional practice, complemented by a return to ethical research.

In the next chapter, we will explore the complexity of thought. We do this in order to demonstrate that attributing one single thing as the cause of abnormal behavior makes little sense when we examine the enormous intricacies that go into the human thinking process. A quasi-mathematical model is presented, not as an accurate model, but merely as a representation of what it takes to have one single thought. When looked at in this way, we learn that understanding cancer eludes us, but we readily see that the mind is even far more complex, and, therefore, is it any wonder that we are having so much trouble deciphering the intricacies of the mind. In addition, we may explore, in a different way, that the mind and brain are really one and the same, but so enormous are the variables and their combinations that how the brain works as a mind may elude us for a very, very long time, or even that it may never be solved.

CHAPTER SEVEN

WHAT IS THOUGHT?

A QUASI-MATHEMATICAL MODEL AS A REPRESENTATION OF THE COMPLEXITY OF THE BRAIN AND THE MIND, ILLUSTRATING WHY CLARITY HAS ELUDED PSYCHOLOGY

This chapter is not an attempt to propose an absolute model of the "mind". It is intended to serve as a demonstrative or conceptual model. It is used here to point out why any singular model of human psychological functioning, such as the disease model or the learning model, is simplistic and completely unrealistic.

The model presented here is also intended to bridge the gap between the mind/body dualism, between mechanism and vitalism, between the phenomenological world and metaphysical explanations, and ultimately between free will and compulsion. All that is stated applies only to the issue of mind and brain and not to the cosmology of the universe or existence.

The difference between the mind and the body, henceforth to be referred to as 'the brain', began with the evolution of civilization. Is the mind something special? Is it something that defies natural rules? Pythagoras (570-497 B.C.E.) may have been the first to believe that, "All things are made up of numbers." He not only believed this to be true for the universe, but for the mind as well. Immediately, the argument for a mind/body dualism began. Plato (427-347 B.C.E.) argued that the mind consisted of ideas which came from a higher authority. One can trace through the millennia that support of this concept permeated through the more theological strains of philosophy. We must have a mind, a soul, and free will in order to justify worshipping the Divine. Thus, metaphysics, at least where applicable to the mind, began. Aristotle (384-322 B.C.E.) countered that all things are subject to natural law, which included the mind or thought. The seed for understanding the physiologically functioning thing called a 'brain' began. The argument strongly erupted during the Age of Enlightenment, during the 16th to the 18th centuries. However, even more recently, the notion that the brain, and, therefore, the mind, could be understood through science, physics, and the application of mathematics to language, grew even stronger with Thomas Kuhn (1922-1996) (1957), Bertrand Russell (1872-1970) (1935), and Ludwig Wittgenstein (1889-1951) (1965). However, the most serious attempts to merge the use of science with mathematically precise theories became earnest with Ebbinghaus (1850-1909) (1885), Thorndike (1874-1949) (1903), Hull (1884-1952) (1933), (1943), Frege (1848-1925) (1903), and Bush and Mosteller (1955). Their models focused on learning concepts, which is the singular concept that learning underlies the functioning of the mind. Ah, were it that simple? Sadly, the well-developed concepts of learning from the early pioneers, when applied to the modification of behaviors, has seemed to disappear, where much of the latest research violates well-established and well-documented principles. (Stein, 2001; 2003; 2004)

The newest Zeitgeist involves the anatomy and chemistry of the brain. Namely, this too is another singular theory that all things of the mind can be explained by understanding its physiology. This school of thought has grown out of the advent of computerized medical machines, such as CT scans, MRIs, electron microscopes, SPECT scans, and PET scans. The number of those currently focusing on this singular theory are far too extensive to attempt an enumeration here. Suffice it to say, this has been discussed in detail in previous chapters. The biggest problem in this arena is the shenanigans of pharmaceutical company moneys compromising the integrity of this research to such an extent that one can no longer trust in the ethics of what is published. The money nexus to promote these concepts is also destroying its legitimacy. It is because of the debacle of bad research, or junk science (DeGrandpre, 1999), that any real or legitimate findings may elude psychology, having been buried in an avalanche of unethical research. These circumstances still exist today and actually hinder finding the real physiological underpinnings of the mind. Everything being produced is not gaining acceptance because of the extent of destroying anything scientific within the study of the brain and mind.

Thus, singular theories, one of language, one of learning, and one of physiology, have been posited, but none has been successful in explaining how the mind works or whether or not the mind and the brain are the same or different.

What Is a Thought?

A thought is the end product of a complex set of events. The occurrence of combining these events has already been covered in the chapter "The Pyramid". Delineated were the five components of "behavior", where anyone can trigger a final behavior, which may be motoric or verbal. The five components are: environmental, i.e., early life through current life, cognitive, behavioral, emotional, and physiological. We explored how any of these variables can initiate or trigger a behavior, and, once initiated, a dance of interactions occurs, leading to the final event, which can also be cognitive, behavioral, emotional, and physiological. We can elucidate this concept into a more specific conceptual model, expressed in mathematical terms.

The Overall Quasi-Mathematical Model of a Thought

It must be explained, in the easiest terms possible, that permutations represent every possible combination within a set. Thus, each of the five variables can be considered five sets, but within each variable are subsets that can combine into a finite number of permutations. Permutations are expressed with the sign "!", which stands for factorial. Thus, the permutations of six variables is expressed as 6!. The solution is 6 x 5 x 4 x 3 x 2 x1 = 720 combinations, which is the totality of all possible outcomes.

In its broadest form, a thought would be represented as:

{E!} x {C!} x {P!} x {B!} x {A!} x {I!} x p! = an extraordinarily large number, indicating a finite number ending in a thought. Each represents sets of the following:

x = multiplication

{ } = represents a set.

E = the set of all environmental experiences in a persons life, from birth rightup to the moment of measurement.

C = the number of cognitive memories stored in the person's memory banks.

P = the physiological responses.

B = the number of possible motoric responses or behavioral responses.

A = the number of affective or emotional responses.

I = the instincts we are born with, perhaps called *a priori* knowledge by some philosophers, or more elaborately and eloquently presented by Piaget as the unlearned, instinctual way we organize information.

The Model in More Detail

The more detailed equation would be represented as:

{E!} x {t! x b! x a! x P! x 5! X L!} x {BC! X N! x ~200NT! X NI!} x {B!} x {A!} x {I!} x {p!} = Thought

Thus, E! = environmental experiences which would number in the millions for a twenty-one-year-old person, more for a forty-year-old person, and so forth.

The Next Set Represents Cognition Subsets:

t! = the number of thoughts which are the most immediately available or surface cognitions that some would call consciousness. These are stored memories composed of neuropeptides. (Chopra, 1993)

B! = the number of beliefs, also neuroptides, stored in long-term memory.

A! = the number of attitudes, i.e., neuropeptides, which are the deepest beliefs about ourselves and others, stored in very-long-term memory.

P! = the number of perceptions, ie., neuropeptides, accurate or inaccurate, that we store in long-term memory.

5! = the permutations of sensory experiences (Note: Early psychology began on the singular notion that if we could understand the senses, or how information is sent to the brain, we could, in turn, understand how the mind functions. Thus, psychology began with a very simplistic singular assumption.)

L! = all the language concepts, i.e., neuropeptides, that a person has learned, which also includes all the rules for semantics, syntax, grammar, and diction.

The next set represents physiological subsets:

BC! = the ten billion, or so, brain cells produced before and after birth, which continue to grow until about age twenty-three.

N! = the trillions of neural connections that continue to evolve throughout life.

The next set represents the individual's behavioral repertoire:

B!

The next subset represents the emotional of affective responses:

A! This represents the combining of affects, such as anger, fear, happiness, guilt, rage, anxiety, and so on. The full spectrum of human emotions is quite large and may not lend itself to a precisely knowable quantity.

The next set includes all of the ways for making choices and assessing the probabilities of outcomes:

This part of the equation represents the fact that we do not make absolute choices where we can consider every possible outcome. As John Nash (1951, 1953) points out, in game theory we think in terms of probabilities. We cannot consider every outcome but can only guess at possible outcomes. A champion chess player can only envision perhaps the possible consequences of a move for six or seven outcomes. Beyond that, he cannot calculate the absolute outcome. Thus, the set represents a probability guess, expressed as:

p! = the probable outcome.

And, the final set includes all of the ways, best elucidated by Piaget, of how the brain instinctively organizes information:

I!

The a priori Debate

Immanuel Kant (1724-1804) (1787, 1788, 1790) proposed the concept of *a priori* knowledge, which is knowledge that is independent of experience, such as the ability to reason. One can argue that reasoning is the result of learning language and is therefore *a posteriori* knowledge. Piaget (1896-1980) (1954, 1976, 1978) argued that we are born with cognitive abilities that organize sensory input:

Schemes – are mental structures to organize concepts.

Assimilation – is the mental structure to modify information to fit into existing schemes, i.e., what is already known.

Accommodation – is the process of modifying schemes to incorporate new information.

Piaget's concepts are fairly consistent with learning theorists, especially for principles early established by Pavlov (1849-1936) (1927) and J. B. Watson (1878-1958) (1924, 1928). These principles have been faithfully adhered to in the modern writings of Stein (2001, 2003, 2004), which demonstrates that if properly applied, they work. The learning or behavioral concepts of *generalization,* which is the ability to comprehend a stimulus as similar to other stimuli and responses as similar to other responses in the presence of similar stimuli, and the concepts of *discrimination,* which is the ability to distinguish one stimulus from another or one response from another, are also unlearned and present at birth. For example, when learning the concept 'chair', a child, after exposure to several different chairs as stimuli, innately organizes the concept 'chair' into a category, and he can thus recognize many forms of chairs as belonging to that category. Discrimination involves the ability to tell the difference of one chair from another, which is also unlearned and innate. Without these abilities, a child would have to relearn the concept of 'chair' for every variety of chair imaginable.

Let us not forget the human ability to think in probabilities. This, too, is a natural predisposition to which we are born. How the brain does this, we do not know.

Thus, when understanding what a thought is, all of these innate abilities must be factored into the equation.

Conclusions

When one multiplies all the possible permutations of the elements which compose a thought, the resulting outcome is an enormous number, perhaps even a number too difficult to conceptualize. Thus, some would say that the mind is more complex than the universe. That number is so vast that one may be fooled into perceiving it as infinity, which is a metaphysical concept and which supports the idea of free will and a vitalistic specialty of the mind. This is not, and cannot, be accurate. The resulting thought comes from the finite number of permutations which have been reviewed in this essay. As science evolves, more elements will have to be added to this equation. But, the number is finite. How the brain navigates through this elaborate maze is, at present, unknown. How the brain does this with incredibly awesome speed is amazing. The vastness, and the speed, gives the illusion of free will. At present, this seems like free will, but over time, as we decipher all the elements of this equation, the illusion of free will one day will have to dissipate. Perhaps the element of free will is that in some manner or form we calculate the probabilities of the best outcome, and this alters the tracks of the thought. In some manner or form, we are active participants in how we navigate our way to our final thought, and, thus, the process of navigating through these vast possibilities is indeed—free will. The physical world and the metaphysical world are really one.

Examining this model demonstrates how complex a thought is. Singularity theories, attributing thought and mind as resulting from one thing or variable, such as the simplistic medical anomaly model or even the behavioral/cognitive model, is naïve and simplistic. The array of things to consider, when examining the mind, is complex, and singular theories are extremely inadequate. This model explains how the brain may work, but it also explains how the mind may work. It helps point the way to what the mind might indeed be and that ultimately the brain and mind might be the same, but with making choices after combining all the variables and thinking in terms of probable outcomes, it is sufficient to conclude that we are mechanistic/deterministic machines that have free will. This means that the brain and the mind may be one and the same, but figuring out the gigantic complexities of the brain may take ages, and, therefore, our ability to equate it to the mind may equally take ages.

In the next chapter, we will review why the scientific integrity of psychology is being compromised. Excessive greed is actually setting us back from making progress in solving the brain/mind mysteries. Science is cumulative, but only when we can rely on the work of others. Science can be mired down in uselessness when the work of others keeps us running in circles. We will see how money, greed, and ambition are helping to keep psychology in the Stone Age.

CHAPTER EIGHT

MONEY, GREED, AND THE LOSS OF SCIENTIFIC INTEGRITY IN PSYCHOLOGY: FURTHER OBFUSCATING THE CLARITY IN PSYCHOLOGY

In the Bible, Timothy wrote, "*The love of money is the root of all evil.*" (6:10). Sophocles wrote in *Antigone,* "Money: There's nothing in the world so demoralizing as money." Noam Chomsky (1986) writes about the evils which countries do to each other over the vicious fight for money. George Seldes, the twentieth century's most crusading reporter, exposed, as far back in the 1940s, the evils of the tobacco companies in their quest for money when they gave free cartons of cigarettes to soldiers boarding the boats for the European theater during World War II, knowing that cigarettes caused cancer and that the nicotine content was addictive. The tobacco companies wanted soldiers to start smoking and become addicted as they nervously waited for combat to commence.

Lucy Johnstone (2000), in her book, *Users and Abusers of Psychiatry,* reports that the pharmaceutical companies internationally rank second in total income, with only the arms companies profiting higher. One of the authors of this book, Stein, at the 2001 New York Ritalin Litigation Conference, where the law firms that prevailed against the tobacco companies and are now targeting the pharmaceutical companies over the issue of giving these drugs to children, verbally confronted the attorneys representing the pharmaceutical companies with the following statement:

"How can you people do this? How can you sleep at night? How can you knowingly support putting this crap [the amphetamine drugs] into the bodies of children? Any one of you can make your million dollar incomes by representing companies that engage in more honest ways of making money. Have you no conscience?"

It is recognized that the pharmaceutical companies deserve much of the money they make. They have supported research in all of medicine, giving us drugs that legitimately combat real diseases. There has been much written about how they have engaged in some questionable research practices even in *real* medicine

(Bodenheimer, and Grumbach, 2004; Valenstein, 1998). However, the key issue here is whether or not they have gone too far promoting stimulant and amphetamine drugs, as well as all psychiatric drugs, as so called treatment for children, knowing that these drugs do not correct chemical imbalances, that these drugs are in fact addicting, and that these drugs have serious short-term and long-term side effects, i.e., health risks. For some companies, one amphetamine drug used for children is the company's primary source of profit. (Valenstein, 1998)

Researchers, attorneys, psychiatrists, and psychologists are participating in this disgrace for money? How does the money flow? How are some *professionals* and executives growing rich from this propaganda campaign? How is it actually being orchestrated?

The Investment Ratio

What would you do if you were asked to invest one dollar today for an almost guaranteed return of one thousand dollars within one or two year? This reflects the formula for the pharmaceutical companies' investment in a well-camouflaged propaganda campaign designed to get as many children on their stimulant and other drugs as possible. Think about the ratio, 1 to 1000. The only difference is the amount of money that the pharmaceutical companies are investing; they operate on a formula of investing millions in order to guarantee returns of billions. The stakes are considerably larger for these giant corporations, where their investment ratio is more like 1 million for 1 billion. These companies are seeding millions of dollars throughout the medical, psychiatric, and psychological communities, as well as the public, in order to convince them that children have diseases that can best be controlled with psychiatric drugs. The Drug Enforcement Agency, DEA, reports that 25% of all children are on some form of psychiatric drug, and if the trend continues, by 2010, the report estimated that 50% of all children would be on these drugs. Anthem, Blue Cross, and Blue Shield in 2010 reported the rate to be at 32%, which still reflects an alarming trend. It is difficult to determine who is most evil, the *professionals* who are deliberately slanting the research which supports claims of nonexistent diseases and false claims about the safety of the drugs, or the overwhelmingly larger number of *professionals* who are increasingly believing this sales campaign.

How the Money Is Being Spread

The pharmaceutical companies are becoming more clever about how to dispense their money to help escalate sales. They are using every avenue possible: direct consumer advertising; contaminating science by investing in research that makes their products look good and makes children look sick; donating money directly to professional associations, such as the American Psychiatric Association; supporting parent groups who receive only biased and slanted information about psychiatric children's diseases and drug effectiveness and safety; routing exorbitant fees to polished speakers who, with great skill, represent the pro-disease and pro-drug points of view to parents and professionals; advertising in medical and psychiatric journals in order to prevent them from going bankrupt; exorbitantly spending money entertaining practicing physicians in exchange for their listening to sales pitches disguised as research presentations designed to get them to prescribe the products; funding the research of professors who desperately need research credits for tenure and promotions and demanding that no research compromise sales of their products or else the professors can forget about ever receiving further research money; financing writers and researchers who favor their products for attendance at conventions or trips to exotic vacations; funding an avalanche of direct public advertising on TV and magazines; and, most recently, turning over research money to so-called independent research companies that are skilled at making products look good. Thus, it is evident that the pharmaceutical companies are using any and every means at their disposal to market their wares. The accuracy and truth of their information does not matter; all that seems to matter is profit. The health and well-being of children is of no consequence, only money matters. Several years ago, Stein (1999) did a radio interview in New York City. The announcer related, while on the air, and there is a taped record of this, that he jogged every day with one of the higher executives from the company that manufactures Ritalin. He said that his jogging companion had been directed to put his own child on Ritalin, but he said, "There was no way I'd ever put my kid on that stuff!" Let's look at the money trail in more detail.

1. *Direct Contributions to the American Psychiatric Association:* The American Psychiatric Association almost ceased to exist during the 1970s (Breggin, 1991). Revelations about the mistreatment of psychiatric patients in hospitals and in the offices of psychiatrists were made public during the late 1960s and throughout the 1970s, which resulted in families seeking help from psychologists or in seeking no help at all. The financial bottom dropped out for psychiatrists. In a desperate attempt to save psychiatry from extinction, pharmaceutical companies began to deposit huge amounts of money directly into coffers of the American Psychiatric Association in exchange for psychiatrists to continue selling their products. It apparently worked, and the tradition of direct deposits continues to this day, where about one-fourth to one-third of the APA's budget still depends on these deposits. (Breggin, 1991)

2. *Advertising in Psychiatric Journals:* Also, during the 1960s and 1970s, the budgets for professional psychiatric journals became bleak. They, too, hovered on the brink of bankruptcy. The pharmaceutical companies, once again, came to the rescue by purchasing advertisements for psychiatric drugs in the journals. This, too, proved successful, because not only did the journals not fail, but also sales of psychiatric drugs escalated (Breggin, 1991; Valenstein 1998). Psychologists are now fighting for the right to write prescriptions for these drugs, and for the first time, in 2001,

advertisements for psychiatric drugs began to appear in psychological journals. These adds place the drug companies in a powerful position of determining the content of professional articles within the journals. If they do not like any research articles that compromises drug sales, all they need to do is threaten to pull their lucrative advertisements. This is an especially heinous conflict of interest, since the wares of the drug companies can effect the health and well-being of our children.

3. *Grant Money:* Part of the job for professors is a fight for survival, known as, *publish or perish.* In most universities and medical schools, professors must conduct research and publish their findings in professional journals and present at professional conventions. Promotions, tenure, and even keeping their jobs heavily depend on publishing. They need research grant money. Not only is grant money necessary to conduct their research, but also a considerable portion of the money is directly or indirectly given to the university or medical school. The indirect route involves the purchase of very expensive research equipment, such as computers, Cat Scans, PET scans, and so forth, eventually becoming the property of the research institute. The direct route involves donating a percentage of the grant money to the teaching institutions. The amounts range between thousands to millions of dollars. A young professor seeking his or her first position will, during the interview stage, have to convey that he or she can readily obtain grant money. You probably have already guessed that the easiest source for grant money is the extremely wealthy pharmaceutical companies. And with grant money comes a hidden and unspoken caveat, namely, that the researcher better not conclude from his or her research anything that will detract from the sales of drugs. If a researcher discovers something adverse to sales, then two things are likely to happen. The pharmaceutical companies are the proprietors of the research, and therefore they can prevent the findings from ever being published, and they can make certain that the professor has great difficulty in ever again getting grant money from any of the pharmaceutical companies. It must also be remembered that there are ways for professors to supplement their incomes from these grants. This is the way the game is played. This game is played even in *real* medicine but is more difficult because most research findings are more concrete, where disease entities are present or they disappear. However, in psychiatry and psychology, where, in most instances, no one can identify specific disease entities, and where terms are poorly defined, there is considerable latitude for unscrupulous researchers to get away with bloody murder, and, indeed, they do. In psychiatry and psychology, there are only a handful of researchers, a few dozen, who are milking this grant business to death and getting away with it. The sad part is that too many other professionals are accepting these highly biased and nebulous findings as

gospel. And, with the health of children at stake, this is a particularly nefarious and deadly game (Breggin, 1991; DeGrandpre, 1999; Johnstone, 1995; Valenstein, 1998). Perhaps an example will demonstrate the seriousness of such out of control research conditions. There is strong suspicion that the FDA, Food and Drug Administration, has in its possession numerous studies indicating that the stimulant drugs used for controlling ADD/ADHD children can cause life threatening liver problems. However, the FDA will not release these studies because of "proprietary rights", which means that the pharmaceutical companies funded the studies and therefore own them, and without their permission, no one may have access to them. The Freedom of Information Act does not apply, because that law is only applicable when the study is funded by a government agency. These studies may only be released if a solid lawsuit against a pharmaceutical company orders them in a subpoena or when a legislative investigative body requires their release to an investigative subcommittee*CHADD:* One of the cleverest marketing strategies ever devised involves organizing parents into a national network of support groups, brainwashing them into believing in non-existent diseases, convincing them that unsafe drugs are safe, and then molding them into a militant campaign group to help with the promotion of mysterious diseases and drugs. This is exactly what is happening with a parenting organization known as CHADD, Children and Adults with Attention Deficit Disorder. Few parent members are aware that the organization is funded mainly by Novarits, the pharmaceutical company that manufactures Ritalin and by all the other pharmaceutical companies that produce drugs which are used to "treat" ADD and ADHD. *All* the brochures, information pamphlets, films, recommended book readings, and guest speakers are slanted to present to the parents one point of view, which is that their children have a disease and that the best course of treatment involves combining behavioral treatments with safe drugs that correct chemical imbalances. The recommended behavioral treatments have been repeatedly proven to work poorly, thereby necessitating the addition of drugs. Truly effective behavioral treatments exist but are remain largely ignored. Most parents are not sophisticated enough to do primary research and assess the accuracy of the materials that are presented. There is no discrediting of their so-called *facts*, and they are never given contrary information, such as: that no disease has ever been identified, that the drugs do not correct a chemical imbalance, that the recommended behavioral treatments do not work and therefore necessitate reliance on drugs, that the drugs are not safe, that all the drugs do is sedate their children, constrain behavior, and give a false feeling of energy, and, finally, that statistically, over the long run, the drugs do not enhance academic performance.

The Americans with Disabilities Act was passed in 1990 in order to allow for special accommodations and benefits for those with real disabilities, such as blindness, deafness, paralysis, and other physical challenges. ADD/ADHD were not included in the original act, but with persistent and militant lobbying by CHADD parents, these were later added. Now, every special help and assistance is given to these children, which Stein (2004) points out, only further handicaps them. By treating them as disabled, they eventually fulfill this expectation by becoming reliant on special help and assistance. They become dependent on others and less and less capable of performing independently. Stein tells the story of one of his college students, who, he discovered, near the end of a semester, had not taken a single note. Upon inquiry, it was discovered that because the student supposedly had ADD, he was provided with a full-time note taker in all of his courses, thanks to the added provisions of the disability act. Stein encouraged the student to take his own notes and utilize the note taker to help him improve his note-taking skills, but the student would not hear of it, especially since he had been provided with years of this special assistance. The student flunked out of college in his first semester. What good did it do to convince this perfectly capable young man that he was diseased, handicapped, and incapable of performing? What good did it do for him to rely on others to do everything for him? In the story *The Miracle Worker*, Helen Keller's teacher taught Helen that she could and should do as much for herself as possible, even with real disabilities. With this "can do" expectation, we have the gift of one of America's greatest writers. What would have happened to Helen if her family had unwittingly prevailed and treated her as diseased, handicapped, and incapable? Thanks to the efforts of CHADD, youngsters who should be expected to perform are taught that they are handicapped, cannot perform without special help and special conditions, and will remain so for the rest of their lives. What a terrible thing it is to convince a youngster that he has a disease, when no such proof exist, when it has been clearly demonstrated (Stein, 1998; 20001; 2004) that they can indeed function on their own, and that they are perfectly capable of leading fruitful and productive lives. CHADD, being duped by the pharmaceutical companies, has naively contributed to millions of children believing that they are sick, always will be, and can never fully function on their own.

CHADD also tried to have Ritalin lowered to a less stringent prescription standard than provided by the Drug Control Act of 1971, revised in 1998. Fortunately, this time they did not succeed. (Breggin, 2002)

It is a shame that these innocent parents do not realize how the pharmaceutical companies are manipulating them.

4. *The American Psychological Association:* Psychologists have not had the power to write prescriptions for psychiatric drugs. However, recently, New Mexico was the first of the fifty states to grant prescription writing privileg-

es for psychologists. The other forty-nine states will soon follow. The ties of psychologists to the pharmaceutical companies are already beginning to appear. For the first time, in November, 2001, a costly add for Concerta, which is time-released Ritalin, appeared in the psychologists newsletter, the *APA Monitor.* There are far more psychologists in practice than psychiatrists, and, therefore, they will provide an additionally gigantic army for the pharmaceutical companies to prescribe their wares. Already, apparently, the money is beginning to flow. In addition, there is considerable controversy within the ranks of psychology about psychologists writing prescriptions. Some psychologists fear that too many psychologists will abandon their tradition of providing psychotherapy for the more lucrative practice of prescribing drugs, thus abandoning the practice of helping patients help themselves, and, instead, they will be helping patients to mask their problems by intoxicating these patients with drugs. One glance at the change in a financial profile that drug writing can offer gives perspective to this concern. In some locales, psychologists earn $75.00 to $90.00 per hour for psychotherapy. If psychologists were to spend the hour performing medical checks for prescriptions, which merely involves, "Hello, Mr. Jones. How are you? Do you need your prescription adjusted?" then the hourly fee for seeing several patients in rapid succession easily escalates to $240.00 per hour. That is quite a temptation. Furthermore, along with prescription privileges, psychologists will be allowed to hospitalize patients and, therefore, collect very heavy fees for making morning hospital rounds. Of course, there will be those psychologists who will not bend to this temptation, but as for the number of how many will, only time will tell. If too many succumb, then it will be difficult for patients and parents to find quality help for their life problems and all too easy to receive drugs to mask over the psychological pains that serve as a warning sign that something in life's problems needs repair. There is too much danger for teens and children that this change will mean that the ultimate solution for emotional and behavioral problems will be drugs, drugs, and more drugs.

5. *Professional Speakers Promoting Nonexistent Diseases and the Wonders of Psychiatric Drugs:* Did you know that doctors, until just a few years ago, received $600.00 merely to attend an extremely lavish dinner and listen to a fifteen minute presentation promoting the existence of nonexistent psychiatric diseases, how wonderful and non-harmful psychiatric drugs are, and, added to that the great lie, that psychiatric drugs correct chemical imbalances? Would it bother you to learn that doctors had to sign a confidentiality agreement to not divulge the fact that she/he had signed that very same confidentiality agreement in order to receive the check at the end of the dinner? This practice has been legally stopped, but the ultra-posh dinners continue. Most physicians do not read the actual research on psychiatric diseases and drugs, but, instead, get most of their

information from these dinners and from office visits by the pharmaceutical company sales representatives (Breggin, 1991). Is it any wonder that physicians are clueless about the real facts pertaining to the safety and addictive properties of the drugs being given to children, teens, as well as to adults?

The speakers themselves are not exempt from the financial reach of the pharmaceutical companies. Many receive in excess of $10,000.00, which is mere pocket change for the pharmaceutical companies, for giving these speeches. Only those who present in the most slick and polished manner and who best represent research slanted to favor the drug companies will be permitted to receive these lucrative fees. Many of these speakers also present to CHADD, and, indeed, they are slick at winning converts.

It may be helpful to give you, the reader, a few specifics about the money trail for grants and speaking engagements. Kean (2004) cites disclosures about a few key players, i.e., those who have received numerous grants, make numerous speeches, and who have had enormous influence in marketing medical diagnoses and prioritizing the drugging of children in this heinous game, from the *The Journal of Clinical Psychology* (2003):

> "Dr. Biederman has received research support from Shire Richwood, Eli Lily, Wyeth, Pfizer, Cephalon, Novartis, Janssen, Noven Pharmaceuticals, Stanley Foundation, National Institute of Mental Health, National Institute of Child Health & Human Development, and National Institute of Drug Abuse; is on the speakers bureaus for GlaxoSmith Kline, Eli Lily, Pfizer, Novartis, Wyeth, Shire Richwood, Alza, and Cephalon; and is on the advisory boards fro Eli Lily, Celltech, Shire Richwood, Novartis, Noven Pharmaceutical, Alza, McNeil, and Cephalon."
>
> "Dr. Farone is a consultant for, has received grant/research support from Ortho-McNeil, Eli Lily, and Shire Richwood; and has received honoraria from and is a member of the speakers/advisory boards for Ortho-Mcneil, Eli Lily, Shire Richwood, and GlaxoSmithKline."
>
> "Dr. Wilens is a consultant for, has received grant support from, and is a member of the speakers bureaus for Abbott, Celltech, Janssen, Eli Lily, Ortho-McNeil, National Institute on Drug Abuse, National Institute of Mental Health, Novartis, Pfizer, Shire Richwood, and GlaxoSmith Kline." (p. 91)

Kean reports that these doctors are now under court indictment, which is finally getting the prestigious schools that they are affiliated with (such as Harvard) to begin looking at the practices which are taking place on their campuses.

6. *Other Perks:* Lucrative speaking engagements are not the only ways that professor-speakers, who would otherwise not be rich, can make fabulous amounts of money. Many receive funding for attending professional conventions and even more money to make professional presentations at these conventions. This is especially tantalizing during a period of time when universities are decreasing support money for professors to attend professional conferences, making it even more burdensome for the professors to have to finance attendance out of their own pockets. It places professors in a dilemma, since tenure and promotions strongly depend on their getting paper presentation credits. The easiest place to be funded for conference attendance and presentations is also the pharmaceutical companies. Therefore, the tentacles of the drug companies are digging deeper and deeper into the pockets of academics, and increasingly causing them to compromise the ethical standards of their research and what they ultimately present to both the professional communities and the public. Vacations, condominiums, and other exotic trips also are provided sometimes for physicians, who only are required to attend brief presentations about make-believe psychiatric diseases and the wonders of psychiatric drugs, in exchange for spending the rest of the day on the golf course, followed by a sumptuous repast. (Vanlenstein, 1998; Breggin, 1991; 2002)

7. *Advertising in Professional Journals:* Medical journals, psychiatric journals, and psychological journals are becoming saturated with ads for not only psychiatric drugs, but for many other types of drugs as well. It is not difficult to calculate how much power this gives the drug companies over the content of those journals. If any unfavorable research articles appear, then the mere threat to pull all these expensive ads can easily bring these journals in line. In addition, the editors of some of the journals serve on the board of directors of some of the drug companies and are well reimbursed for their time. Is it any wonder that science is being seriously compromised in psychiatry and psychology? Is it any wonder that with increasing amounts of tainted literature appearing in the professional journals, more and more physicians, psychiatrists, and psychologists, are slowly evolving as believers in the content of this massive propaganda campaign? Is it any wonder that both the professional community and the public are rapidly becoming converts and believers in that which is not true? Conditions are such that psychology and psychiatry can no longer police themselves, and only legal or government intervention will change things. It is equally problematic that this will not happen, since the coffers of many politicians are handsomely supplemented from the drug companies. With the enormity of their profits, it seems that they are leaving no stone unturned and no corner untouched in order to guarantee the continuation of their massive profits. Is the reader beginning to dis-

cover that part of the reason we consumers are paying increasingly large amounts for our prescriptions is not just to supplement the research of drug companies, but to help with the growing expenses of their propaganda war on us.

8. *Advertising in Magazines and on Television:* Have you noticed the increasing adds for all types of drugs appearing in magazines and on television? Pay careful attention to the wording of these adds. They do not overtly state that psychological problems "are" diseases, instead, they state, "You *may* have a medical condition known as depression [or whatever]." Then, notice how quickly they review that, "Side effects may include, blah, blah, blah." They skim over the side effects so fast that few people pay attention. Direct marketing is not only selling drugs to the public and working extremely well, but it is also providing a powerful lever for the pharmaceutical companies to control the content of news articles which or speakers who may say anything detrimental about their products. It is a hell of a lot of power when the media becomes compromised, because a free press is supposed to be a fundamental policing agency for protecting the public. With enormous amounts of money changing hands, it will become increasingly difficult for the media to fulfill this important role.

Loss of Policing

Historically, America is a complex nation, with all forms of diversity and differing opinions. Systems or institutions were set in place to protect one segment of society from dominance and control by other systems and institutions; namely, politicians represent the people and protect us from such things as abuses by industry, and the newspapers and media served as our ultimate policing agencies, protecting us from corporate or political abuses by exposing any wrongdoings. However, as Kean (2004), and Chomsky and McChesney (1992) point out, self-monitoring and policing of abuses is rapidly eroding. Globalization and the growth of megacorporations have led to industry controlling, influencing, and sometimes outright owning politicians, newspapers, and other media. Therefore, corporations are increasingly free to do as they wish without fear of sanctions. This is what is now taking place with the pharmaceutical companies. Their monies now control too many politicians, newspapers, media, physicians, psychiatrists, psychologists, and even government agencies. Greed and profit are now the values *du jour* (Chomsky and McChesney, 1992; Kean, 2004), and nowhere is this more evident than the subject of this book, the drugging and exploitation of children. Lies, misinformation, and disinformation are rampantly out of control to convince the public and professional communities of the existence of make-believe psychiatric diseases and of the safety of psychiatric drugs in the bodies of our children. Look at the interconnected selling practices owned, strongly influenced, and/or controlled by the pharmaceutical companies: politicians, newspapers, propaganda distributed to CHADD, grant money, professional speakers, physicians, psychiatrists, and psychologists (individually and by contributions to their respective organizations). The protection of parents and their children is disappearing.

Is Aldous Huxley's *Brave New World* becoming a reality? Are we loosing our own and our children's humanity to powerful psychiatric drugs? Don't forget to take your "Soma" so that you will soon feel better. In *Brave New World*, the entire population loses its ability to feel anything by taking the fictitious drug known as "Soma". If we and our children lose God's gift of feeling, we then lose our souls and our humanity.

CHAPTER NINE

Psychologists Can Serve Important Roles

Are there important roles for practicing psychologists? Do people have a need for their services? Without reservation, the answers are "Yes". However, psychologists must recognize their limits and abandon the magical, wishful, and blind thinking that has permeated the profession for far too long.

Ellis and Harper (1975) question the existence of something called "*therapy*". They view the therapist's role as that of a teacher and the patient's role as that of a student. This is perhaps the accurate portrayal of what goes on behind the closed door of a therapist. Cognitive/behavioral therapies seem to offer a somewhat better treatment efficacy rate (Lipsey and Wilson, 1993) than other modalities, and it is more transparent, which means it is not filled with convoluted, obscure, and mystical theoretical concepts shrouded in fancy vocabulary about what is abnormal and what is therapy. Basically, cognitive /behaviorism focuses on faulty thinking and beliefs, which is simple and straightforward, and, most importantly, appeals more to good common sense than the myriad of fanciful theories that have permeated psychology for far too long. If the reader understands this, then it becomes clear that we teach healthier ways of thinking and behaving. What therapists can teach in this arena can be expanded by more in-depth readings on the part of therapists in the specifics of the wide variety of human problems, and as pointed out by Stein and Foltz (2009), better doctoral training in specific human problems. There are still other roles that psychologists can play.

Soothing Emotional Pain – Affective Therapy – or "How do you feel about that?"

Affective therapies are those modalities which involve therapists constantly asking, "Well, how do you feel about that?" This is a nondirective, non-teaching form of therapy, pioneered by Carl Rogers (1951). This form of therapy may be useless when people are facing some of life's most difficult problems, such as with marriage counseling or anger management (Hagen, 1997). In fact, Rogers was completely wrong to believe that this form of so-called therapy, with an unconditional positive regard by the therapist, no matter how stupid a patient may behave, would cure everything and would subsequently return the patient to the path of self-actualization. What rubbish! How many research protocols must it take to point out that, overall, this form of therapy does not work? However, there may be a place for it in some instances, but not for the reasons proposed by Rogers. When someone is dealing with loss, trauma, or grief, then this form of therapy often proves helpful for alleviating extreme emotional pain (Fisher, 1981). The therapist provides a shoulder upon which to rest one's head. The therapist can understand the pain, commiserate with the person, show empathy, and offer a comforting friendship. In other words, the therapist fulfills the role of "*The paid friend*" (Dineen, 2000). The therapist can validate what the person is feeling when and if it is appropriate and fits the circumstance (Fisher, 1981). Whereas, ordinary friends who have not gone through a similar circumstance may be unable to understand the intensity of the pain and may even have unrealistic expectations for how long it should take to recover. They may even impose unrealistic pressure for the person to recover too soon. (Fisher, 1981)

Grief

When there is the major loss of a loved one, then the work of the therapist is fairly obvious: listening and listening endlessly to the person's heartache. This is one area where affective therapy serves an excellent purpose. Friends and relatives may commiserate with the grieving person for a short period of time, but it does not take long before they tire of it (Fisher, 1981). The therapist, as a *paid friend,* may serve one of his or her most meaningful roles. The patient must go through the grieving period, and this may take considerable time. Most therapists understand this and can console the patient for as long as necessary. Even though therapist training is lacking in many areas, this is one area where therapists seem to understand their purpose, i.e., being a supportive, empathetic, and patiently listening friend who makes no demands for the patient to recover in an unrealistically short time. Some therapists even form grief support groups. These groups surround the patient with others who are also grieving and who can be trained to be supportive without time constraints.

Posttraumatic Stress Disorder

Most people, at some time in their lives, will be faced with a life-threatening stress and will react with posttraumatic stress disorder, PTSD. Recovery from such stress, like grief, also takes a long time. One can think of PTSD as a prolonged period of emotional shock that takes considerable time from which to recover. Here, too, affective therapy is the treatment of choice, and, once again, there is nothing wrong with the therapist serving the role as the paid friend. Ventilation is necessary over a long time period if the patient is going to get past the horrors which he or she had undergone. The therapist can be patient, placing no time constraints for the patient to recover. Both listening and empathizing are easy to do, and most therapists seem to understand this. Once again, a group setting is perhaps ideal, and once again therapists can organize such groups.

But, Affective Therapy Can Make Matters Worse

The "How do you feel about that?" form of therapy is often overdone. In Rogerian Therapy, it is a basic premises that the patient will eventually come up with solutions, but the reality is that this typically does not happen (Dawes, 1994). One may be reminded of the commercial for a television show called *American Chopper,* when the father of the repair team says to the female therapist, "If you tell me to get in touch with my feelings one more time, I'm going to shove this boot up your ass!" This portrays how unsuitable this type of approach is for this type of patient and for the presenting problem of a father and son who argue a lot.

In marriage counseling, this approach is often inappropriate and potentially harmful. Psychologists seem to have forgotten the research on communication and affective styles so long ago presented by Byrne (1964) and made more popular by Brendan Maher (1966). Byrne distinguishing two feeling and communication styles:

The repressor is a more factual person who does not experience feelings much of the time. They make good pilots and good physicians. They do not care to discuss feelings but may prefer discussing baseball scores.

The sensitizer is constantly in touch with their feelings and desires to talk about his or her feelings much of the time. They make good writers or literature teachers. They do not understand the importance of baseball scores and prefer to discuss a good book or a good play.

Marriage counselors all too often target the repressor and coerce him or her into discussing his or her feelings. The patient, in the interest of trying to save the marriage, may try hard, but, eventually, he or she will revert to the natural tendency of being a repressor. It is then that the repressor may be made to feel as if he or she were a complete boob and a failure, when it is the therapist who is conducting a destructive therapeutic approach. It may be simpler to make the couple aware of this basic difference and then work on ways to deal with it that are constructive, such as the sensitizer learning to enjoy playing golf and the repressor learning to enjoy a play every now and then. Unfortunately, when the therapist goes in the wrong direction, probably because he is not familiar with this research, then therapy will precipitate the divorce.

The Therapist as a Parental Figure

Levinsohn and Rosenbaum (1987) offered copious research to support the idea that people with recurring depressions may have had more difficult childhoods, often with cold, un-reinforcing, and non-nurturing parents who were excessively punitive. Many of these people may have been so harmed by prolonged childhood trauma that they will never be able to be emotionally strong. They may not be good candidates for the more stoical therapies espoused by the cognitive therapists (Ellis, 1961). They may require the presence of a nurturing, supportive type of therapist in order to march their way through life with less pain. Indeed, this may be an expensive way to get through life, but at least the person's life can be more comfortable. The parent therapist may have to constantly reassure the person that they are okay (Berne, 1964), which is, according to Steiner (1974), a core existential position or attitude that is established during the first years of life and that directs the entire life of the person. The person may not ever be able to extricate him or herself from this position and may, therefore, always be dependent on the need for a nurturing parent. It is important that the therapist not delude himself into believing that he is doing therapy. What he is really doing is being more than a mere friend; he is serving an ongoing role as an ever-present parent figure. Perhaps there are many therapists who would like a practice filled with such patients who guarantee a lucrative practice. Rather than being judgmental, it is recognized that this may be a legitimate role for therapists to play. Easing others' pain can be a noble vocation.

In a similar fashion, some people develop little or no confidence in themselves, which Bandura (1969) terms as 'low self-efficacy'. Individuals manifesting this type of personality often seek out dependent relationships, and therapists often fill that need. This is such an ingrained attitude that it is unlikely the patient may ever change, in which case the therapist may be necessary to play a role of constant reassurance, i.e., a sage advisor who is always there to guide and reassure the patient. Steiner (1974) indicates that dependent people rarely change. There is nothing wrong for therapists to provide comfort for people such as these, even though this relationship may last a very long time. It would indeed be better if the therapist could persuade patients such as these to become independent, but it is unlikely this will ever occur, so why not give them comfort?

The Therapist as a Teacher – Philosopher

Ellis and Harper (1975) and Beck (1961, 1979) view therapists as a teachers and remove much of the magic and mystic, powers that therapists all too often believe they have. Ellis sometimes changed the number of basic irrational beliefs upon which people function ranging from ten to thirteen. Research on cognitive therapy has expanded this to many, many more (Kendall and Hollon, 1981; Meichenbaum, 1979). However, Stein and Foltz (2009) points out that what is most needed for a meaningful improvement in cognitive-behavioral therapies is for therapists to be thoroughly trained in all the dynamics involved in the vast myriad of human problems, such as marriage and relationships, communication and social skills, alcohol and drugs, and so forth. Stein and Foltz (2009) have identified over forty-one human problems for most of which therapists receive little or no training. If a therapist is to understand how people think and what they believe, then they must fully understand the dynamics of all human problems.

This requires extensive reading and learned discussion beginning in doctoral training and continuing throughout a therapist's career.

In addition, many human issues involve things best addressed not by the so-called science of psychology but perhaps more by the disciplines of philosophy and theology. This means that therapist, when faced with existential issues by patients, must be prepared to offer educated ideas and insights. Thus, instead of the term addressing the psychologist as *the scientific practitioner* (Lefton, 2000), it may be a better descriptor to address them as *the well-read psychologist.* If we are to teach, then knowing must come first.

Pragmatics

There are tons of textbooks out there roughly called something like *Theories of Personality.* Historically, the most popular is Hall and Lindsey's *Theories of Personality* (1957), through which many aspiring psychologists had to suffer. Stein and Foltz (2009) point out that too much doctoral training time is spent on abstract, arcane, pedantic, obscure, mystical, magical tripe, whereas, little or no training time is spent in the understanding of the practical, everyday problems that people face throughout their lives. Thus, the highly educated therapist is, in reality, hardly educated at all. Without knowing much about specific human problems, is it any wonder that treatment efficacy rates are extremely poor (Stein and Foltz, 2009). Psychologists have, for too long, hidden behind a mask of erudite clouds, while failing to understand the pragmatics of living.

However, there are those few psychologists who are well read and pragmatic, who have much to offer their patients. It is hoped that this essay will serve as a stimulus for there to be many more. It is hoped that the American Psychological Association shifts its accreditation standards away from abstract theories and excessive research method courses to courses requiring intense reading and discussion in many specific human problems, with an emphasis on the cognitive patterns and behaviors that accompany these problems, and, oh yes, the feelings, of course.

Physio-therapy or Psychiatric Drugs or Pharmacotherapy

There are two camps on the issue of psychiatric drugs, and both seem to lie at the opposite extremes:

1. On the one side are the liars who permeate the psychiatric literature with claims of false psychiatric diseases and who view drugs, not only as the treatment of choice, but as the treatment that will have to be sustained year after year, with little or no plan to wean patients off of drugs within a reasonable length of time. This side includes the American Psychiatric Association, APA, the American Psychological Association, also APA—a recent convert to this side, and the American Association of Pediatricians.

a) They seem to care little about the iatrogenic illnesses these drugs can cause, such as nerve and brain damage, heart damage, liver damage, and reduction of protection by the immune system.
b) They claim that drugs correct chemical imbalances or restore balance to a nervous system impaired by some type of neurological anomaly.

2. On the opposite side are those who believe that psychiatric drugs should never be used, since they present too great a threat to health because of the iatrogenic risks just mentioned. While there are several organizations on this side, the three that are most prominent are The International Center for the Study of Psychiatry, or ICSPP, Psychology and the Citizen's Commission on Human Rights, or CCHR, and International Society For Ethics in Psychology and Psychiatry, or ISEPP.

The Truth – Once and For All!

There is a judicious and defensible use for psychiatric drugs. They can help alleviate pain. The Roman writer Syrus wrote, "The pain of the mind can be greater than the pain of the body." Psychiatric drugs, whether they are the stimulants or the tranquilizers, reduce anxiety. All categories! Plus, they do a bit more. The tranquilizers produce sedation. The stimulants allay anxiety and produce a feeling of energy. The antidepressants allay anxiety and gradually produce a feeling of energy, thus, in most cases, reducing the pain of depression.

Fact 1. None of the psychiatric drugs correct chemical imbalances. (Jackson, 2005; Valenstein, 1998)

Fact 2. None of the psychiatric drugs correct some anomaly of the nervous system or brain. (Jackson, 2005; Valenstein, 1998)

Fact 3. Concluding that because they do as indicated, whether it be to allay anxiety, reduce depression, or reduce schizophrenic symptoms, is not accepted in the science of pharmacology as proof that they are correcting a chemical imbalance or anatomical anomaly. This is called *allopathic logic* (Baldessarini, 1985) or *ex juvanitibus reasoning* (Valenstein, 1998). Perhaps the example easiest to understand is that alcohol reduces anxiety and alleviates feelings of depression, but this does not prove that alcohol is correcting chemical imbalances or anomalies of the nervous system.

Fact 4. These drugs do cause iatrogenic illnesses (Breggin, 1991, Jackson, 2005: Valenstein, 1998), especially when taken for a long time. The percentages of risk vary but should be taken seriously. Therefore,

Fact 5. When used to reduce the pain and suffering of a patient, they should be given for the shortest time period, such as perhaps a year or two until the crisis has passed. The patient should be weaned off the drugs gradually to avoid a sudden and dramatic return of the emotional pain, called a rebound effect. The patient's health should be monitored more closely, such as high blood pressure problems, liver problems, cardiac problems, and many more. Thus, the consideration for using drugs should be predicated on whether or not the patient's pain is so severe that it would be remiss to allow them to continue intense suffering. However, it should be noted that sometimes a really skilled therapist may be able to break the stranglehold of pain with just the right formula of words. If this can be done successfully, then the use of drugs can be completely avoided, and, subsequently, the health risks can also be completely avoided. It is preferable to avoid us of these drugs as much as possible.

Stated succinctly, psychiatric drugs should be used with great moderation to ease pain, instead of the current trend to use them as artillery against so-called mental illnesses that no one has identified is actually there, and this statement is irrefutable and easy to support, should any of the liars scream foul play! These arguments include the treatment of schizophrenia. The drugs used to treat this problem, the anti-psychotics or major tranquilizers, will produce irreversible brain damage in most patients. These patients need help to solve the life problems that are overwhelming them and should be taken off the drugs as soon as possible. I stated early in the book that acute, or fairly rapid onset schizophrenia, seems to be a loss of cognitive functioning when a person is faced with what they believe is insurmountable and overwhelming stress. The brain seems to go haywire for a period of nine months to a year. Chronic schizophrenia seems to appear more like a patient presenting symptoms of brain damage, where they are listless and non-responsive to the environment. Many writers (Breggin, 1991; Valenstein, 1998) believe that this is indeed brain damage that is caused by the major antipsychotic drugs themselves. There is ample research from the 1970s that schizophrenics can be successfully treated with the less dangerous minor tranquilizers, but in higher doses. Reduction of overwhelming anxiety seems to underlie schizophrenic attacks, and minor tranquilizers can allay that quite well. However, even the so-called minor tranquilizers present numerous iatrogenic health risks, and, if taken, they too should only be taken for as brief a period as possible. This begs an intriguing question: Why would insane patients or schizophrenics respond well to anti-anxiety drugs?

Fact 6. Psychiatric drugs often have numerous potential side effects. Short-term side effects can appear within minutes, days, or even weeks. Sometimes these effects will be mild, and sometimes they can be life threatening. Long-term side effects usually result from years of accumulated damage, and some forms of these side effects can produce irreversible nerve and brain damage or even death. If a patient is considering taking a psychiatric drug, then he should be told the whole truth about all of the potential side effects. In addition, these effects should be stated and written in plain and easy to understand language, i.e., full disclosure, which allows the patient to make an informed decision. *The patient, and not the doctor, can then be the one to weigh the benefit of pain reduction against the health risks.* This means a much more ethical approach for drug use would be in place, with the patient being a full participant in the decision-making process.

Psychologists and Prescription Privileges

Psychologists are lobbying for prescription writing privileges throughout the United States. Two states, New Mexico and Louisiana, and the territory of Guam, currently allow psychologists to prescribe psychiatric drugs. Presently, nine other states are battling over this as legislation. It is inevitable that eventually psychologists will prevail in all fifty states. Does it matter? Not really! Psychiatrists, for the most part, are already misusing and mis-prescribing the privilege (Breggin, 1991, 2002). Too many patients are on far too many drugs at one time. Too many patients are being prescribed these drugs for a lifetime, with little or no effort being made to get them off the drugs as soon as possible. Rarely are patients who are on the drugs given proper medical checks to make certain that side effects are being carefully monitored. Medical checks by psychiatrists usually consist of, "Hello, how are you?" and, "Good by." This is all done within a span of ten minutes. It is expected that not only will psychologists become equally as careless and indifferent about patient care, but there are so many more psychologists than psychiatrists, the problems will escalate.

The safest approach would be to help patients identify the problems and work with well-educated psychologists to solve them, and get the patients off the drugs as quickly as possible.

A Word about Behavior Modification

The issues surrounding behavior modification are somewhat complex.

In the child arena, behavioral techniques are usually poorly designed and rely heavily on an overrated method called 'The token economy'. Token economies do not work well, and they are a ridiculous way to advise parents on how to raise children. The methods developed by Stein (1998, 2001a, 2001b, 2004) have won numerous awards, work extremely well, but have not gained popularity. They are correctly designed based on theory, and in reality they work, but the quest for higher drug sales seems to have undermined popularizing these methods.

Effective child behavioral interventions have been compromised by the pharmaceutical companies and their large supply of lackeys who invent childhood mental diseases that cannot be replicated from neutral outside experts. Therapies are based on the core belief that children have diseases and handicaps for which there is no cure (Barkley, 1995). Barkley (1995) has pieced together a hodgepodge of behavioral interventions which are designed to help and assist the handicapped child. These behavioral interventions are loaded with reminders, prompts, coaching, assisting, helping, and so forth. Unfortunately, these methods increase children's dependencies and make them more handicapped than before intervention even began. In addition, because these techniques theoretically should not work and realistic do not work, the inevitable conclusion is to put them on drugs. How convenient, and how suspicious! Are these techniques designed because of stupidity, or are they deliberately in use to foster the Machiavellian sale of drugs?

Only the forces on the dark side know for certain. Most of the books on the subject of treating children are variations of Barkley's folly (Stein, 2001a, 2001b). The reader is asked to make a direct comparison of Barkley's methods with Stein's methods. Try them and discover for yourself which really gets results?

Behavior Modification with Adults

Behavior modification with adults only offers very few promising approaches. Wolpe's (1958) desensitization methods seem to provide an adequate treatment for phobias. Bandura's (1969) modeling methods are comparable. Behaviorists may argue that they successfully treat other problems, such as anger management, anxiety reduction, alcohol and drugs addictions, paraphilias, and social skills training, but treatment efficacy studies do not support these claims (Lorandos and Cambell, 2005). Perhaps, a large part of the problem lies in the inability to control the environments of adults, while with children, the environment can be completely controlled (Stein, 2001, 2004). Eisler (2000, in a personal communication, October 15) summed up the steady decline of behaviorism for the last thirty years as a promising treatment modality when he said, "They ran out of ideas!"

Psychology and the Courts

It is without any doubt that psychologists should be banned from the fact-finding or substantive stages of trials (Lorandos and Cambell, 2005). They should also be banned from custody cases or any part of cases that directly effect lives, since they are wrong two out of three times in threat assessment (Hagen 1997; Lorandos and Campbell, 2005). Can they serve a purpose? Yes, but only in suggestive roles, such as competency to stand trial and jury selection. It is apparent that the courts are fed up with psychologists and psychiatrists mucking up the judicial system with large vocabulary words and convoluted, confusing, and incorrect assumptions (Hagen 1997; Lorandos and Campbell, 2005), most of which no one seems to understand.

Better Therapists

Psychology cannot go much lower. The documentation for the compilation of this book is out there for any psychologist to read. What has been written between the covers of this book is not opinion, but fact. It is time that psychologists face the issue that *they do not know, what they do not know.* It is time for a revolution in the training, thinking, and ongoing scholarly reading for psychologists. They must recognize their limits, and, at the same time, expand their skills. The doctoral programs can abandon their Stone Age mentality and offer more progressive, pragmatic, and accurate courses of study. They can train clinicians who graduate with solid clinical skills. Currently practicing psychologists are required to take continuing education courses, and perhaps now they will focus on those courses that train them to deal with specific human problems rather than the same courses that perpetuate and bolster their arcane therapy approaches. Clinicians can read, read, and read material that is more germane to patient care and better clinical practice.

Thus, a better definition for psychology is proposed here for introductory textbooks: "Psychology is the Science, Philosophy, and Art for Human Behavior and Human Problems!"

My fellow psychologists, the time is at hand for us to begin the revolution!

References

Adler, A. (1927). The practice and theory of individual psychology. New York: Harcourt.

Akbarian, S., Bunney, W. E., Potkin, S. G., Wigal, S. B., Hagman, J. O. Sandman,C. A. & Jones, E. G. (1993). Altered distribution of nicotinamide-adenine dinucleotide phosphate-diaphorase cells in frontal lobe of schizophrenics implies disturbances of cortal development. Archives of General Psychiatry, 50, 169-177.

Allport, G. W. (1937). The functional autonomy of motives. American Journal of Psychology, 50, 141-156.

Amen, K. G., Paldi, J. H. & Thisted, R. A. (1993). Brain SPECT imagining. Journal of the American Academy of Child and Adolescent Psychiatry, 32, 1080-1081.

American Educational Research Association, American Psychological Association, National Council on Measurement in Education (1999) Standards for educational and psychological testing. Washington, D.C.: American Psychological Association.

American Heritage Dictionary (2000). Boston, MS: Houghflin Mifflin Company.

American Psychiatric Association, (1957). Diagnostic and statistical manual of mental disorders. Washington, D. C.: Author.

American Psychiatric Association, (1968). Diagnostic and statistical manual of mental disorders II. Washington, D. C.: APA.

American Psychiatric Association (1980). The diagnostic and statistical manual of mental disorders, III. Washington, DC: APA.

American Psychiatric Association (1994). The diagnostic and statistical manual of mental disorders, IV. Washington, DC: APA.

American Psychiatric Association, (1994). Diagnostic and statistical manual of mental disorders IV. Washington, D. C.: Author.

American Psychiatric Association, (1994). Diagnostic and statistical manual of mental disorders (4th ed.). Washington, D. C.: Author.

American Psychiatric Association, (2000). Diagnostic and statistical manual of mental disorders - TR. Washington, D.C.: Author.

Anastasi, A. (1988). Psychological testing. New York: Macmillan Publishing Company.

Arnold, L. E., Kleykamp, K., Votolato, N. & Gibson, R. A. (1994). Potential link between dietary intake of fatty acids and behavior: Pilot exploration of serum lipids in attention deficit hyperactivity disorder. Journal of Child and Adolescent Psychopharmacology, 4, 171-182.

Athens, L. (1992). The creation of violent criminals. Urbana, IL: University of Illinois Press.

Athens, L. (1997). Violent criminal acts and actors revisited. Urbana, IL: University of Illinois Press.

Bachrach, L. L. (1984). Asylum and chronically ill psychiatric patients. American Journal of Psychiatry, 141(8), 975-978.

Baldessarini, R.J. (1985). Chemotherapy in psychiatry: Principles and practice. Cambridge, MA: Harvard University Press.

Baldwin, S. (1990). Alcohol education and offenders. London: Batsford.

Baldwin, S. (1991). Alcohol education and young offenders: Medium and short-term effectiveness of education programs. New York: Springer-Verlag.

Baldwin, S. & Jones, Y.(1996). ECT and minors: When more is less. Behavioural and Cognitive and Psychotherapy, 24, 319-322.

Baldwin, S. & Anderson, R. (2000). The cult of methylphenidate: clinical update. Critical Public Health, 10(1), 81-86.

Baldwin, S. & Oxlad, M. (2000)._Electroshock and minors: A fifty-year review. Westport, CT: Greenwood Press.

Bandura, A. (1969). Principles of behavior modification. Lanham, MD: Holt, Rinehart, and Winston.

Bandura, A. (1977). Social learning theory. New York: Prentice Hall.

Bandura, A. (1997). Self-efficacy: The exercise of control. New York: Walter H. Freeman and Company.

Barkley, R. A. (1992). (Video). Attention Deficit Hyperactivity Disorder: What can we do? New York: Guilford Publications, Kevin Dawkins, Producer.

Barkley, R. A. (1995). Taking charge of ADHD: The complete authoritative guide for parents. Nebraska: Boys Town Press.

Barlow, D. Leitenberg, H. & Steinbook, R. M. (1969). Experimental control of sexual deviation through manipulation of the noxious scene in covert sensitization. J. Abnormal. Psych., 1969, 74, 596 – 601.

Barlow, D. (1988). Anxiety and its disorders: The nature and treatment of anxiety and panic. New York: Guilford Press.

Barlow, D. H. & Durand, V. M. (1999). Abnormal psychology: An integrative approach. Pacific Grove, CA: Brooks/Cole Publishing Company.

Barlow, D. H. & Durand, V. M. (2002). Abnormal psychology: An integrative approach. Pacific Grove, CA: Brooks/Cole Publishing Company.

Barlow, D. (2004). Anxiety and its disorders: The nature and treatment of anxiety and panic. New York: The Guilford Press.

Barlow, D. and Durand, V. W. (2006). Abnormal psychology: An integrative approach. New York: Brooks/Cole Publishing Company.

Barlow, D. and Durand, V. W. (2008). Abnormal psychology: An integrative approach. New York: Brooks/Cole Publishing Company.

Bateson, G., Jackson, D. D., Haley, J. & Weakland, J. (1959). Toward a theory of schizophrenia. Behavioral Science, 1, 251-264.

Baughman, F. (2006). The ADHD fraud: How psychiatry makes patients of normal children. Victoria, BC: Trafford Publishing.

Beck, A. (1961). A systematic investigation of depression. Comprehensive Psychiatry, 2, 163 – 170.

Beck, A. T. (1967). Depression. New York: Hoeber-Harper.

Beck, A. (1979). Cognitive therapy and the emotional disorders. New York: Meridian Books.

Becker, W. C., Engelmann, S., and Thomas, D. R. (1971). Teaching: A course in applied psychology. Chicago, IL: Science Research Associates, Inc.

Begley, S. (2009). Ignoring the evidence: Why do psychologists reject science? Newsweek, October, 2.

Berkow, R. (1997) (Ed.). The Merck manual of medical information: Home edition. Whitehouse Station, NJ: Merck Research Laboratories.

Berman, K. F. & Weinburger, D. R. (1990). Lateralization of cortical function during cognitive tasks: Regional cerebral blood flow studies of normal individuals and patients with schizophrenia. Journal of Neurology, Neurosurgery and Psychiatry, 53, 150-160.

Berne, E. (1964). Games people play. New York: Grove Press.

Bodenheimer, T. & Grumbach, K. (2004). Understanding health policy: A clinical approach. New York: McGraw-Hill Publishers.

Boyle, M. (2002). Schizophrenia: A scientific delusion. London, UK: Routledge.

Boyle, M. (2002). Schizophrenia: A scientific delusion. New York: Taylor and Francis.

Coffin v. United States, 156 U.S. 432; 15 S. Ct. 394

Daubert v. Merrell Dow Pharmaceuticals, 509 U S 579, 113 S Ct 2786 (1993).

Bradley, C. (1937). The behavior of children receiving Benzedrine. American Journal of Psychiatry, 94, 577-585.

Brasfield, W. (1999). The effects of environment, drugs, and cognitions on receptor sites. A paper presented at the Conference of the Virginia Psychological Association, October, in Williamsburg, VA.

Breggin, P. (1991). Toxic psychiatry: Why therapy, empathy, and love must replace drugs, electroshock, and biochemical theories of the "new psychiatry." New York: St. Martin's Press.

Breggin, P. (1998). Talking back to Ritalin: What doctors aren't telling you about stimulants for children. Monroe, ME: Common Courage Press.

Breggin, & Cohen, D. (1999). Your drug may be your problem: How and why to stop taking psychiatric drugs. Cambridge, MA: Perseus Publishing.

Breggin, P. (2002). The Ritalin fact book: What your doctor won't tell you about ADHD and stimulant drugs. Cambridge, MA: Perseus Publishing.

Brehm, J. W. (1966). A theory of psychological reactance. New York: Academic.

Buchanan, R. W., Vladar, K., Barta, P. E. & Pearlson, G. D. (1998). Structural evaluation of the prefrontal cortex in schizophrenia. American Journal of Psychiatry, 155 (8), 1049-1055.

Bush, R. R. & Mosteller, F. (1955). Stochastic models for learning. New York: Wiley Publishing.

Buss, A. H. (1966). Psychopathology. New York: John Wiley & Sons, Inc.

Butler, G. & Mathews, A. (1983). Cognitive processes in anxiety. Advances in Behavior Therapy and Research, 5, 51-62.

Butler, G., Duran, R. E., Jasiukaitis, P., Kopman, C. & Spiegel, D. (1996). Hospitalizatility and traumatic experience: A diathysis stress model of dissociative symptomatology. American Journal of Psychiatry, 153, 42-63.

Byrne, D. (1964). Repression-sensitization as a dimension of personality. In B. A. Maher (Ed.), Progress in Experimental Personality Research, Vol. 1. New York: Academic.

Cannon, W. B. (1927). The James – Lang theory of emotion: A critical examination and an alternative theory. American Journal of Psychology, 39, 106-127.

Carlson, G. A. & Kashani, J. H. (1988). Phenomenology of major depression from childhood through adulthood: Analysis of three studies. American Journal of Psychiatry, 145 (10), 1222-1225.

Carlsson, A. (1995). The dopamine theory revisited. In S. R. Hirsch and D. R. Weinburger (Eds.), Schizophrenia (pp. 379-400). Oxford, England: Blackwell Science Limited.

Castellanos, F. X., Giedd, J. N., Eckburg, P., Marsh, W. L., Vaituzis, C., Katson, D., et al. (1994). Quantitative morphology of the caudate nucleus in attention deficit hyperactivity disorder. American Journal of Psychiatry, 151, 1791-1796.

Castellanos, F. X. (2006). "The brain size of ADHD children are smaller than normal's." A speech presented before a hearing on black box warnings for stimulant drugs with children for the federal FDA, Food and Drug Administration.

Chomsky, N. (1986). What Uncle Sam really wants. Tucson, AZ: Odoman Press.

Chomsky, N. & McChesney, R. (1992). Profit over people. New York: Seven Stories Press.

Chompsky, N. (1999). Profit over people: Neoliberalism and global order. New York: Seven Stories Press.

Chopra, D. (1989). Quantum healing: Exploring the frontiers of mind/body medicine (CD recording). New York: Bantam audio Publishing.

Chopra, D. (1993). Ageless body, timeless mind. New York: Harmony Books.

Clare, A. (1976) Psychiatry in dissent. London: Tavistock

Colbert, T. C. (1995). Depression and mania, friends or foes? A new "non-drug" model of hope for depression, mania, and compulsive disorders. Santa Ana, CA: Kevco Publishers.

Comings, D. E., Comings, D., Muhleman, G., Dietz, B. et al. (1996). The dopamine D2 receptor locus as a modifying gene in neuropsychiatric disorders. Journal of the American Medical Association 266: 1793-1800.

Cook, E. H. Jr., Stein, M. A., Leventhal, B. L. (1997). Family based association of attention-deficit/hyperactivity disorder and the dopamine transporter. In K. Blum & E. P. Noble (Eds.), Handbook of psychiatric genetics (pp. 297-310). Boca Raton, FL: Crc Press, Inc.

Damjanov, I. (1995). Disease: The encyclopedia Americana international edition. Connecticut: Grolier, Inc.

Daubert v. Merrell Dow Pharmaceuticals, Inc, 509 US 579; 113 S Ct 2786 (1993).

Davison, G. C. & Neale, J. M. (1994). Abnormal psychology (6th ed.). New York: John Wiley & Sons, Inc.

Dawes, R. M. (1994). House of cards: Psychology and Psychotherapy built on myth. New York: The Free Press.

Dawes, R. M. (1996). House of cards: Psychology and psychotherapy built on myth. New York: The Free Press.

DeGrandpre, R. (1999). Ritalin nation: Rapid fire culture and the transformation of human consciousness. New York: W. W. Norton.

Depue, R. A. & Spoont, M. R. (1986). Conceptualizing a serotonin trait: A behavioral dimension of constraint. Annals of the New York Academy of Sciences, 487, 47-62.

Depue, R. A. & Iacono, W. G. (1989). Neurobehavioral aspects of affective disorders. Annual Review of Psychology, 40, 457 – 492.

Dershowitz, A. M. (1994). The abuse excuse: And other cop-outs, sob stories, and evasions of responsibility. New York: Little Brown and Company.

Dietz, P. E. (1986). Mass, serial and sensational homicides. Bulletin New York Academy of Medicine, 62 (5), 477-491.

Dineen, T. (2000). Manufacturing victims: What the psychology industry is doing to people. New York: Robert Davies Multimedia Publishing.

Dollard, J. & Miller, N. E. (1950). Personality and psychotherapy: An analysis in terms of learning, thinking, and culture. New York: McGraw-Hill Book Company.

Douglas, J. E., Burgess, A. W., Burgess, A. G. & Ressler, R. K. (1992). Crime classification manual: A standard system for investigating and classifying violent crimes. San Francisco, CA: Jossey-Bass Publishers.

Douglas, J., Burgess, A., Burgess, A. G. & Ressler, R. (1997). Crime classification manual: A standard system for investigating and classifying violent crimes. San Francisco: CA: Jossey-Bass Publishers.

Durant, W. (1961). The story of philosophy: The lives and opinions of the great philosophers of the western world. New York: Touchstone Books.

Ebaugh, F. G. (1923). Neuropsychiatric sequelae of acute epidemic Encephalitus in children. American Journal of Disease in Children, 25, 89-97.

Ebbinghaus, H. (1885). Psychology, an elementary textbook. New York: Dissertation Abstracts International, 37, 286B.

Edwards, A. (1967). Statistical methods. New York: Holt, Rinehart, and Winston, Inc.

Ellis, A. & Harper, R. A. (1961). A new guide to rational living. New York: Wiley Publishing.

Ellis, A (1962). Reason and emotion in psychotherapy. New York: Lyle Stuart Press.

Ellis, A. and Harper, R. A. (1975). A new guide to rational living. Englewood Cliffs, NJ: Prentice Hall.

Ellis, A. & Harper, R. A. (1975). A new guide to rational living. Englewood Cliffs, NJ: Prentice Hall.

Eysenck, H. J. (1952). The effects of psychotherapy: An evaluation. Journal of consulting Psychology, 16, 319 – 324.

Eysenck, H. J. (1961). The effects of psychotherapy. In H. J. Eysenck (Ed.), Handbook of abnormal psychology: An experimental approach. New York: Basic Books, Pp. 697-725.

Faries, D., Helligenstein, G., Tollefson, G., and Potter, W. (2001). The double blind variable placebo lead in period: Results from two antidepressant clinical trials. Journal of Clinical Psychopharmacology, 21, 561-568.

Faust, D., Anderer, D. & Ziskin, J. (2001). Ziskin's coping with psychological testimony. Cambridge, MA: Oxford University Press.

Festinger, L. (1957). A theory of cognitive dissonance. Stanford, CA: Stanford University Press.

Festinger , L. (1977). Leon Festinger. In David Cohen, Psychologists on psychology. New York: Taplinger Publishers. (pp. 262-266)

Fisher, B. (1981). Rebuilding when your relationship ends. San Luis Obispo: CA: Impact publishers.

Fisher, B. (1992). Rebuilding when your relationship ends. San Luis Obispo, CA: Impact Publishers

Fisher, M. P. (1997). Living religions. Upper Saddle river, NJ: Prentice Hall.

Flick, G. L. (2004). How to reach and teach teenagers with ADHD: A step-by-step guide to overcome difficult behavior at school and at home. West Nyack, NY: The Center for Applied Research in Education.

Frege, G. (1903). The foundations of arithmetic: The logical-mathematical Investigation of the Concept of Number. Grundgesetze der Arithmetik, Band I (1893); Band II (1903). Jena: Verlag Hermann Pohle.

Frye v. United States, 54 US App 46, 293 F 1013 (1923).

General Electric v. Joiner, 864F. Supp. 1310-1314 (N.D., Ga., 1994).

Gibbons, J. L. (1964). Cortisol secretion rates in depressive illness. Archives of General Psychiatry, 10, 572-575.

Giedd, J. N., Castellanos, F. X., Casey, B. J., Kozuch, P., King, A. C., Hamburger, S. D., et al. (1994). Quantitative morphology of the corpus callosum in attention deficit hyperactivity disorder. American Journal of Psychiatry, 151, 665-669.

Glasser, W. (1965). Reality therapy: A new approach to psychiatry. New York: Harper Trade.

Glasser, W. (1998). Choice therapy: A new psychology of personal freedom. New York: Harper PerennialGlasser, W. (2003). Warning: Psychiatry can be hazardous to your health. New York: Harper Collins Publishers.

Goodwin, F. K. & Jamison, K. R. (1990). Manic depressive illness. New York: Oxford University Press.

Greenblatt, J. M., Huffman, L. C. & Reiss, A. L. (1994). Folic acid in neurodevelopment and child psychiatry. Progress in Neuropsychopharmachology and Biological Psychiatry, 18, 647-660.

Gruenberg, E. (1966). Evaluating the effective of community mental health services. New York: Milbank Publishers.

Gur, R. E. & Pearlson, G. D. (1993). Neuroimaging in schizophrenia research. Schizophrenia Bulliten,19 (2), 337-353.

Hagen, M. A. (1997). Whores of the court: The fraud of psychiatric testimony and the rape of American justice. New York: Regan Books.

Hall, C. & Lindzey, G. (1957). Theories of personality. New York: John Wiley & Sons, Inc.

Halperin, J. M., Newcorn, J. H., Kopstein, I., Mckay, K. E., Schwartz, S. T., Siever, L. J., et al. (1997). Serotonin, aggression, and parental psychopathology in children with attention-deficit hyperactivity disorder. Journal of the American Academy of Child and Adolescent Psychiatry, 36 (10), 1391-1398.

Hanson, G. & Venturelli, P. J. (1998). Drugs and society. Boston, MA: Jones and Bartlett Publishers.

Hanson, G. & Venturelli, P. (1998). Drugs & society. Boston, MA: Jones and Bartlett Publishers.

Hanson, G. & Venturelli, P. (2001). Drugs & society. Boston, MA: Jones and Bartlett Publishers.

Hazelwood, R. & Michaud, S. G. (2001). Dark dreams. New York: St. Martin's Press.

Heather, N. & Robertson, I. (1983) Controlled Drinking. London: Methuen.

Heilman, K. M., Voeller, K. K. & Nadeau, S. E. (1991). A possible pathophysiologic substrate of attention deficit hyperactivity disorder. Journal of Child Neurology, 6, 576-581.

Holmes, R. M. & Holmes, S. T. (2002). Profiling violent crimes: An investigative tool. London, UK: SAGE Publications.

Hull, C. L. (1933). Hypnosis and suggestibility: An experimental approach. New York: Apleton-century-Crofts.

Hull, C. (1943). Principles of behavior: An introduction to behavior theory. New York: Appleton-Century Crofts.

Huxley, A. (1976). Brave new world. New York: Hodder Arnold Publishers.

Jackson, G. (2005). Rethinking psychiatric drugs: A guide for informed consent. Bloomington, IN: Authorhouse.

James, W. (1884). What is an emotion? Mind, 9, 188 –205.

Jellinek, E. M. (1960). The disease concept of alcohol. New Haven: CT: Hillhouse Press.

Johnstone, L. (1995). Users and abusers of psychiatry: A critical look at psychiatric practice. London, UK: Routledge.

Johnstone, L. (2000). Users and abusers of psychiatry: A critical look at psychiatric practice. Philadelphia, PA: Taylor and Francis.

Joseph, J. (1999). The genetic theory of schizophrenia: A critical overview. Ethical Human Sciences and Services, 1(2), 119-145.

Joseph, J. (2003). The gene illusion: Genetic research in psychiatry and psychology under the microscope. Herefordshire, UK: PCCS Books.

Julien, R. M. (1998). A primer of drug action: A concise, nontechnical guide to the actions, uses, and side effects of psychoactive drugs. New York: W. H. Freeman & Co.

Kanfer, F. H. & Phillips, J. S. (1970). Learning foundations of behavior therapy. New York: John Wiley & Sons, Inc.

Kant, I. (1787). Critique of pure reason. New York: American Dome Library.

Kant, I. (1788). The critique of practical reason. New York: Forgotten Books.

Kant, I. (1793). Kritik der urteilskraft. Germany: F. T. Lagarde.

Kaplan, D. and Sandock, B. (1995). Synopsis of psychiatry: Behavioral sciences, clinical psychiatry. Baltimore, MD: Lippincott Williams & Wilkins.

Kazdin, A. E. (1994). Behavior modification in applied settings (5th ed). Belmont: Brooks Cole.

Kean, B. (2004). The Risk Society and Attention Deficit Hyperactivity Disorder (ADHD): A critical social research analysis concerning the development and social impact of the ADHD diagnosis. Southern Cross University, Australia, doctoral dissertation.

Kendall, P. C. & Hollon, S. D. (1981). Assessment strategies for cognitive-behavioral interventions. New York: Academic Press.

Kendall, P. (1998). Cognitive therapy. Workshop presented at a meeting of the Virginia Psychological Association, Richmond, VA.

Kennedy, D. M. (2002). The ADHD autism connection: A step toward more accurate diagnosis and effective treatment. Colorado Springs, CO: Waterbrook Press.

Khan, A., Warner, H., and Brown, W. (2000). Symptom reduction and suicide risk in patients treated with placebo in antidepressant clinical trials. Archives of General Psychiatry, 57, 211 – 217.

Klonsky, E. D. (2000). The DSM classification of personality disorder: Clinical wisdom and empirical truth?, 56 Journal of Clinical Psychology 1615-1616.

Kluft, R. P. (1984). Treatment of multiple personality disorder. Psychiatric Clinics of North America, 7, 9-29.

Kraeplin, E. (1883). Clinical psychiatry. Leipzig, Germany: A. R. Diefendorf.

Kraepelin, E. (1898). The diagnosis and prognosis of dementia praecox. Paper presented at the 29th Congress of Southwestern German Psychiatry, Heidleburg.

Kraepelin, E. (1899). Kompendium der psychiatrie (6th ed.). Leipzig: Abel.

Krishnamurti, J. (1973). The awaking of intelligence. New York: Harper and Row.

Kumho Tire Company, Ltd. v. Carmichael, 526 U S 137; 119 S. Ct. 1167 – 1171.

Kushner, H. (2004). When bad things happen to good people. New York: Anchor Publishing.

Kuhn, T. (1957). The Copernican revolution: Planetary astronomy in the development of western thought. Cambridge MA: Harvard University Press.

Lahat, E., Avital, E., Barr, J., Berkovitch, M., Arlazoroff, A. & Aladjem, M. (1995). BAEP studies in children with attention deficit disorder. Developemental Medicine and Child Neurology, 37, 119-123.

Laing, R. D., (1969). The divided self. New York: Pantheon Books.

Lang, C. G. (1985). The emotions. Baltimore, MD: Williams & Wilkins.

Lavin, M. (1985). Doctors, psychiatrists and disease. Social Science & Medicine, 20(5), 535 - 543.

LeDoux, J. (1996). The emotional brain: The mysterious underpinnings of emotional life. New York: Simon and Schuster.

Lefton, L. A. (2000). Psychology. Boston, MA: Allyn and Bacon.

Levy, F. (1991). The dopamine theory of attention deficit hyperactivity disorder. Australian and New Zealand Journal of Psychiatry, 25, 277-283.

Lewinsohn, P. M. & Talkington, J. (1979). Studies on the measurement of unpleasant events and relations with depression. Applied Psychological Measurement, 3, 83-101.

Lewinsohn, P. M. & Rosenbaum (1987). Recall of parental behavior by acute depressives, remitted depressives, and nondepressives. Journal of Personality and Social Psychology, 52(3), 611-619.

Lilienfeld, S. O., Wood, J. M. & Garb, H. N. (2000). The scientific status of projective techniques. Psychological Science in the Public Interest, 1, 27 – 66.

Lilienfeld, S. O., Wood, J. M. & Garb, H. N. (2001a, May). What's wrong with this picture? Scientific American, 284(5), 80 – 87.

Lilienfeld, S. O., Lynn, S. J. & Lohr, J. M. (2003) (Eds). Science and pseudoscience in clinical psychology. New York: The Guilford Press.

Lipsey, M. W. and Wilson, D. B. (1993). The efficacy of psychological, educational, and behavioral treatment: Confirmation from meta-analysis. American Psychologist, Vol. 48(12), 1181-1209.

Lorandos, D. & Campbell, T. W. (2005). Benchbook in the behavioral sciences.

Durham, NC: Carolina Academic Press.

Lovaas, O. A. (1987) Behavioral treatment and normal educational/intellectual functioning in young autistic children. Journal of Consulting and Clinical Psychology, 55, 3-9.

Maher, B. (1966). Principles of Psychopathology. New York: McGraw-Hill, Inc.

Marbin-Miller, C. (2009, February 19). The story of Gabriel Myers. Miami Herald, p. 1.

Martin, I. (1983). Human classical conditioning. In A. Gale & J. A. Edward (Eds.), Physiological correlates of human behavior: Vol. 2. Attention and performance. London: Academic Press.

Maultsby, M. C. (1984). Rational behavioral therapy. Englewood Cliffs, NJ: Prentice Hall.

Mayberg, H. (1998, May 7). Today [Television broadcast]. New York: National Broadcasting Network.

McGraw, P. (2000). Relationship rescue: A seven step strategy for reconnecting with your partner. New York: Hyperion.

Meichenbaum, D. (1977). Cognitive-behavioral modification: An integrative approach.

New York: Plenum Press.

Melton, G. B., Pertrila, J., Poythress, N. G. & Slobogin, C. (1997). (2nd ed.). Psychological evaluations for the courts. New York: Guilford Press.

Meltzer, H. Y. (1992). The importance of serotonin-dopamine interactions in the action of clozapine. British Journal of Psychiatry Supplement, May (17), 22-29.

Miller, G. A., Galanter, E. H. & Pribrma, K. H. (1960). Plans and the structure of behavior. New York: Holt, Rinehart & Winston.

Miller, W.R. & Heather, N. (1999). Treating addictive behaviors. New York: Plenum.

Mischel, W. (1996). Personality and assessment. Mahwah, NJ: Lawrence Erlbaum Associates, Publishers.

Moncrieff, J. (2003, April 4). Is psychiatry for sale? An examination of the influence of the pharmaceutical industry on academic and practical psychiatry. Healthy Skepticism International News, 22.

Morgan, T. & King, R. (1966). Introduction to psychology. New York: McGraw Hill Education books.

Mosby's 2008 Drug Guide. St. Louis, MO: Elesvier.

Nash, J. (1951). Non-cooperative games. Annals of Mathematics 54 (1951), 286–295.

Nash, J. (1953). Two-person cooperative games. Econometrica 21, 128–140.

National Institute of Health (1998). A summary of the NIH consensus committee. Bethesda, MD: An NIH Publication.

National Institute of Health Conference, 1998, in Bethesda, MD.

NDA (1996). Review and evaluation of clinical data. A review given to the Department of Health and Human Services, and FDA. (pp. 20-592)

NIH (1998). A summary of the findings of the NIH consensus on ADHD. National Institute of Health, Bethesda, MD: National Institute of Health.

Odell, J. D., Warren, R. P., Warren, W. L., Burger, R. A. & Maciulis, A. (1997). Association of genes within the major histocompatibility complex with attention-deficit hyper activity disorder. Neuropsychobiology, 35 (4), 181-186.

Osgood, C. E. (1953). Method and theory in experimental psychology. New York: Oxford University Press.

Oxlad, M. & Baldwin, S. (1996) The use of ECT in older people: Risks, rights and responsibilities. Health Care in Later Life, 1(1), 39-49.

Papolos, D. & Papolos, J. (1999). The bipolar child: The definitive and reassuring guide to childhood's most misunderstood disorder. New York: Broadway Books.

Papolos, D. & Papolos, J. (2002). The bipolar child: The definitive and reassuring guide to childhood's most misunderstood disorder. New York: Broadway Books.

Patterson, G. R. (1971). Families: Applications of social learning theory to modern life. Chicago, IL: Science Research Associates, Inc.

Pavlov, I. (1927). Conditioned reflexes. London: Oxford University Press.

Peele, S. (1989). Diseasing of America: How we allowed recovery zealots and the treatment industry to convince us we are out of control. San Francisco: Jossey-Bass Publishers.

Peele, S. (1995). Diseasing of America: How we allowed recovery zealots and the treatment industry to convince us we are out of control. San Francisco, CA: Jossey-Bass Publishers.

Piaget, J. (1954). The construction of reality in a child. New York: Basic Books.

Piaget, J. (1976). Judgment and reasoning in a child. New York: Littlefield Adams.

Piaget, J. (1978). The development of thought: Equaliberation of cognitive structures. New York: Littlefield Adams.

Puttnam, F. W. (1989). Diagnosis and treatment of multiple personality disorder. New York: Guilford Press.

Radfield, J. (1993). The Celestine prophecy: An adventure. New York: Time Warner, Inc.

Ray, W. (1962). Statistics in psychological research. New York: The MacMillan Company.

Ray, W. (1968). Basic statistics. New York: Appleton – Century – Crofts.

Roback, A. A. & Kierman, T. (1969). Pictorial history of psychology and psychiatry. New York: Philosophical Library.

Robins, L. N. & Helzer, J. E., (1986). Diagnosis and clinical assessment: The current state of psychiatric diagnosis. Annual Review of Psychology, 31, 409.

Rogers, C. (1951). Client centered therapy: Its practice, implications, and theory.. New York: Houghton Mifflin.

Rogers, C. (2004). Client-centered therapy: Its current practice, implications and theory. New York: Constable Publishers.

Rosemond, J. (2001). New parent power. Kansas City, MO: Andrew McMeel.

Rosenberg, K. E. (1989). Disease in history: frames and framers. The Milbank Quarterly, 67, 1 -15.

Rossi. P. and Wright, J.D. (1984). Evaluation research and assessment. Annual Review of Sociology, volume (10), 331-352.

Russell, B. (1935). Religion and science. New York: Home University Library.

Sackeim, H. A. & Devanand, D. P. (1991). Dissociative disorders. In M. Hersen & Turner, S. M. (Eds.), Adult psychopathology & diagnosis (2nd ed., pp. 279-322). New York: John Wiley.

Samango-Sprouse C. (1999). Frontal lobe development in childhood. In B. L. Miller & J. L. Cummings (Eds.), The human frontal lobes: Functions and disorders (The science and practice of neuropsychology series) (pp. 584-603). New York: The Guilford Press.

Samenow, S. (2004). Inside the criminal mind. New York: Crown Business.

Samenow, S. (2007). The myth of the out of character crime. New York: Praeger Publishing.

Samson, J. A., Mirin, S. M., Hauser, S. T., Fenton, B. T. & Schidkraut, J. J. (1992). Learned helplessness and urinary MHPG levels in unipolar depression. American Journal of Psychiatry, 149(6), 806-809.

Santrock, J. W., Minnett, A. M. & Campbell, B. D. (1994). The authoritative guide to self-help books. New York: The Guilford Press.

Schacter, S. & Singer, J. E. (1962). Cognitive, social, and physiological determinants of emotional state. Psychological Review, 69, 379-399.

Schildkraut, J. J. (1965). The catecholamine hypothesis of affective disorders: A review of supporting evidence. American Journal of Psychiatry, 122, 509-522.

Schlesinger, L. (1998). The Dr. Laura radio show [Radio broadcast]. Richmond, VA: WRIC Broadcasting.

Schmalleger, F. (2006). Criminology today: An integrative introduction. Upper Saddle River, NJ: Pearson, Prentice Hall.

Schnert, K. W. (1981). Stress/unstress: How you can control stress at home and on the job. Minneapolis, MN: Augsburg Publishing House.

Schreiber, F. R. (1989). Sybil. New York: Grand Central Publishing.

Sedvall, G. (1997). The current status of PET scanning with respect to schizophrenia. Neuropsychopharmacology, 7 (1), 41-54.

Seligman, M. E. P. (1975). Helplessness: On depression development and death. San Francisco: W. H. Freeman.

Seligman, M. E. P. (1975). Helplessness. San Francisco, CA: Freeman.

Seligman, L. (1994). DSM-IV: Diagnosis and treatment planning [Audio Cassette]. Arlington, VA: American Counseling Association.

Seligman, L. (2004). Diagnosis and treatment planning in counseling. New York: Springer Publishing.

Sgori, S. (1982). Handbook of clinical intervention in child sexual abuse. New York: The Free Press.

Shafii, M. & Shafii, S. L. (1998). Melatonin in healthy and depressed children and adolescents. In M. Shafii & S. L. Shafii (Eds.), Melatonin in psychiatric and neoplastic disorders (pp. 149-167). Washington, DC: American Psychiatric Publishing, Inc.

Shannon, J. (2001). We Will Sue You! A statement made at the Ritalin Litigation Conference, New York.

Sidman, M. (1960). Tactics of scientific research: Evaluating experimental data in psychology.. New York: Basic Books, Inc. Publishers.

Silverstone, T. (1985). Dopamine in manic depressive illness: A pharmacological synthesis. Journal of Affective Disorders, 8(3), 225-231.

Sizemore, C. (1989). A mind of my own: The woman known as 'Eve' tells the story of her triumph over multiple personality disorder. New York: William Morrow and Company.

Skinner, B. F. (1953). Science and human behavior. New York: MacMillan.

Skinner, B.F. (1957) Science and human behavior. New York: MacMillan.

Skinner, B. F. (1963). Behaviorism at fifty. Science, 140, 951-958.

Smail, D. (1998). Taking care: An alternate to therapy. London, UK: J. M. Dent & Sons Ltd.

Snyder, C. R. & Elliott, T. R. (2005). Twenty-first century graduate education in clinical psychology: A four level matrix model. Journal of Clinical Psychology, 61, 1033 – 1054.

Spitzer, R.I., Forman, J. B. W. & Nee, J. (1979). DSM-III field trials: Initial inter-rater diagnostic reliability, 136 American Journal of Psychiatry 815.

Stein, D. B. (1977). Principles of conflict: Revision and reconceptualization.

Dissertation Abstracts International, 37, 286B.

Stein, D. B. (1998, October). Effective Behavioral Treatment of ADD/ADHD Without Psychaitric Drugs. A paper and award winning media presentation made at the convention of the American Psychological Association in San Francisco, CA.

Stein, D. B. (1998a). Lies about child mental diseases and psychiatric drugs. A statement made at a press conference for award winners at the American Psychological Association Conference in San Francisco, CA.

Stein, D. B. (1998b). Ritalin is not the answer: A drug-free, practical program for children diagnosed with ADD or ADHD. San Francisco, CA: Wiley, Jossey-Bass Publishers.

Stein, D. (1999). What Ritalin Is Not the Answer is all about. The shocking truth.
Radio Broadcast – WFAS, William O'Shea, New York City, NY, January 9.

Stein, D. B. (2000). What psychology is and isn't. Paper presented at the annual conference for The International Center for the Study of Psychiatry and Psychology, New York.

Stein, D .B. & Baldwin, S. (2000). Toward an operational definition of disease in psychology and psychiatry: Implications for diagnosis and treatment. International Journal of Risk and Safety in Medicine, August.

Stein, D. B. (2001a). The Ritalin is not the answer action guide: An interactive companion to the best-selling drug-free ADD/ADHD parenting program. San Francisco, CA: Wiley, Jossey-Bass, Publishers.

Stein, D. (2001b). Unraveling the ADD/ADHD fiasco: Successful parenting without drugs. Kansas City, MO: McMeel Publishing.

Stein, D. B. (2001c). Prescription privileges for psychologists, ethical issues. A
symposium presentation at the Virginia Psychological Association Conference, Roanoke, VA.

Stein, D. B. (2003). The truth about ADD/ADHD and stimulant drugs. Testimony presented before the Virginia State Legislative Subcommittee investigating schools diagnosing children and recommending psychiatric drugs.

Stein, D. B. (2004). Stop medicating/start parenting: Real solutions for your 'problem' teenager. Lanham, MD: Taylor Publishers.

Stein, D. B. (2005). A new diagnostic system based on cognitive patterns. Paper presented at the Conference of the International Center for the Study of Psychiatry and Psychology, New York.

Stein, D. B. (2006). How the chemical imbalance trick is done. Testimony before the Food and Drug Administration, Washington, DC.

Stein, D. B. (2007). Profiling rampage school shooters. A presentation made at the Crime Solvers Conference, Richmond, VA.

Stein, D. B. (2009). The need to operationally define 'disease' in psychiatry and psychology. Ethical Human Psychology and Psychiatry, Vol. 11, 2, 120-141.

Stein, D. B. & Foltz, R. (2009a). An operational definition of 'disease' in psychiatry and psychology. Ethical Human Psychology and Psychiatry, 11, 2, 120-141.

Stein, D. B. & Foltz, R. (2009b). Choosing a psychologist? What the shrinks don't know, and what they need to fix. Frederick, MD: Publish America Publishers.

Stein, D. B. & Fotlz, R. (2009c). The Course Content of APA Accredited Doctoral Programs: If the Use of Psychiatric Drugs Is to Be Challenged Then a Road to Better Psycho-social Treatments Needs to Be Paved! Ethical Human Psychology and Psychiatry: An International Journal of Critical Inquiry, 11, 4.

Steiner, C. M. (1974). Scripts people live: Transactional analysis of life scripts. New York: Grove Press.

Still, J. M. (1902). The Coulstonian lectures on some abnormal physical conditions in children. Lancet,1, 1008-1082.

Strauss, A. & Lehtinen, L. W. (1947). Psychopathology and education of the brain impaired child. New York: Greene & Stratton.

Swanson, J. (1998, October). The biological basis of ADHD. Paper presented at the National Institute of Health ADHD consensus conference, Bethesda, MD.

Szasz, T. S. (1961). The myth of mental illness: Foundations of a theory of personal conduct. New York: Hoeber – Harper.

Szasz, T. (1974). Ceremonial chemistry: The ritual persecution of drugs, addicts, and pushers. Garden City, NY: Anchor Press/Doubleday.

Szasz, T. (1976). Schizophrenia: The sacred symbol of psychiatry. New York: Basic Books, Inc. Publishers.

Thigpen, C. H. & Cleckley, H. (1957). The three faces of Eve. New York: McGraw Hill.

Thorndike, E. L. (1903). Educational psychology. New York: The Science Press.

Time Magazine, December 2, 1985.

Torrey, E. F. (1988). Stalking the schizovirus. Schizophrenic Bulletin, 14, 223 – 229.

Trachtenberg, P. (1989). The Casanova complex: Compulsive lovers and their women. New York: Poseidon Press.

United States (1990). The Americans with Disabilities Act. US Congress: Washington, DC.

United States v. Downing, 733 F2d 1224, 1237 – 42 (3rd Cir. 1985).

Valenstein, E. (1998). Blaming the brain: The truth about drugs and mental health. New York: Free Press.

Watson, J. B. (1928). Psychological care of infant and child. New York: Norton.

Watson, J. B. (1924). Psychology from the standpoint of a behaviorist. Philadelphia, PA: Lippincott.

Wedding, D. & Mengel, M. (2004). Models of integrated care in primary care settings. In L. Haas (Ed.). Handbook of psychology in primary care. (pp. 47-62). New York: Oxford University Press.

Whitaker, R. (2002). Mad in America: Bad science, bad medicine, and the enduring mistreatment of the mentally ill. Cambridge, MA: Perseus Publishing.

Wilson, J. W. (2002). The marriage problem: How our culture has weakened families. New York: Harper Collins Publishers.

Wittgenstein, L. (1965). Philosophical investigations. Ondon, UK: Basil Blackwell.

Wolpe, J. (1958). Psychotherapy by reciprocal inhibition. Stanford, CA: Stanford University Press.

Wolpe, J. (1958). Psychotherapy reciprocal inhibition. Stanford: Stanford University Press.

Wolpe, J. & Lazarus, A. (1966). Behavior therapy techniques: A guide to the treatment of neuroses> New York, Pergamon Press.

Wolpe, J. (1958). Psychotherapy by reciprocal inhibition. San Francisco, CA: Stanford University Press.

Wood. J. M., Nezworski, M. T., Lilienfeld, S. O. & Grab, H. N. (2003). What's wrong with the Rorschach? San Francisco, CA: Wiley, Jossey-Bass.

Wrightsman, L. S., Nietzel, M. T. & Fortune, W. H. (1994). Psychology and the legal system. Pacific Grove, CA: Brooks/Cole Publishing Company.

Yalom, I, & Leszcz, M. (2005). Theory and practice of group psychotherapy. New York: Basic Books.

Zametkin, A. J., Liebenauenauer, L. L., Gitzgerald, G. A. & King, A. C. (1993). Brain metabolism in teenagers with attention deficit hyperactivity disorder. Archives of General Psychiatry, 50, 330-340.

Zametkin, A. J., Nordahl, T., Gross, M., King, A. C., Semple, W. C., Rumsey, J., et al. (1993). Cerebral glucose metabolism in adults with hyperactivity of childhood onset. New England Journal of Medicine, 323, 1361-1366.

Zemishlany, Z., Alexander, G. E., Prohovnik, I., Goldman, R. G., Mukherjee, S. & Sackeim, H. (1996). Cortical blood flow and negative symptoms in schizophrenia. Neuropsychobiology, 33 (33), 127-138.

Zieler, D. & Phillips, P. (1961). Psychiatric diagnosis and symptomatology. Journal of Abnormal and Social Psychology, 63, 61-70.

Zimbardo, P., Weber, A. & Johnson, R. (2000). Psychology. Boston, MA: Allyn and Bacon.

Zubin, J. & Spring, B. (1977). Vulnerability – a new view of schizophrenia. Journal of Abnormal Psychology, 86, 103-126.

Biographical Summary

David B. Stein, Ph.D., DACFE

Dr. David B. Stein is a Professor of Criminal Justice at Virginia State University, in Petersburg, Virginia and a former Professor of Psychology at Longwood University, a state college in Central Virginia. He teaches Abnormal Psychology, Child Psychopathology, Applied Behavior Analysis (Behavior Modification), Psychopharmacology, Psychology and Law, The Psychology of Terrorism and Homeland Security, Psychological Profiling, and, of course, Introduction to Psychology. Currently, he is the Director of Criminal Justice Intern Training at Virginia State. He has an extensive list of research publications and professional presentations. He is a best-selling author, and his books include: Ritalin is Not the Answer: A Drug-free, Practical Program for Children Diagnosed with ADD or ADHD; The Ritalin is Not the Answer Action Guide: An Interactive Companion to the best-selling Drug-Free ADD/ADHD Parenting Program; Unraveling the ADD/ADHD Fiasco: A Guide for Successful Parenting; Stop Medicating/Start Parenting: Real Solutions for Your Problem Teenager; *and* Controlling the Difficult Adolescent: The REST Program (Real Economy Program for Teens).

He has won numerous honors and awards for his thirty years of devoted work in offering drug-free treatment and parenting alternatives for the most difficult and out-of-control children and teens. He has been listed in Who's Who Among America's Teachers for many years; he is a Diplomate as a Forensics Examiner; he was awarded the 2000 outstanding teacher and scholar at Longwood, and his research on ADD/ADHD treatment was selected as one of the top ten for Media Coverage Award at the 1998 American Psychological Association convention; he was awarded the Outstanding Achievement Award in 2005 from The International Center for the Study of Psychiatry and Psychology; and his most recent award was in 2008 for Human Rights Achievements from The Citizens' Commission on Human Rights. His book, Ritalin is Not the Answer, was endorsed as required reading by all parents, educators, and doctors at the 2001 Ritalin Litigation Conference in New York. His work was featured in the 2001 text, Advances in Medicine.

Dr. Stein is also a criminologist, was a former credentialed consultant to the Virginia State Police, and served as a sheriff's deputy for Prince Edward County, Virginia. His duties included criminal profiling, crisis and hostage negotiations, critical incident responding, crime scene investigations, and threat assessment. He has written numerous criminal justice and police journal articles and book chapters, and has made numerous presentations to law enforcement agencies. He is the founder and senior partner of Legal/Psych Training and Consulting, a company unlike any other.

Contact:
Office e mail: dstein@vsu.edu
Web sites: www.drdavestein.com and www.legalpsychexperts.com

Dr. David Stein, Ph.D.
Virginia State University
Criminal Justice
Petersburg, VA 23806

INDEX

www.ingramcontent.com/pod-product-compliance
Ingram Content Group UK Ltd.
Pitfield, Milton Keynes, MK11 3LW, UK
UKHW041628031026
15587UKWH00001B/153

9 780761 859567